29861

COUNTY OF SOUTH GLAMORGAN LIBRA

This book is due for return on or before the last date st
e for each week or part of week overdu
urrent scale of

EI OCT 1977

D0655722

THE ACHIEVEMENT OF
E. M. FORSTER

By the same Author

*

COLERIDGE THE VISIONARY

THE
ACHIEVEMENT OF
E. M. FORSTER

J. B. BEER
Lecturer in English in the
University of Manchester

1962
CHATTO & WINDUS
LONDON

797 823.912
FOR-BEE

X

Published by
Chatto & Windus Ltd
42 William IV St
London WC 2
*
Clarke, Irwin & Co Ltd
Toronto

AA 6820 17a

© J. B. BEER 1962
Printed in Great Britain by
T. & A. Constable Ltd.
Hopetoun Street, Edinburgh

For
CHARLES PARKIN

CONTENTS

Preface   *page* 9

     I Aspects of a Novelist   11

    II The Earth and the Stars   31

   III From a View to a Death   53

   IV Flame Boats on a Stream   77

    V In Country Sleep   101

   VI The Undying Worm   131

  VII Serving the World   166

 VIII In and Out of Time   177

Notes   209

Bibliography   218

Index   220

PREFACE

IT is a pleasure to acknowledge several debts: to the British Council, Newcastle-upon-Tyne, and the Manchester Branch of the English Association, for commissioning lectures which enabled me to give an airing to some of the themes presented here; to the Librarians of the English Faculty in the University of Cambridge; to the Librarian and staff of the Manchester Public Libraries for making available special facilities for study and research; to Messrs Edward Arnold Ltd. for permission to quote extensively from the works of E. M. Forster; to Mr Angus Wilson for allowing me to quote extensively from a published interview and for a stimulating correspondence on one or two points in it; and to the many friends and colleagues with whom I have had the opportunity of discussing Forster's work at various times.

Manchester, 1961   J. B. B.

CHAPTER I

Aspects of a Novelist

THE account of E. M. Forster which has reached more readers than any other appears on the cover of a paper-back edition of his works:

> He is one of those rare authors whose books are kept and re-read, not only for their stories, but for the wise sayings which crowd their pages and the gentle humanist philosophy which they reveal.

A general comment like this, addressed as it is to the reader who likes a good story, seasoned with occasional wisdom, might be allowed to stand. It is more disquieting to find the author of the *Concise Cambridge History of English Literature*, which ought to have a different audience in view, writing of the 'shy, unworldly quality' of work 'almost diffidently presented' by a man who is 'at heart a scholar'.[1] As Lionel Trilling points out, the author of such a comment has taken an irony literally and has misinterpreted a manner.[2]

One reason for the diverging views of critics in dealing with Forster's work is a basic uncertainty as to how the novels ought to be read. There is a deceptive directness about them—a concentration on events, which encourages the reader to read them 'for the story'.

Forster himself has never forgotten the truth which he reiterated painstakingly in his Clark Lectures: 'Yes—oh dear yes— the novel tells a story.'[3] Yet it would be foolish to see in this statement more than a basis on which to build. For example, there is a good deal of attention to plot in the novels: but it is evidently not aimed at creating the normal relationship between author and reader. An author whose main concern is to entertain his audience will sometimes surprise them—but he will also take care not to jar them. At the point of surprise, the reader will begin to recognize that preceding events contained the seeds of the surprise. Forster's surprises, on the other hand, do sometimes jar—particularly those irruptions of death or violence which break suddenly into a prevailing atmosphere of domestic comedy. On examining the context of such passages, indeed, one sometimes discovers that Forster has been deliberately leading his readers in a different direction: that the irruption of violence has actually been preceded by a letting down of tension in the narrative. The result is that sudden death enters the novel with the jarring quality that it has in real life. The harmonic pattern within which we were comfortably established suddenly gives way. There is a moment of unreality which we then recognize to be in point of fact a moment of reality—but the reality of everyday life, not of art.

Such intrusions of an unartistic 'reality' should in themselves convince the reader that this is no ordinary story-teller. If he is used to reading detective stories he may well draw the same conclusion still more strongly after reading *A Passage to India*. A novel which has the air of a good mystery story, with a succession of exciting events and promise of an unexpected dénouement, turns out to be nothing of the sort. Long before the novel ends, the woman around whom the plot revolves suddenly withdraws the charge that she has been assaulted by a young Indian doctor. The case is dropped, and apart from desultory discussion, we hear no more of the events that gave rise to it. There is no final twist of events, no sudden revelation. Many readers must have laid down the novel with feelings of disappointment or even of disgust.

Nor is it enough to read Forster for his social comedy alone. The late Rose Macaulay produced a critique of the novels which dwelt mainly upon these features. She had shared and knew well the background from which Forster came and described, with an assurance touched by nostalgia, his natural ancestors—'philanthropists, bishops, clergy, members of parliament, Miss Hannah More'. But her familiarity with the scene and her enjoyment of Forster's skill in evoking it also blinkered her. It was the natural corollary of her views that she should conclude by preferring the earlier novels, 'the three commentaries on then contemporary life that appeared from thirty to forty years ago—and have, with the years, taken on a delightful period flavour— *The Longest Journey*, *A Room with a View* and *Howards End*. . . .'[4]

The reader who comes to Forster looking for social comedy, however, will also meet with disappointments. He will be put out by the fact that the novels are not only serious in basic intention but sometimes deliberately flat in their immediate effect. The attractiveness is there, but it has a habit of disappearing round the corner at moments when one most expects it to be present.

A more promising line is taken by those critics who look at Forster's work against the moral traditions of the English novel. While acknowledging the high quality of plot and characterization, they see that the author is not simply aiming to make his readers turn the pages. He is inviting them to pause and reflect from time to time: to see in the events as they are described patterns which constantly recur in our world and to judge them by moral principles which are sensitive to the full implications of each particular situation.

For many critics this is a very satisfactory art-form, combining a number of virtues. There is a concentration on actions, presented in some sort of serial continuum, which gives an immediate reference to reality. The element of universality in the action makes for seriousness. And the fact that the reader is at one and the same time being entertained and reacting morally provides the work with a complexity of effect which challenges analysis.

So far as Forster's work is concerned, however, there are draw-backs to a strictly moral approach. For one thing, the social issues which are being discussed in moral terms are now somewhat dated. Forster's examination of the British Raj in India may attract American critics by its relevance to their persisting anti-colonial tradition. For British readers, the novel loses some of its point in a world where India is independent. Similarly, the unexpected eclipse of the old middle class and its power, to be replaced by a more amiable but less principled attitude in society at large, makes one less inclined to laugh at the absurdities of Sawston. It is too much like hitting a man when he is down.

Of course, this is not the whole story. So long as people have to live together in social relationships the sort of problems which come to a head in Sawston or British India will continue to exist. The moral element in the novels in fact burrows beneath particular issues towards ultimate human problems.

The 'moral' approach at its best can be found in Lionel Trilling's study. In his examination of Forster's work, he has been concerned with two objects: to test the novels by the touchstone of human experience and to match them against the best that has been thought and written during the period. The result is a highly intelligent evaluation of the novels in terms of the liberal humanist tradition. His concluding judgment has the weight of the whole book behind it:

> Forster reminds us of a world where the will is not everything, of a world of true order, of the necessary connection of passion and prose, and of the strange paradoxes of being human. He is one of those who raise the shield of Achilles, which is the moral intelligence of art, against the panic and emptiness which make their onset when the will is tired from its own excess.[5]

For many readers, this sums up certain positive effects of the novels with economy and deftness. It defines the 'singleness' of them.

But if there is a singleness in the novels, there is also a complexity: and that complexity is not simply, shall we say, the result of interweaving prosaic and passionate elements. It is a complexity which reminds us that Forster is ultimately a romantic writer and that his work reflects some of the tensions and conflicts peculiar to romanticism.

Nothing has yet taken the place of romanticism in the West. We are still romantics by birth, however much we may disguise our romanticism by devices such as cynicism or understatement. But since 1914 much of the original impetus of romanticism has been lost. It has lost its innocence in the face of Freud, its idealism in face of the events and policies of two world wars, and its positiveness in face of a world that becomes steadily more complex. It is not dead: most modern attitudes are romantic attitudes. But the fact that we describe them as 'attitudes' betrays the difference.

The peculiar forces which drove romanticism between the French Revolution and the First World War, enabling it to inspire a whole way of life, have gone. They will hardly combine again in a similar pattern.

To understand Forster fully, one has to see him at the end of that earlier phase, the spiritual heir of Blake, Coleridge and Shelley, of Beethoven and Wagner. He shares their aspirations and their struggles, while counterpoising them with his grasp of human affairs. The fact that both factors are present in his thinking inevitably affects his work. The straightforward run of the plot is not usually disrupted, but is sometimes diverted or distorted by this very individual attitude of the author's.

The exact nature of his romantic struggle will emerge later. It is sometimes critical, but rarely agonizing. His sense of reality is always vigilant, curbing his inward vision: and this sense of reality includes certain inbred attitudes which mediate between warring elements or damp their effect.

Forster was brought up within that stratum of the upper middle class which prides itself on its sense of humour and tends to view human affairs with an amused detachment. At its extreme, indeed, it might be said to cultivate the wit of Jane Austen while ignoring the serious purpose behind her humour. Forster himself, who is a master of ironic comedy, admires Jane Austen particularly when her humour is directed to a moral end, as when it points to a failure of love. For example, he likes the description of Mr John Dashwood in the opening chapter of *Sense and Sensibility*:

> He was not an ill-disposed young man, unless to be rather cold-hearted, and rather selfish, is to be ill-disposed: but he was, in general, well respected; for he conducted himself with propriety in the discharge of his ordinary duties.

Those who sit down to read Forster in the comfortable frame of mind that they associate with Jane Austen, however, are due for a shock. For instance, his developed moral seriousness emerges at times into direct utterances which she would not have used and which are calculated to attack the reader's complacency. He is also aware of violence and death with an immediacy that is absent from her works. This second factor may account for the shock which many readers experience at one of the famous sudden deaths. They are not expecting such directness to interfere with their comfort.

There is yet another side to Forster which makes it still more difficult for him to combine his forces. A combination of comedy and moral seriousness is an acceptable mixture, with an honourable ancestry in English satire; but Forster is also strongly emotional and imaginative. His devotion to love is backed by an admiration for spontaneous passion which finds its best model in the culture and mythology of ancient Greece. This element fits even less readily into the world of Jane Austen, and from this fact many of Forster's difficulties derive. But his truth to himself demands that he include this imagination and passion also, in his total vision.

Forster's difficulties as a moralist thus come second to his difficulties as an artist. His chief qualities are his gift for domestic humour, his moral seriousness, and his admiration for open-hearted passion. Normally one expects the last two to come into conflict. There are occasions when passionate behaviour is also immoral behaviour, and an author often has to occupy himself with the conflict. But Forster's difficulties spring less commonly from this than from the conflict between his gift for domestic comedy and his admiration for spontaneous emotional behaviour. By nature, the two are not ideal companions, and it requires a good deal of skill to prevent passion from either breaking so crudely upon a more delicate scene that it devalues itself, or restraining itself to the point of insignificance. Locally, Forster is usually successful, but occasionally an uneasiness in the total effect of a novel, or even more a short story, can be traced to the difficulty of making these two forces live together.

If justice is to be done to Forster's work, weight has to be given to each element in this nexus: comedy, moral seriousness and imaginative passion. And we are justified in asking how, in the first place, the juxtaposed elements should have come to exist together in his personality.

Again, the main reason lies in his background. As he has explained in the biography of his great-aunt Marianne Thornton, his mother came from a family that was closely associated with the Clapham Sect, the group responsible for many organizations associated with nineteenth-century piety. He himself characterizes the group by its 'affections, comfort, piety, integrity, intelligence, public activity, private benevolence'.[6]

His own attitude to the group has always been ambivalent. He saw in the mental attitudes which it fostered the root of much that was obtuse and unsympathetic in English middle-class life—that narrow patriotism and incapacity for personal relationships beyond a restricted circle which he was to satirize in his descriptions of Sawston. But he also has a feeling for it. Writing of the prayers of Henry Thornton, he says:

> What can the words have conveyed to the reader or to the family and the servants who listened to them from opposite ends of the great library at Battersea Rise? To us they mean nothing at all. We get something quite different out of them: no meaning, but an aroma, the aroma of a vanished society, the sense of well-to-do people on their knees, the solid chairs into which the elbows dig, the antimacassared backs against which the foreheads rest, the voice of the master of the house, confronting his Maker in a monotone, and, if the hour be morning, the great virgin breakfast table, clothed all in white like a bride. For three generations it was a problem to religious Englishmen whether the breakfast dishes should come in before prayers and so get cold, or should come in after, which meant a wait, and an unpleasant sense of hanging in a void between two worlds. I do not know which decision my great-grandfather took, but there is a story that in later years his daughter Marianne read the same passage out of the Bible again and again, because she was paralysed by the sight of the cat eating the ham, and felt unable to stop either the cat or herself.[7]

It is a good example of Forster in intimate vein. The serious criticism of Thornton's attitude is followed by a steady let-down towards affectionate whimsy in which Forster's highly developed sense of the ridiculous plays an increasing part. But in the middle, between the social criticism and the affectionate whimsy, there comes that recollection of an Evangelical breakfast-time which is neither critical nor ridiculous, but for a moment, almost in parenthesis, imaginative. Despite everything, there is a touch of nostalgia.

A similar fleeting moment occurs in the essay on Mrs Hannah More:

> In her later life she wished to dine out less, became intimate with the Clapham Sect, and ended by thinking nearly everything sinful: 'The word Trinity, you know, means three. I once lived in a street called Trinity Street. I do think it very wrong to give such sacred names to common things.' And 'He who is taught arithmetic on a Sunday when a boy, will, when a man, open his shop on a Sunday.' For my own part I prefer her like this. She gained nothing by being broad-minded; what is the point of just being able to tolerate Gibbon? She is more herself in the country, shocked and busy, and surrounded by her sisters.[8]

Once again the note of affection dominates. If we prefer her like this, no ultimate condemnation is made. It is being qualified by the fact that even Mrs Hannah More, in the midst of her scruples and prejudices, has her vision.

The sentiment has increased, if anything, with the years. He reproduces criticisms of William Wilberforce, for example, including Francis Place's phrase, 'ugly epitome of the devil', but continues:

> I agree with the above line of criticism. But I do not share the moral indignation that sometimes accompanies it. The really bad people, it seems to me, are those who do no good anywhere and help no one either at home or abroad. There are plenty of them about, and when they are clever as well as selfish they often manage to slip through their lives unnoticed, and so escape the censure of historians.[9]

This persisting respect and affection suggests a long-standing influence. Overtly, his sympathies would be aligned with Marianne Thornton, who could view the clergymen and pietists around her with a detached amusement, and whose accounts of religious meetings are flecked with descriptions of some of the more absurd participants and their activities. He moved beyond her, to reject Evangelical Christianity altogether: but certain basic attitudes of mind persist beyond the rejection.

This is no new phenomenon. It has been noticed before that the rise of the novel took place at a time when the more moralizing forms of Christianity were also moving into popularity. Constant emphasis on self-examination, and even more on the importance of motives rather than results in judging actions, encourages personal introspection and the habit of analysing other minds. It is a good training ground for the novelist who is to deal with psychological states as well as actions.

This type of religious attitude is also an enclosing one. It encourages privacy and the sheltered life. A good deal of the obtuseness and vulgarity in Sawston springs from the narrow outlook of its inhabitants. But narrowness can also produce an intensity of feeling which Forster finds sympathetic. 'People today,' he remarks, 'love each other from moment to moment as much as ever their ancestors did, but loyalty of soul, such as the elder Thorntons possessed, is on the decrease.'[10]

The intensity can be a characteristic of mental states, too. The enclosing forces of Evangelical Christianity encourage a tendency to hysteria, and it is probably no accident that some of Forster's most original writing occurs in his descriptions of hysterical states. Rickie's nightmares in *The Longest Journey* and Mrs Moore's experiences in the caves in *A Passage to India* linger in the mind long after reading.

Forster also retains some of the moral earnestness which one associates with the Clapham Sect. A recurring phenomenon in nineteenth-century religious life was the tendency of young men to take over the earnestness and love of truth which characterized their elders and then to turn them against the very doctrines which had been handed down to them. Forster is typical of a still later generation. His moral earnestness, duly taken over, rejects not only religious dogmas but specific moral codes. His chief moral demand is that men should be true to themselves—that they should not confuse either themselves or their memories of themselves in the past. A prime count in the case against Mr Herbert Pembroke in

The Longest Journey was that 'it never took him long to get muddled, or to reverse cause or effect'.[11] Mrs Munt, the foolish aunt of *Howards End*, 'possessed to a remarkable degree the power of distorting the past'. In the same novel, it is claimed for Leonard Bast that of this fault, at least, he was never guilty:

> He never confused the past. He remained alive, and blessed are those who live, if it is only to a sense of sinfulness. The anodyne of muddledom, by which most men blur and blend their mistakes, never passed Leonard's lips—
>
> > 'And if I drink oblivion of a day,
> > So shorten I the stature of my soul.'
>
> It is a hard saying, and a hard man wrote it, but it lies at the root of all character.

Forster normally avoids direct moral statements. That he is so open here is an indication of the strength of his conviction on this point. It is reiterated in *A Passage to India*, when Mrs Moore is repelled by the idea that India may be a muddle—preferring to think of it as a mystery.

A morality which lays so much stress on the importance of not getting muddled evidently owes something to the popularity of G. E. Moore's philosophy. *Principia Ethica* was published in 1903, two years after Forster graduated, and was widely discussed in Cambridge. Moore's chief point was that in our search for goodness we ought continually to be asking, 'What is a good state of mind?' And one very evident prerequisite of a good state of mind is that it should not be muddled.

The pursuit of honesty also links Forster's moral seriousness with his approval of spontaneous passion. An honest mind must acknowledge its awareness of passionate impulses. If it does not, it will eventually find itself in the unfortunate position of Mr Herbert Pembroke:

> . . . once he had been in love, violently in love, but had laid the passion aside, and told it to wait till a more convenient season. This was, of course, the proper thing to do, and prudence should have been rewarded. But when, after the lapse of fifteen

years, he went, as it were, to his spiritual larder and took down Love from the top shelf to offer him to Mrs Orr, he was rather dismayed. Something had happened. Perhaps the god had flown; perhaps he had been eaten by the rats. At all events, he was not there.[12]

Forster's morality is more likely to guide his characters towards passion than to lead them away from it. But that does not involve the condemnation of those who control passion. His satire is directed against those who try to ignore it, to forget its existence. Such characters are muddling themselves, and their muddling will lead them into triviality and peevishness.

There is also an important qualification. Old Mr Emerson, attempting to make Lucy Honeychurch see clearly in *A Room with a View*, stresses one point above all others: 'love is of the body; not the body, but of the body'. The converse is equally important. Love is not simply a bodily urge: it has a visionary, imaginative dimension that takes hold of all the bodily faculties and unites them.

The imagination confirms the validity of passion. Nor is the transformation which it effects to be regarded as a momentary, isolated, heightening of feeling. On the contrary, in the moment of exaltation, reality is revealed. We have thus moved, by scarcely perceptible stages, away from the run of normal human thinking. The moment of exaltation is being presented not as a welcome high point in a human life which finds its natural level in lower spheres, but as the reality by which other states of human existence are to be judged and against which they sink into various modes of unreality.

Were it not for this fact, the reader could afford to glide over the moments of heightened passion in Forster's novels with no more attention than he gives to the rest of the narrative. But if imaginative passion is to be identified with true reality, vigilance is called for. It is by such moments that other moments in the novel will be judged: and in some cases the judgment will be crucial.

Forster also recognizes the dangers of the visionary moment, of course. The experience of reality which it brings is a subjective revelation: and a character must beware of identifying it too hastily with the object which called it forth. Rickie's downfall in *The Longest Journey* springs from this mistake. But a recognition of the implications of this factor also helps to throw light on events and minor characters in the novels. The imagination, as the instrument of true reality, will always be on the side of life: and many characters will be dealt with less severely in their imaginative moments. The religious characters, for instance, have this saving grace: their view of life is, at least in part, an imaginative one. An ascetic young man will look at a young girl in the same way that he looks at a Leonardo da Vinci, ignoring her human passions and vitality: he will lose the girl, but will not be damned. And sometimes Forster goes further and suggests that despite the moral orientation of a character, his imagination still retains its proper nature, subconsciously ministering to the forces of life. So in *A Room with a View*, Miss Bartlett, always among those who are ranged against the forces of life, 'brown against the view' when Lucy and George tumble into each other's arms, acts twice in ways which guide events towards the very conclusion that she is striving to avoid. She describes the embrace to Miss Lavish (who subsequently incorporates it into a novel) in a way that shows, as Lucy says, that it must have burnt into her. And towards the end of the novel, though fully aware that George's father is in Mr Beebe's study, she fails to divert Lucy from entering. These unexpected touches make Miss Bartlett a 'round' character in Forster's sense of the word: they also suggest that even if her muddled beliefs have enrolled her in the 'armies of the benighted', her unconscious imagination remains, however obliquely, on the side of life.

Forster's imagination involves itself in his novels in a much deeper way, however, by giving rise to symbolic patterns within the works as a whole. The word 'symbol' is not one with which Forster himself is entirely happy. In *Aspects of the Novel*, for example, he discusses the ways in which rhythm can be produced in a novel by discreet use of *leitmotivs*, but goes on to warn that 'Done badly, rhythm is most boring, it hardens into a symbol and instead of carrying us on it trips us up.' Several exchanges with him, recorded in the *Paris Review* interview, help to bring out his views more fully, and may be quoted in succession:

INTERVIEWERS: . . . Would you admit to there being any symbolism in your novels? Lionel Trilling rather seems to imply that there is, in his books on you—symbolism, that is, as distinct from allegory or parable. "Mrs Moore," he says, "will act with a bad temper to Adela, but her actions will somehow have a good echo; and her children will be her further echo. . . ."

FORSTER: No I didn't think of that. But mightn't there be some of it elsewhere? Can you try me with some more examples?

INTERVIEWERS: The tree at Howards End? (A wych-elm, frequently referred to in the novel.)

FORSTER: Yes, that was symbolical; it was the genius of the place.

. . . . .

INTERVIEWERS: Do you have any Wagnerian leitmotiv system to help you keep so many themes going at the same time?

FORSTER: Yes, in a way, and I'm certainly interested in music and musical methods. Though I shouldn't call it a system.

. . . .

INTERVIEWERS: Is there a hidden pattern behind the whole of an author's work, what Henry James called "a figure in the carpet"? (*He looked dubious.*) Well, do you like having secrets from the reader?

FORSTER (*brightening*): Ah, now, that's a different question. . . . I was pleased when Peter Burra noticed that the wasp upon which Godbole meditates in *A Passage to India* had already appeared earlier in the novel.

INTERVIEWERS: Had the wasps any esoteric meaning?

FORSTER: Only in the sense that there is something esoteric in India about all animals. I was just putting it in; and afterwards I saw it was something that might return non-logically in the story later.

INTERVIEWERS: How far aware are you of your own technical cleverness in general?

FORSTER: We keep coming back to that. People will not realize how little conscious one is of these things; how one flounders about. . . .[13]

The last remark is a warning against reading too much into the novels, but not against finding symbolic meanings in them. Even when the pattern is not intentional, it is common experience that symbolic meanings may emerge subconsciously—that a writer may feel the 'rightness' of what he is doing long before conscious analysis (his own or someone else's) reveals to him the nature of the pattern which he has created. Symbolism, in its proper function, is not a set of counters for the author to play with. It is at one and the same time there, for his use, and yet thrusting unperceived roots into his subconscious because it partakes of the reality which he takes for granted. It is this interplay of 'realities' which makes the subject so slippery to deal with.

And to explore this sort of element in a novel means going behind the words on the presented page—a practice which is sometimes regarded as reprehensible nowadays. Surely, it is said, the critic's task is to examine the work as it is finally set down in print, without introducing any knowledge of the writer and his background. The point of view is a valuable one: it guards us, for instance, against the fatuities of those who imagine that they can explain a work of literature purely in terms of the author's biography. But it also raises many difficulties. What is the intelligent reader to do with *The Waste Land*, for instance? Should he simply read it at its face value, or may he resort to a commentary which will explain the relevance of Eliot's references to earlier literature? Should he read Yeats's 'Byzantium' alone and in itself as a single poem, or would he be justified in gaining additional illumination by reading 'Sailing to Byzantium'? And if he is, must he stop there, or may he go on to learn more about Yeats's personal mythologies?

Once a reader has been allowed to refer to any external source in trying to understand a work of literature, a new principle has been admitted, and it becomes difficult to know where to draw the line. How far may the scholar go in his search for references and parallels?

Common sense is the best guide here, and common sense

suggests that exploration of the world behind the work may continue so long as any light at all continues to be shed upon the finished work itself. After that, if it is still of value, it must be transferred to the sphere of biography or the history of ideas and not allowed to clutter pages which are meant for an illuminating interpretation and criticism. A way still has to be left open for oblique illumination, however, For instance, an item of information may help us to understand not the novel but the novelist. Yet the novelist may be present in his own novel to an extent that to know him is also to know his work.

This is the sort of problem which is likely to occupy literary critics increasingly in coming years. Under the persuasive arguments of Richards, Leavis and others, we have learnt to examine works with an analytic eye fixed firmly on the page. We have learnt to look closely at the texture of a work, asking at each point whether the author is realizing the scene or the emotion which he has set out to depict—whether the result that he offers represents a true exercise of the creative human intelligence. The approach, and the questions asked, are of major importance, but there are times when they do not altogether suit the works under discussion. There are cases where the reader may agree with everything that has been said in criticism of a poem or a novel, yet still be left with a feeling that the work is greater than the sum of the criticisms would imply. In particular, a number of works by romantic artists fall into this category.

To say this is not to underestimate the achievement of the critics involved, but to suggest that their examination does not take account of certain other factors. Their analysis is in no way crude. When they look for 'realization' and exercise of creative intelligence, they are not asking for any sort of naïve realism. They are looking rather for work where realism and inward imagination are brought together so tightly that they fuse into an artistic whole.

But many romantic writers do not and cannot attain this fusion. There is a split between their sense of reality and their sense of inward vision which obstinately refuses to close. It reflects a similar split in the world around them, which has little place for the human imagination except as a decorative accessory to life, preferring either to fix its eye stringently on the object or else to indulge its illusions uncritically. This split means that the author is conscious of a variance between the demands of his audience and the demands of his own intelligence. And in such a situation, a work which manages to satisfy both demands is liable to possess a peculiar ambiguity: to appear in one light to the common reader and in quite another to the critic who is aware of the artist behind the work. Vision and reality cannot quite fall into a single pattern.

The prime example of an artist in this condition is that of Blake. Some of his poems yield directly to the analytical approach, but in comparison with the complete body of work they are few. Elsewhere in his work, one becomes conscious of a split between what he actually succeeds in saying and the extraordinarily intense power of vision playing *behind* what is said, the imaginative background. Sometimes he even tries to convey this imaginative background through another medium, in his illuminations to the printed text.

A similar split between vision and realism is displayed by poets such as Coleridge, Shelley and Yeats. It has to be taken into account as part of their 'total statement'—and the failure to do so seems to account for the fumblings of analytic critics in dealing with them. For a part of the time, their work is moulded by consciousness of the audience: for a part, they are trying to render something which may be personal to the point of obscurity: and their triumphs are realized somewhere between these two extremes. 'The Ancient Mariner' is a good case in point. At first sight it is an elegant and fanciful ballad, composed for ladies of sensibility in Unitarian drawing-rooms. This façade drops away to reveal an achievement of 'pure imagination' which makes an immediate appeal to any reader in whom the sense of wonder is not dead. And at a further level it turns out to be a piece of symbolism in which Coleridge is trying to express his inward vision of the nature of the universe. Analytic criticism can reveal the presence of eighteenth-century sensibility in the poem, and can recognize, with respect, the less analysable imaginative achievement. But the shaping vision which gives the poem its inward meaning—that can be revealed only by study of and sympathy with the poet himself.[14]

The stature of such works is thus greater than analytical criticism might suggest. The artist's failure to communicate simply is due to his positive awareness of all the other things that might have been said. Romantic artists who create successfully in such a situation often do so because they have adopted some sort of mask which enables them to concentrate upon a single view: but there are other artists, and Forster is among them, for whom such a device would amount to self-betrayal.

As a result of his imaginative endowment and moral background, Forster finds himself at times confronted by the problem in its central form—the puzzling relationship between the inward imagination and the outer world of sense-perception. It is a problem that had occupied several of his predecessors and links him with a strain of nineteenth-century thought that leads back eventually to Wordsworth. The problem is particularly pressing to those who have lost their religious faith: the writers who most acknowledge a debt to Wordsworth are those in the tradition of George Eliot, Mark Rutherford and Thomas Hardy. Their moral seriousness makes them peculiarly aware of those situations in which the world appears for a time without that imaginative light that normally links us to it. And this state of 'visionary dreariness' can be connected to that conflict between rational analysis and imaginative vision which is responsible for so much in romantic thinking.

It is a familiar conflict. The imaginative man walks out on a summer's night and looks at the stars. His mood is probably like that of Shakespeare's Lorenzo:

> Look how the floor of heaven
> Is thick inlaid with patens of bright gold.
> There's not the smallest orb which thou beholdest
> But in his motion like an angel sings,
> Still quiring to the young-eyed cherubins;
> Such harmony is in immortal souls,
> But whilst this muddy vesture of decay
> Doth grossly close it in, we cannot hear it.[15]

Yet the same man knows, if he pauses to rehearse facts in the light of cold reason, that the specks of light at which he is looking come from dead worlds revolving through space. He himself and every other human being who looks at the sky on a night like this is by comparison no more than a speck of dust, created to flourish for a span of time which is less than a moment in the annals of the stars. He may enjoy that moment's life as much as he likes, but the overwhelming fact in the universe is the fact of death.

The gap between these two universes of imaginative life and scientific analysis seems unbridgeable except by an act of faith in some metaphysical order transcending the universe, for which there is no positive and convincing evidence in the world around us.

For those who reject such a solution, the only alternative is to look at the world itself and to look for any positive facts which might suggest an interpretative pattern. There is, for example, the fact of order. The stars may be worlds of death, but they are not in disorder. Century after century the same patterns appear in the sky.

And there is a psychological fact to be set at the side of this. Not only do these patterns appear in the sky, but they are seen by men, generation after generation, as pictures. One constellation is seen as a splendid man with armour and a sword. Myths are created about him. This sort of imaginative projection is also a fact, to be laid at the side of other facts: it tells us something about man that he should project his own ideal of himself upon the stars in the sky. There is a reality in 'shared vision' which is as true in its way as other sorts of reality.

Shelley would have argued the point vehemently: Forster is less vehement, but still sees the ancient mythology of the stars as symbolizing humanity's enduring vision of its own glory. He goes on to compare the glory-giving imagination of the ancients with a world in which development of the machine threatens man with meanness and loss of stature. And he is constantly, though unobtrusively, looking for other symbols which give an imaginative dimension to the world around us—symbols which will take their place quite naturally in the narrative of a novel, yet also fit a pattern of imaginative interpretation. The search for a pattern where the two forms of realism will interlock, where symbolism and plot will be perfectly reconciled, is one of the urges that leads him from exploration to exploration in successive novels.

There is more than one way of reading Forster's novels, but to read them with this point in mind helps to explain some features of them more fully. It shows that uneasinesses at some points are due to a jarring between symbolism and plot. It also illuminates his greatest single gift as a novelist. He has been rightly praised for his skill in plot-construction, in characterization and in satirical comedy. But in the end one is driven to agree with Rex Warner that his most distinctive gift is his power to evoke states of vision and nightmare.[16]

The nightmare states bear a strange relation to the state produced by overindulgence in scientific analysis—the state described so brilliantly by Coleridge in *Dejection: an Ode*.

> For not to think of what I needs must feel,
> But to be still and patient all I can;
> And haply by abstruse Research to steal
> From my own Nature all the Natural Man—
> This was my sole Resource, my wisest plan!
> And that, which suits a part, infects the whole,
> And now is almost grown the Temper of my Soul.[17]

In this state, values and imaginative experiences disappear or exist only as dead facts, identical with other dead facts. But as Coleridge recognizes, it is not scientific analysis that *produces* this state. The habit of exclusive analysis is itself a symptom, the result of an emotional failure to live satisfactorily in the world at large. Forster goes further than Coleridge in his exploration of the psychological conditions surrounding such states and his investigation is both subtle and profound.

In other states, imagination is so tuned to the outside world that the perceiver is filled with a complete and satisfying sense of reality. Such states may exist diffusely over a period of time: or they may be concentrated into a single moment, in which case they may appear as a revelation, important enough to interpret all other experiences and throw them into perspective. The idea is familiar to us from the writings of many mystics and particularly from the descriptions of the 'timeless moment' in Eliot's *Four Quartets*. Its importance in Forster's thinking can be measured by the fact that he called one of his collections of short stories after the story in it which is entitled 'The Eternal Moment'.

. . . .

It is not these elements in Forster's work that have most influenced the writers who came after him. In fact, some of his most enthusiastic admirers have deplored his tendency towards 'mysticism'. Cyril Connolly has pointed out the pioneering importance of his style: the extreme simplicity, the absence of relative and conjunctive clauses and the choice of everyday words marking the evolution of a more radically simplified, dis-integrated and colloquial form of art which appeals to the reading public of the twentieth century and has steadily ousted the 'mandarin' style of the nineteenth.[18] M. D. Zabel, on the other hand, is more preoccupied with Forster's moral tone and describes him, with his 'English' qualities, as the greatest single influence on writers of the thirties—'the one most clearly stamped by the peculiarly English skeptical sensibility and moral passion that has survived two wars with sanity and made possible the reassessment of the tradition and delusion that made those wars and their con-sequences possible in the Twentieth Century'.[19]

These qualities of style and content will speak for themselves in the pages that follow. The reason for probing further is that not all the writing is in everyday style and not every event or comment relatable directly to skeptical sensibility and moral passion. There are moments (often marked by a heightening of the style) when Forster reaches out to a sphere where sensibility is transcended by imaginative passion, and where his moral serious-ness is so dominated by an awareness of love and death that moral values lose their definition, their place being taken by a spirit which is less easy to describe, but which is nearer to the condition of music.

CHAPTER II

The Earth and the Stars

FORSTER has recorded some recollections of his childhood in the biography of his great-aunt, Marianne Thornton. There is no need to transcribe them in full: they convey events common to sensitive children brought up in predominantly feminine households. Some features, however, betray the future man. He was highly imaginative, and it is no surprise to find that at an early age he was writing stories—usually with a background of home or animals. One, of which he gives a brief analysis, treats religion in a similar domestic way: it is called 'Chattering Hassocks'. 'Fifty lions and as many unicorns sit upon hassocks, and the lions put forward a plea for tolerance and for variety of opinion which I still support.'[1]

Other reminiscences show a more individual taste. There was the house itself:

The garden, the overhanging wych-elm, the sloping meadow, the great view to the west, the cliff of fir trees to the north, the adjacent farm through the high tangled hedge of wild roses were all utilized by me in *Howards End*, and the interior is in the novel too. The actual inmates were my mother, myself, two maids, two or more cats, an occasional dog; outside were a pony and trap with a garden boy to look after them. From the time I entered the house at the age of four and nearly fell from its top to its bottom through a hole ascribed to the mice, I took it to my heart and hoped, as Marianne had of Battersea Rise, that I should live and die there. We were out of it in ten years. The impressions received there remained and still glow— not always distinguishably, always inextinguishably. . . .[2]

Perhaps it was the great view to the west that encouraged, even at this age, his great love for the stars. His mother writes, in a letter, 'he is determined the maids shall look for nineteen constellations this evening, poor things. He is quite annoyed with frivolous Emma for calling Jupiter a star.' Another letter relates that he has been teaching Emma the Great Bear and Little Bear.[3]

This love has never left him. In India, many years later, he wrote:

> One is starved by the absence of beauty. The one beautiful object I can see is something no Indian has made or can touch— the constellation of the Scorpion which now hangs at night down the sky. I look forward to it as to a theatre or picture gallery after the constant imperfections of the day.[4]

The stars, as we have seen, became more than beautiful objects to him. They came to stand for an ideal beauty, a perfection rarely attainable on the earth beneath: and man's devotion to the stars seemed in itself a recognition that all human beings found mirrored in them an ideal for which they were striving. Stars are common in romantic symbolism; with Forster, however, one is conscious that the symbol is not second-hand but an expression of personal feeling.

Forster's latent romanticism was more fully awakened by music, another lifelong passion. In his childhood and youth, the late German romantics were in fashion and he developed a taste for Wagner. Such music spoke immediately to his feelings: one of Wagner's operas provides a visionary scene in a short story[5] and it is against a background of Wagnerian music that Rickie makes his fatal, romantic misjudgement in *The Longest Journey*. In 1954, Forster returned to the Bayreuth festival and reported his criticisms of present-day methods of producing Wagner. Beethoven was another composer who appealed to him, with his constant note of heroism and even of triumph.

But meanwhile he was making another discovery of equal importance. Heroism and beauty might be attractive, but ordinary human beings often turned out to be neither heroic nor beautiful. Yet their lives and behaviour might attract by what they were in themselves, their very humanity. A number of relationships in the novels are adumbrated in his friendship with other children in the village:

I depended a good deal for company upon the garden boys. With one of them, William (Mr Taylor), I am still in touch and he remembers, as I do, how he led me on the pony into the wilds of Botany Bay. But it is Ansell whom I remember best. This was a snub-nosed pallid even-tempered youth who came to us shortly before Aunt Monie died. He was reliable but not too reliable; ' 'e done it isself' was his explanation when the puppy was patterned in tar. My mother in her kindness let Ansell off every Wednesday afternoon so that he could play with me. We mostly played on a straw-rick which Mr Franklin abandoned to our fury. More kindness. We slid and we shouted. Ansell hid and left his billy-cock as a decoy. Not finding him I jumped on it and stove it in, and this did ruffle him. Once we built a hut between the rick and the hedge: ' 'ow 'ot it is in 'eer, I've got the 'eerdache already' said he. We stored apples there, and could not think what ate them.

Nor was his education neglected. I neglected no one's education. Each week, as we walked round the edges of the fields, I recounted to him what last I had read of the Swiss Family Robinson, and he retold it to me fairly well, except that he would call Fritz Frizz. Arithmetic defeated him. He never could state how many chickens his mother had, however much he waved his arms, and 'Ansell and the Chickens' survived as a family saying long after we left Hertfordshire. For me he has survived in other ways. He was the good sweet side of the odious Blowdy Wags, and probably did more than anyone towards armouring me against life. That is why I bring him in. He faded when a professional armourer was introduced in the person of a snobbish Irish tutor who prepared me for a preparatory school which was to prepare me for a public school which was to prepare me for the world, and who supposed he had obliterated the world of Emma and Ansell for ever.[6]

From this carefree world, where human relationships were limited by few rules or social codes, Forster passed to the very different world of Tonbridge School, which he attended as a day boy. There is every indication that the more disagreeable features of Sawston School in *The Longest Journey*, including the contempt displayed by some masters for day boys, reflect a dissatisfaction with features of his own education. A particularly angry irony is reserved for the attitude which could turn schooldays into a miniature hell, the like of which the children would probably never experience again, on the bland assumption that 'school is the world in miniature'. Worse still, such educationists might succeed in making their belief come true: children who believed that school was the world in miniature might go out to create a world in the image of their school. They might remember all too well the guidance of Mr Herbert Pembroke, addressing his house on the first day of term.

Taking a wider range, he spoke of England, or rather of Great Britain, and of her continental foes. Portraits of empire-builders hung on the wall, and he pointed to them. He quoted imperial poets. He showed how patriotism has broadened since the days of Shakespeare, who, for all his genius, could only write of his country as—

"This fortress built by Nature for herself
Against infection and the hand of war,
This happy breed of men, this little world,
This precious stone set in the silver sea."

And it seemed that only a short ladder lay between the preparation-room and the Anglo-Saxon hegemony of the globe. Then he paused, and in the silence came "sob, sob, sob," from a little boy, who was regretting a villa in Guildford and his mother's half acre of garden.[7]

In such a passage one sees the germ of later discussions of British imperialism and of the suburban society which produced so many imperialists.

From his school, Forster proceeded to Cambridge, where he read classics and history. He found the contrast striking. The impact of Edwardian Cambridge on the young is described in his biography of Goldsworthy Lowes Dickinson:

He had no idea what Cambridge meant—and I remember having the same lack of comprehension about the place myself, when my own turn came to go up there. It seems too good to be real. That the public school is not infinite and eternal, that there is something more compelling in life than team-work and more vital than cricket, that firmness, self-complacency and fatuity do not between them compose the whole armour of man, that lessons may have to do with leisure and grammar with literature—it is difficult for an inexperienced boy to grasp truths so revolutionary, or to realise that freedom can sometimes be gained by walking out through an open door.

And later,

As Cambridge filled up with friends it acquired a magic quality. Body and spirit, reason and emotion, work and play, architecture and scenery, laughter and seriousness, life and art—these pairs which are elsewhere contrasted were there fused into one. People and books reinforced one another, intelligence joined hands with affection, speculation became a passion, and discussion was made profound by love. When Goldie speaks of this magic fusion, he illumines more careers than his own, and he seems not only to epitomise Cambridge but to amplify it, and to make it the heritage of many who will never go there in the flesh.

In *The Longest Journey*, similarly, there is a tribute to the tenderer side of Cambridge.

[Rickie] had crept cold and friendless and ignorant out of a great public school, preparing for a silent and solitary journey, and praying as a highest favour that he might be left alone. Cambridge had not answered his prayer. She had taken and soothed him, and warmed him, and had laughed at him a little, saying that he must not be so tragic yet awhile, for his boyhood had been but a dusty corridor that led to the spacious halls of youth.[8]

Society and gaiety were evidently important features of his Cambridge career. Intellectually, it is less easy to discover the patterns of thought or the writers who were influencing him at this time. There is, for example, a surprising statement in his biography of Lowes Dickinson. Having mentioned Dickinson's love for Plato, Goethe and Shelley, he goes on to say that these three writers have never particularly appealed to himself, so that he can only divine by analogy what he found in them.[9] Yet there is a platonic strain in his own work, and Shelley is an insistent presence. It is Shelley who plants the sign 'To Heaven' in 'The Celestial Omnibus'; he appears, with 'particularly bright eyes' in the essay 'Art for Art's Sake'; he is quoted with the highest approval in two other essays, and provides both title and key quotation for *The Longest Journey*.[10] It seems as though influences have often come to Forster broadly, through living among people who are steeped in a particular tradition of thought.

We have already referred to the interest which greeted the publication of Moore's *Principia Ethica* a little later, with its stress on the importance of considering states of mind when discussing questions of conduct. Another pervasive influence of the time was that of idealist philosophy. It would be almost impossible to avoid absorbing the habit of thinking dialectically. There is a strong dialectical element beneath the plot of Forster's novels which no doubt owes a good deal to such influences.

But he was not all passiveness. In this atmosphere of earnest truth-seeking and ruthless analysis he would also become aware that in certain important respects his mind refused to run in the channels prescribed for it by academic philosophers.

The first chapter of *The Longest Journey* is relevant here. Several undergraduates are discussing a familiar philosophical problem. Do objects exist only when there is someone to perceive them? Or have they a real existence of their own? They have chosen a cow as a focusing-point for their discussion. Does the cow exist when there is no one to look at her? Rickie, hero of the novel, is more intent on looking out of the window and enjoying the evening atmosphere, but at last he tries to address his mind to the problem. Either possibility strikes him as attractive. 'If she was there, other cows were there too. The darkness of Europe was dotted with them, and in the far East their flanks were shining in the rising sun.' Or, if the other possibility were true, 'A cowless world, then, stretched round him on every side. Yet he had only to peep into a field, and, click! it would at once become radiant with bovine life.'

At this point, Rickie pulls himself up with the reflection that he has missed the whole point and is, as usual, overlaying philosophy with gross and senseless details. Yet, for all the lightness of his fantasy, it has to be observed that he has brought to the discussion an element which is being ignored by the others. Not only is he aware of the evening outside (evidently invisible to the ardent philosophers) but he reveals a strong and vivid imagination. And between them the world of sense and the world of imagination can make the world of the philosophers seem a rather shadowy place. Forster never loses his respect for those who devote themselves to the path of strict reasoning, but it seems fair to identify Rickie's position with his own at this point. When the question of 'reality' is being discussed, it may be less important to consider the function of objective and subjective factors in perception than to consider the rôle of the imagination. For so far as the 'sense of reality' is concerned, the function of the imagination is vital. It is less important whether a cow exists when there is no one there to see it than whether the particular person who does see it sees it as a 'flat' object or surrounded by that aura of feeling-tone which is a feature of normal sensation and which can, in moments of heightened sensibility, give correspondingly greater pleasure.

Forster's career as a writer began soon after he left Cambridge, and during the next ten years he published a succession of novels and short stories. The short stories appeared in magazines. It cannot be assumed, of course, that the date of publication corresponds to the date or order of writing. The only clear indication of date from the author himself is his statement that the short stories were all written before the First World War. The first story to be published was one which has never appeared in the collections, 'Albergo Empedocle'.[11] Its theme is generic with those of other stories. A young man on holiday in Greece falls asleep in a Greek temple and awakens as an ancient Greek, with ancient Greek ideals and behaviour. Unfortunately, such behaviour forces his companions to have him locked up as insane. The story is amusing, but slightly cruder in construction than later ones.

Forster himself recalls, however, that the first story to be actually written was 'The Story of a Panic', which was not

37

published until a year after the other. He recalls, too, the circumstances of its composition.

> After I came down from Cambridge—the Cambridge to which I have just returned—I travelled abroad for a year, and I think it was in the May of 1902 that I took a walk near Ravello. I sat down in a valley, a few miles above the town, and suddenly the first chapter of the story rushed into my mind as if it had waited for me there. I received it as an entity and wrote it out as soon as I returned to the hotel. But it seemed unfinished and a few days later I added some more until it was three times as long; as now printed. Of these two processes, the first—that of sitting down on the theme as if it were an anthill—has been rare. I did it again next year in Greece, where the whole of The Road from Colonus hung ready for me in a hollow tree not far from Olympia.[12]

He had a third inspiration, equally vivid, equally strong—and this time the story was a total flop. He has never sat down on a theme since.

The two stories which did succeed are particularly important, for they contain themes and situations which recur in later stories, but are here to be found in a very pure form.

The first theme is that of Greek mythology. Lionel Trilling points out that Forster is a Hellenist, not a 'classicist', but also remarks, 'Surely the Greek myths made too deep an impression on Forster.' Elsewhere he complains that Forster's mythology is inappropriate to his theme. 'It is the most literary and conventionalized of all mythologies and in modern hands the most likely to seem academic and arch, and it generates a tone which is at war with the robust invention of the stories.'[13]

To one reader, at least, the truth is different. When the Greek myths are really at work, there is no war between their vigour and 'robust invention' of any sort—any suggestion that there is must surely spring from a memory of pale academic pastiches of Greek mythology rather than from the myths themselves. But it is true that an attempt to fit these myths with the circumstances of modern life runs into several dangers, and Forster is sometimes driven to a compromise and modification of tone. In *A Room with a View*, for example, he says of a bewildering afternoon, 'Pan had been among them—not the great god Pan, who has been buried these two thousand years, but the little god Pan, who presides over social contretemps and unsuccessful picnics.'[14]

To discuss this problem is to mention something that is central to the Short Stories. They have a particular 'period' flavour to them. They indulge that taste for fantasy which characterized the Edwardians and which died with the First World War. The figure of Pan was a familiar one. In delicate sketches of the period, gentle figures with sharp features play pan-pipes in the midst of delicate greenery. Behind them stands the final absurdity— Barrie's Peter Pan.

Dissentient voices were heard, however. Saki, in his short stories, dwells upon the essentially pagan, terrible qualities of Pan.[15] Forster goes a stage further. He sees the difficulty of introducing the real Pan into the cultivated Edwardian scene which he likes to satirize. His way of meeting the difficulty is to have the events of the story related by some slightly pompous and idiotic person, who cannot quite see the point of what is happening. The narration distances the events, while the implied satire on the narrator makes their seriousness more real.

This is the method which is employed in 'The Story of a Panic'. A party of English visitors decide to go out for a picnic in a wooded valley near the Italian town where they are staying. Among their number is a disagreeable boy named Eustace, who is busy making himself a whistle. Gradually a feeling of foreboding is introduced, first by the description of the shape of the valley ('the general appearance was that of a many-fingered green hand, palm upwards, which was clutching convulsively to keep us in its grasp') then by the strange silence which descends, followed by the noise of Eustace's whistle and the running of a wind through the trees. The adults take to their heels in uncontrollable fear.

It was not the spiritual fear that one has known at other times, but brutal overmastering physical fear, stopping up the ears, and dropping clouds before the eyes, and filling the mouth with foul tastes. And it was no ordinary humiliation that survived; for I had been afraid, not as a man, but as a beast.

The story continues with the strange behaviour of Eustace. He smiles, races about 'like a real boy', whoops like a wild Indian, imitates a dog, kisses and offers flowers to an old woman and, worst of all, fraternizes with the boy waiter at the hotel. His older companions decide that he must be lectured on the subject of intercourse with social inferiors.

But that night, the narrator is wakened by a strange noise. Eustace is down in the garden, running and cavorting. When his companions try to induce him to come into the house, he refuses and makes a long speech.

He spoke first of night and the stars and planets above his head, of the swarms of fireflies below him, of the invisible sea below the fireflies, of the great rocks covered with anemones and shells that were slumbering in the invisible sea. He spoke of the rivers and waterfalls, of the ripening bunches of grapes, of the smoking cone of Vesuvius and the hidden fire-channels that made the smoke, of the myriads of lizards who were lying curled up in the crannies of the sultry earth, of the showers of white rose-leaves that were tangled in his hair. And then he spoke of the rain and the wind by which all things are changed, of the air through which all things live, and of the woods in which all things can be hidden.

More attempts to make him come into the house follow, but all fail until the Italian boy is bribed into attracting him. He is then brought in by main force—but against the protests of the Italian boy, who declares vehemently that Eustace will die if he is shut in. In the event, Eustace succeeds in escaping again, and it is the Italian boy who collapses and dies. The story ends with the screams of the landlady and, in the distance, the shouts and laughter of the escaping boy.

Two elements stand out in the story. One is the visionary state of Eustace when he has come under the spell, as shown in the speech just quoted. When he is returning towards the house, he says to Gennaro, "I understand almost everything. The trees, hills, stars, water, I can see all. But isn't it odd! I can't make out men a bit. . . ." And when he has been brought in by force, he says, "I nearly saw everything, and now I can see nothing at all."

This idea of a total vision which is shut out by the constrictions of polite society, of an 'earth' which is hostile to all except a few spirits, is reinforced by the strong sense of place and pagan presence. The story, Forster says, was produced as a result of an encounter with the *genius loci*[16]: and almost all the later novels contain some such encounter: with Wiltshire in *The Longest Journey*; with the house in *Howards End*; with the Marabar caves in *A Passage to India*.

The 'sense of place' has haunted Forster throughout his writings, and he has never finally come to terms with it. He attempts to express his feelings, and his misgivings about his feelings, in an essay entitled 'The Last of Abinger', which records several meditations near his house at Abinger. The first deals with a landscape which, in the past, he has found sinister.

> Evening Walk round by the yew-wood on the Pilgrims Way that I have kidded myself into thinking terrifying. It isn't. The junipers looked like men, the yew-roots were silvery in the last light, and resembled skeletons or snakes, a ghostly little plant or two waved at the entrance of the great warm cave. . . . Yet it isn't, it isn't. And a rabbit moving suddenly in the dark as I came down—it isn't either. The really terrifying things are bacteria or the small trefoil that spoils my rockery. I have not time to see or feel this. I waddle on under a ruck-sack of traditional nature-emotions, and try to find something important in the English countryside—man-made, easily alterable by man. George Meredith, my predecessor on these downs, could upset himself with a better conscience.[17]

By now he seems to have laughed himself out of his former emotions, and to see himself clearly as a sentimental old man who is in danger of making a fool of himself. Yet the mood is not really destroyed, and in a later note he returns to treat it more subtly. He describes the feeling that oppresses him at Blind Oak Gate:

> No peace here. Only a sense of something vaguely sinister, which would do harm if it could, but which cannot, this being Surrey; of something muffled up and recalcitrant; of something which rises upon its elbow when no one is present and looks

down the converging paths. Anyone who knows the novels of Forrest Reid will realise what I am trying to say. He, better than any living author, can convey this atmosphere of baffled malevolence, this sense of trees which are not quite healthy and of water which is not quite clear. Yes—something is amiss. Our parish ingredients have been wrongly combined for once, and I can't honestly say I am sorry.

The last sentence is telling. Forster is now recognizing the emotions themselves as important. They have for him the same intangible reality as his feelings for Wiltshire or for the house in *Howards End*. Such emotions for particular places are part of his essential imaginative universe, of the reality by which he lives: and if they are destroyed, a part of his permanent life is destroyed with them. With characteristic acuteness, however, he now turns on these emotions to explore them further and question their validity in wider terms.

My head and deepest being said, 'We approve of your heart— *it* is important—but why exercise it over nonsense? Only those who want, and work for, a civilisation of grass-grown lanes and fallen crab-trees have the right to feel them so deeply.' Most people who feel as I do take refuge in the 'Nature Reserve' argument, so tastelessly championed by H. G. Wells. The moment nature is 'reserved' her spirit has departed for me, she is an open-air annex of the school, and only the semi-educated will be deceived by her. The sort of poetry *I* seek resides in objects Man *can't* touch—like England's grass network of lanes a hundred years ago, but to-day he can destroy them. The sea is more intractable, but it too passes under human sway. Peace has been lost on the earth, and only lives outside it, where my imagination has not been trained to follow, and I am inclined to agree with Gerald Heard that those who do follow will abandon literature, which has committed itself too deeply to the worship of vegetation.[18]

At this point he is confronting his emotions with the realism that his head insists on presenting. The emotions are important, they have their reality, but in one sense they are not 'real'. Any attempt to objectify them in the outside world by the creation of nature reserves or the encouragement of movements 'back to nature' necessarily creates something which is artificial, separated from the genuine emotions of those who are linked with the land by a living tradition. One is reminded of Wordsworth's objections to the presence of tourists in the Lake District: he argued that they would gain nothing, and only corrupt those who had truly gained from living in such an environment.[19]

This combination of genuine emotion with a sense that there is no practical method of making it real in the modern world is one of the permanent features of Forster's thought, and accounts for the impression of weary pessimism which he sometimes conveys. But the pessimism is only one side of the picture, for the emotion which cannot be given objective status in the modern world is preserved in the work of art. And the struggle between head and heart which is responsible for his occasional pessimism is also the touchstone of his integrity as an artist.

As it happens, his next story, 'The Road from Colonus', contains this conflict between imagination and a trivial world in clear-cut form. Mr Lucas is an elderly man who has at last come to visit the Greece which inspired him in his youth. But he has not found his dreams realized in the way that he had hoped. 'Athens had been dusty, Delphi wet, Thermopylae flat, and he had listened with amazement and cynicism to the rapturous exclamations of his companions.' The one thing which Greece has done for him, although he does not appreciate the fact, is to awaken his discontent.

His discontent drives him to hurry ahead of his party at one point, with the result that he discovers first a mysterious stream and then a hollow plane tree which contains its spring. The trunk is a local shrine and after a little hesitation he enters it. The experience which follows surprises him.

Others had been before him—indeed he had a curious sense of companionship. Little votive offerings to the presiding Power were fastened on to the bark—tiny arms and legs and eyes in tin, grotesque models of the brain or the heart—all tokens of some recovery of strength or wisdom or love. There was no such thing as the solitude of nature, for the sorrows and joys of humanity had pressed even into the bosom of a tree. He spread out his arms and steadied himself against the soft charred wood, and then slowly leant back, till his body was resting on the trunk behind. His eyes closed, and he had the strange feeling of one who is moving, yet at peace—the feeling of the swimmer, who, after long struggling with chopping seas, finds that after all the tide will sweep him to his goal.

So he lay motionless, conscious only of the stream below his feet, and that all things were a stream, in which he was moving.

He was aroused at last by a shock—the shock of an arrival perhaps, for when he opened his eyes, something unimagined, indefinable, had passed over all things, and made them intelligible and good.

There was meaning in the stoop of the old woman over her work, and in the quick motions of the little pig, and in her diminishing globe of wool. A young man came singing over the streams on a mule, and there was beauty in his pose and sincerity in his greeting.The sun made no accidental patterns upon the spreading roots of the trees, and there was intention in the nodding clumps of asphodel, and in the music of the water. To Mr Lucas, who, in a brief space of time, had discovered not only Greece, but England and all the world and life, there seemed nothing ludicrous in the desire to hang within the tree another votive offering—a little model of an entire man.

Mr Lucas continues rapt, but when his companions reach him, he speaks in his normal, settled, careful manner.

"I am altogether pleased with the appearance of this place. It impresses me very favourably. The trees are fine, remarkably fine for Greece, and there is something very poetic in the spring of clear running water. The people too seem kindly and civil. It is decidedly an attractive place."

He speaks pompously, but also with truth. His companion Mrs Forman responds with enthusiasm and insincerity: for she merrily urges Mr Lucas and his daughter to stay there for a week, but hurries them impatiently on when they show signs of complying. Mr Lucas displays remarkable stubbornness, however, and is only put back on his mule by main force.

In the sequel, Mr Lucas and his daughter are back in London, a foggy London where the light is still burning in the morning, and where he complains that he cannot sleep. Ethel, who is about to be married, receives some asphodel bulbs from Mrs Forman in Greece, and turns to read the Greek newspaper in which they are wrapped. To her surprise she reads that the little Khan where Mr Lucas had wanted to stay has been destroyed by the very tree in which he stood—and then that the event took place during the night following their visit. She congratulates her father on his escape. But Mr Lucas is busy composing a letter to the landlord, listing the reasons why he cannot sleep in the house at night, and he does not reply.

He does not even seem to recall their visit, and perhaps he does not recall it consciously. Yet when we look at the reasons for his complaints more closely, something else emerges. The incidents about which he complains to his daughter are the cries of the dog and the cat, a young hooligan who passes in the night, singing, and the water gurgling in the pipe above his head. Clearly, although he does not remember the fact, these correspond to the woman with her little pig, the young man who came singing over the waters and the music of the stream. It is the subconscious link with what he has lost that makes these things so irritating to him.

The point has been missed by critics, but it reinforces the story as a whole. Refracted through Forster's irony is the implication that Mr Lucas might have done better to stay and die in his moment of vision rather than return and live out an irritable existence which has no coherence or beauty.

This gives the 'moment of vision' a tragic undertone. The vision cannot last (even if Mr Lucas had stayed in Greece without being killed it could hardly have lasted for very long) and for an old man the only fitting complement to it is death. Mr Lucas ought to have stayed and been killed in the place of his vision.

The relationship between the visionary moment and death occurs again in Forster's writing and springs partly from an aesthetic necessity. Once a character has found reality in a moment of time, his creator is faced with a dilemma. If he does not die at that moment, fulfilled, he is almost bound to pass into a condition of steady degradation. One alternative has been explored in 'The Road from Colonus', the second is the theme of 'The Point of It'.

In this next story the visionary moment occurs at the beginning. Two young men, Micky and Harold, are rowing back into an estuary at sunset. The fields are shining and the windows of a farmhouse are glowing as if filled with fire, but the tide is against them and they are in danger of being carried out to sea. Micky is in roaring spirits and incites his companion (who is recovering from an illness) to greater efforts, shouting:

> "It may be that the gulfs will wash us down,
> It may be we shall touch the Happy Isles,
> And see the great Achilles, whom we knew."

Harold enters into the same spirit, shouting also.

> He made himself all will and muscle. He began not to know where he was. The thrill of the stretcher against his feet, and of the tide up his arms, merged with his friend's voice towards one nameless sensation; he was approaching the mystic state that is the athlete's true though unacknowledged goal: he was beginning to be.

Micky, enjoying himself to the full, begins to see the farm as a star and the boat as its attendant satellite, with the tide as the rushing ether stream of the universe, the interstellar surge that beats for ever. But meanwhile Harold has strained his heart. 'Half in the boat and half out of it, he died, a rotten business.'

The rest of the story concerns the later life of Micky, who remembers Harold's last words: 'Don't you see the point of it? Well you will some day.'

He does not see the point of it, for Harold was a young man of athletic gifts and aimless good temper: and it is difficult to see what is left when such a man dies young. Micky himself is intellectual, warmed by the love of humanity. He hopes to leave more behind him. He enters the British Museum, where he pursues a career 'that was rather notable and wholly beneficial to humanity'. He also marries. His warm devotion to humanity is matched by his wife's cool devotion to truth and it is a sufficiently happy marriage. Micky turns into Michael, then Sir Michael: he is benevolent, sympathetic, even serene. Only a single tiny criticism is offered: 'and if love had been modified into sympathy and sympathy into compromise, let one of his contemporaries cast the first stone'.

After death, he wakes in a dusty, degraded and senile landscape which he comes to recognize as Hell. With a neighbour he praises the restfulness of the place, and deplores the energy and restlessness of his youth. They proclaim their pleasure at not seeing the stars any more: Micky at not seeing Orion, who would recall adventure and his youth, his neighbour at not seeing Gemini.

"Ah, but it was worse," cried the other, "to look high leftward from Orion and see the Twins. Castor and Pollux were brothers, one human, the other divine; and Castor died. But Pollux went down to Hell that he might be with him."

"Yes; that is so. Pollux went into Hell."

"Then the gods had pity on both, and raised them aloft to be stars whom sailors worship, and all who love and are young. . . ."

The symbolism here throws a side-glance at the central theme of the story. But meanwhile a surprise awaits him. His wife is cut off from him, for there are two Hells: one reserved for those who love humanity and grow soft, and one for those who love truth and grow hard. His wife lies among mountains of stone. He begins to see the shortcomings of his own life. 'He had mistaken self-criticism for self-discipline, he had muffled in himself and others the keen, heroic edge.'

While they are lying there, a spirit comes to speak to them, a spirit which most of the souls try to silence and drive away. He is a spirit of light and song who reminds them of what they wish to forget.

"I was before choice," came the song. "I was before hardness and softness were divided. I was in the days when truth was love. And I am."

His last sentence reveals that he can heal the ruinous dialectic between the warm who grow soft and the cold who grow hard. He announces that their present state need not be permanent:

"Who desires to remember? Desire is enough. There is no abiding home for strength and beauty among men. The flower fades, the seas dry up in the sun, the sun and all the stars fade as a flower. But the desire for such things, that is eternal, that can abide, and he who desires me is I."

Micky accepts the challenge and dies a second death, a death of pain but also of desire. He stands up and soon finds himself by the infernal stream, then back in the boat. He goes again through the experience that opened the story, he hears a voice say 'The point of it . . .' and then he is restored to the golden evening on which the tragedy took place. What was then a visionary moment, not even understood, has been revealed as the eternal moment, the one that gives meaning to all the others.

In the third story to deal with this theme, the important experience is distanced by having happened long before the events described. The story itself is called 'The Eternal Moment' and concerns a popular lady novelist who writes a successful novel about a small Italian village, with the theme 'that man does not live by time alone, that an evening gone may become like a thousand ages in the courts of heaven—the idea that was after-wards expounded more philosophically by Maeterlinck'. The consequences of the novel's success are, however, fraught with irony. 'Idle people interpreted it to mean that there was no harm in wasting time, vulgar people that there was no harm in being fickle, pious people interpreted it as an attack upon morality.' The worst consequences are reserved for the village described in the novel. It becomes a commercialized tourist centre, and the peace and happiness described by the novelist are destroyed for ever.

In spite of that Miss Raby, the novelist, returns to the scene and tries to discover someone in the village who has not been hardened and coarsened as a result of her work. Eventually she recognizes in the concierge the young porter who, many years before, had tried to express love for her. Only now does she realize that in that distant moment she had experienced a love which had never been repeated. The man himself is by now as corrupt as everyone else; he is frightened by her discussion of the subject, afraid that she is trying to ruin him. Yet in the evocation of that moment Miss Raby, who has failed in everything else, discovers in herself a success which she had never previously grasped.

The dark irony of 'The Eternal Moment' indicates a theme which dominates in other stories. If Forster is preoccupied with the eternal significance of single moments in time, he is also aware that the trend of modern civilization is to produce people whose minds are closed to the imaginative and visionary. The idea is used with effect in a story entitled 'The Other Side of the Hedge'.

The story opens with a pleasantry which proves by its double layer of meaning to be typical of Forster. 'My pedometer told me that I was twenty-five.' At first sight this looks like a piece of rather tiresome, maidenly humour. But it turns out to have more significance than at first appears, when we discover that the road is in fact the organized road of modern life, and that the statement 'I was twenty-five' is literally true. Along this road everyone travels as fast as possible; it is never admitted in conversation among them that there can be anything on the other side of the parched brown hedges that line it. But the narrator decides to break through the hedge and finds himself in a timeless country. He goes on murmuring the beliefs on which he was brought up: ' "Give me life, with its struggles and victories, with its failures and hatreds, with its deep moral meaning and its unknown goal!" ' But slowly he comes to realize that this peaceful country, devoid of hurry and progress, is the country in which men were intended to live.

Forster has always been suspicious of the idea of progress and its vociferous supporters. In a broadcast talk he remarks that when he was young everyone spoke of problems, evidently on the assumption that problems were the stepping-stones over which progress was made.[20] The First World War killed the complacency of this attitude without substituting any other belief.

'The Other Side of the Hedge' is thus a counterpart to 'The Road from Colonus'. The landscape on the other side of the hedge is intended to give some sort of permanence to that which Mr Lucas saw when he entered the hollow tree. It offers the possibility of 'timeless living' over a longer span.

'The Machine Stops', on the other hand, explores the time-ridden, enclosed road of modern life more fully. This story, which owes something to Wells's *Time Machine*, depicts a world in which mechanical progress has been completed, so that all men live underground in air-conditioned comfort. Only one man and his mother have any feeling for the old days, a sense that something essentially human has passed from the earth.

Of the remaining stories, most are nearer in tone to 'The Story of a Panic'. 'The Celestial Omnibus' is a fantasy about a boy who finds himself able to travel on an omnibus to a scene closely resembling one in Wagner's *Rheingold*. The omnibus comes to a flaming rainbow; as the sun strikes down into the everlasting river beneath, maidens rise to the surface, playing with a ring and singing 'Truth in the depth, truth on the height'. But as in the earlier story, only the boy sees: the adults cannot understand, and the one man who tries to accompany him perishes in the attempt. 'Other Kingdom' and 'The Curate's Friend' both use the earlier device for incorporating Greek mythology into an Edwardian scene. The first story is about a girl who becomes a dryad and enters a tree, the second about a curate who is befriended by a Wiltshire faun. In the first case the girl is running away from convention to be at one with nature, in the second the curate receives unexpected help in the carrying out of his conventional ministrations from his pagan friend. In both cases a simulation of truth is gained by setting the story on the lips of a slightly pompous, self-centred and conventional narrator until the reader is driven to prefer the supernatural to his inanity. 'Co-ordination' is a pleasant story, notable for an ending which proclaims the twin values of Melody and Victory and for a strong reference to Beethoven and Napoleon which reflects Forster's romantic interests.

.   .   .   .

The stories have one aim in common: the presentation of some serious truth, within a body of fantasy, against the background of

contemporary life. Again and again, one particular method is used
for this. Domestic comedy provides the running plot but encloses
some fantastic incident which is intended, by allegorical significance, to give meaning to the whole story. Unfortunately, however,
the chosen method sometimes results in a flawed effect. Forster is
excellent as a writer of domestic comedy—he has an acute eye for
satirical incident, a close ear for the inanities of middle-class talk.
But once an atmosphere of domestic comedy has been established,
it tends to undermine the seriousness of the rest of the story. The
fantastic incidents which follow are liable to be read as part of the
full light effect of the story as a whole, not as events by which the
domestic comedy is itself to be judged.

One of the most successful stories in the volume avoids this
flawed effect by adopting a more conventional method to achieve
the same end. It opens, as so often, with light comedy, when the
narrator's notebook on the Deist Controversy falls into the waters
of the Mediterranean and is dived for by a boatman.

> "Holy Moses," cried the Colonel. "Is the fellow mad?"
> "Yes, thank him, dear," said my aunt: "that is to say, tell
> him he is very kind, but perhaps another time."
> "All the same I do want my book back," I complained.
> "It's for my Fellowship Dissertation. There won't be much left
> of it by another time."

The book is rescued, and the narrator left alone in a grotto with
the boatman, who proceeds to tell him the story of the Siren who
has appeared to one or two people in the district. He ends with the
solemn prophecy that when a man who has seen the Siren marries
a girl who has seen the Siren,

> ". . . that child can be born, who will fetch up the Siren from
> the sea, and destroy silence, and save the world!"
> ". . . Silence and loneliness cannot last for ever. It may be a
> hundred or a thousand years, but the sea lasts longer, and she
> shall come out of it and sing."

The style of this story, the last to be published, is an improvement on that of the others. The story-telling is tight, the humour

drier. There is no archness to war with the serious point, and the story of the Siren, coming from the lips of another man, avoids the awkwardness of making supernatural events appear in an actual scene. The ending of the story, in particular, compares favourably with the endings of the others.

Nevertheless, this story is successful mainly because Forster has here shelved his recurrent problem. He has distanced the supernatural story, making it a story within a story. His central problem of this early period remains: to find a way of combining a sense of the banality and reality of everyday life with some element which will lend depth and substance to his story. The method of fantasy within domestic comedy was bold but flawed in effect: and it throws back to a basic difficulty. Domestic comedy is essentially a realistic mode, allegorical fantasy a visionary mode. It was difficult for Forster to make the two modes live side by side and yet to be true to each, for he is aware that the modern world has little place for the imagination as a power in its own right. Meanwhile, in his novels, he was looking for methods of giving his work imaginative depth without recourse to supernatural events of any sort.

CHAPTER III

From a View to a Death

ALTHOUGH not published until later, *A Room with a View* was begun before Forster's other novels. Compared with the short stories, it seems at first sight to be straightforward social comedy. Lucy Honeychurch, a young girl of conventional up-bringing and romantic leanings, is being escorted to Italy for the first time by her cousin, Miss Bartlett. Miss Bartlett takes her responsibilities seriously, and is worried by an elderly man and his son who constantly appear on the scene. The elder Mr Emerson is a man of liberal inclinations who says what he thinks and whose thoughts are often unconventional. His son George, a pleasant young man, is beset by a *fin de siècle* melancholy.

The novel opens when the two ladies arrive at a pension in Florence to find that the signora has not kept her promise of 'a room with a view'. Mr Emerson, out of the goodness of his heart, offers to exchange with them the rooms which he and his son are occupying. Miss Bartlett is assailed by scruples, but eventually accepts the offer. From this moment, the paths of the four seem fated to cross: as, for example, when Lucy, torn between the bouncing life of the city and the aesthetic values which her guide book tells her to look for, meets the elder Mr Emerson in the church of Santa Croce. She says,

> "I like Giotto. It is so wonderful what they say about his tactile values. Though I like things like the Della Robbia babies better."

to which he replies,

> "So you ought. A baby is worth a dozen saints."[1]

Soon afterwards, two crises occur. The first comes when Lucy sees two men fighting, faints at the sight of blood and falls into the arms of George Emerson. The second comes during a drive to see the view from Fiesole. Lucy, looking for Mr Beebe, an English clergyman, loses her way, falls on to a little terrace and is embraced by George Emerson. The incident is witnessed by Miss Bartlett, who immediately whisks her off to Rome.

The scene changes to Surrey. Lucy has returned home and is on the point of becoming engaged to Cecil Vyse, a young man of aesthetic tastes whom she met in Rome. She begins to fall in with the life of the Vyses—as exemplified by a dinner party arranged by Mrs Vyse which consists entirely of the grandchildren of famous people.

> The food was poor, but the talk had a weary wittiness which impressed the girl. One was tired of everything, it seemed. One launched into enthusiasms only to collapse gracefully, and pick oneself up amid sympathetic laughter.[2]

Meanwhile Cecil, who believes with George Meredith that the cause of Comedy and the cause of Truth are the same, and who has also met the two Mr Emersons, in the National Gallery, decides, 'in the interests of the Comic Muse and of Truth', to bring them as unconventional tenants to a house near by. Lucy is worried by the thought of this fresh meeting and carefully rehearses the bow with which she will greet George when she sees him again. But she is not prepared for the actual meeting, which takes place when she and her mother interrupt a bathing party and George Emerson, running past her naked, greets her 'with the shout of the morning star'. Then, at a tennis party, George kisses her again. She tries to speak to him firmly afterwards, but he replies with a long impassioned speech of declaration and leaves Lucy and Miss Bartlett agreeing with each other about his impossibility. Nevertheless, when Lucy sees Cecil a few moments later, the scales drop from her eyes and she breaks off her engagement. She passes into a mood of detachment and decides to join a small party which is about to visit Greece and Constantinople. When she is on the point of going, she visits Mr Beebe's rectory and in his study finds old Mr Emerson, who makes one last impassioned plea for his son. The pretences which she has been adopting fall away, and in a last scene she is back in Florence with George, to whom she is now happily married.

The main theme is familiar and presents no difficulties to the commentator. We have simply to see George as protagonist of Life, Cecil of Art, and Miss Bartlett of Anti-life, for the main struggle in the novel to be evident. Lucy thinks that she loves Cecil, being ashamed of her franker love for George. Cecil, who thinks that he loves Lucy, really loves her as a work of art, not as a person.

But there are further subtleties in Forster's portrayal. Love, for him, is not a simple passion; it is a state in which the demands of head and heart are both satisfied emotionally. When Lucy refuses George, she is not simply turning away from bodily desire. Forster's description makes it clear that her refusal goes deeper.

> It did not do to think, nor, for that matter, to feel. She gave up trying to understand herself, and joined the vast armies of the benighted, who follow neither the heart nor the brain, and march to their destiny by catch-words. The armies are full of pleasant and pious folk. But they have yielded to the only enemy that matters—the enemy within. They have sinned against passion and truth, and vain will be their strife after virtue. As the years pass, they are censured. Their pleasantry and their piety show cracks, their wit becomes cynicism, their unselfishness hypocrisy; they feel and produce discomfort wherever they go. They have sinned against Eros and against Pallas Athene, and not by any heavenly intervention, but by the ordinary course of nature, those allied deities will be avenged.
>
> Lucy entered this army when she pretended to George that she did not love him, and pretended to Cecil that she loved no one. The night received her, as it had received Miss Bartlett thirty years before.[3]

The statement is central, and reverberates through the novel. Miss Bartlett is one of those who follow neither heart nor head, and Lucy is in danger of following her example. The indications of the danger are introduced subtly, for Forster hardly mentions his theme in the early part of the novel. But whenever his characters fail with their hearts we find that they become 'peevish'; whenever they fail with their heads they are in a 'muddle'. The two words recur at strategic points in the novel. Lucy and Miss Bartlett are peevish when they arrive at the pension; Mrs Honeychurch disapproves of music, declaring that it makes her daughter peevish, unpractical and touchy; and when Cecil tells her that the Emersons are coming to live near her, he notices that 'her face was inartistic—that of a peevish virago'.[4] Each is a situation in which her heart is unable to respond to the demands which are being made upon it.

In the same way, the word 'muddle' rings with insistency through the novel.[5] It occurs first in Santa Croce, when Mr Emerson says to Lucy, almost in passing, "You are inclined to get muddled, if I may judge from last night. Let yourself go. Pull out from the depths those thoughts that you do not understand, and spread them out in the sunlight and know the meaning of them." Some time later, when Charlotte is whisking Lucy off to Rome, she protests late at night, "It isn't true. It can't all be true. I want not to be muddled. I want to grow older quickly." The word recurs in George's long speech to her: ("That's why I'll speak out through all this muddle even now") and again in her doubts after her rejection of both men ('Was it possible that she had muddled things away?'). And the last doubt is followed immediately by old Mr Emerson's impassioned plea in which the word tolls like a bell:

> "Take an old man's word: there's nothing worse than a muddle in all the world. It is easy to face Death and Fate, and the things that sound so dreadful. It is on my muddles that I look back with horror—on the things that I might have avoided. We can help one another but little. I used to think I could teach young people the whole of life, but I know better now, and all my teaching of George has come down to this: beware of muddle."

and,

> "You can transmute love, ignore it, muddle it, but you can never pull it out of you."

To this plea, Lucy can only reply

"Give George my love—once only. Tell him 'muddle'."

As a touchstone of mind and heart, the two words, 'peevishness' and 'muddle' recur in later novels—both words describe Mr Pembroke in *The Longest Journey*, for instance.[6] And the true point of *A Room with a View* lies in this complex idea that there is a truth of the mind and a truth of the heart; both must take their part in the birth of true love, which unites the two of them, transfiguring them into a single, imaginative passion.

It is this central complexity of meaning which raises the novel above those romances which employ the idea of love frequently and uncritically to express an experience which, although vague, is represented as overwhelming and absolute. And the plot is tightened and stiffened by the fact that so many events and actions minister to a precise undercurrent of meaning.

The complexity also helps to explain the attitude which is taken towards some of the minor characters. In *Aspects of the Novel*,[7] Forster has made a rough division of fictional characters into 'flat' and 'round'. An example of a 'flat' character is Mrs Micawber, with her recurring 'I never will desert Mr Micawber'. The test of a round character, on the other hand, is 'whether it is capable of surprising in a convincing sort of way'. In an interview, Angus Wilson suggested that with Mr Micawber, we could guess at his inner being although he was drawn in the flat. Forster replied, "Yes, but we couldn't guess that he would make good in Australia, could we?"[8]

The unexpected action, which yet turns out to be evolved from the character's inner life, is a sure guide to the 'round' character. And the whole distinction helps towards an understanding of Forster's view of character. Does he in fact make a firm moral division into sheep and goats, as so many critics have suggested? Angus Wilson questioned him directly on the point, suggesting that his characters presuppose the idea, in humanistic terms, that human virtue and salvation are not a matter of works but an expression of an inner grace.

. . . There are no external distinguishing marks between your goats and your sheep—they cannot help themselves, they are either fundamentally good or they are not. Would you comment?

E. M. F. (*receiving this without enthusiasm*). The goats and sheep are too plain, surely. At least, many people have said so. No external sign? No. The goats are ... Well, failure to love marks them.

Forster's lack of enthusiasm for the classification into sheep and goats may well spring from a feeling that his characters are more subtly drawn than that, so that the goats are at one and the same time condemned, yet placed within a pattern of meaning which makes their evil comprehensible, not merely a causeless malevolence. Commentators point to Cecil Vyse, for example, as an unsympathetic character, and mention Forster's description of him as 'medieval'. Yet a second look shows that Forster does not regard him with extreme antipathy. At the point when Lucy rejects him, indeed, he rises to unexpected nobility. '. . . Nothing in his love became him like the leaving of it.' He displays unselfishness and lack of rancour.[9]

When Lucy tells Mr Beebe about her broken engagement, his streak of asceticism comes out:

His belief in celibacy, so reticent, so carefully concealed beneath his tolerance and culture, now came to the surface and expanded like some delicate flower. 'They that marry do well, but they that refrain do better.' So ran his belief, and he never heard that an engagement was broken off but with a slight feeling of pleasure.[10]

Yet Mr Beebe, too, is not an unsympathetic character. He is something of a man's man, yet has a particular interest in maiden ladies and a more restrained interest in young girls. His feeling for the open air actually aligns him at one point with Freddy Honeychurch and George Emerson in a woodland bathing party.[11]

We have already mentioned the twist in Miss Bartlett's character, which suggests that in the last analysis, and in her deepest heart, she too is on the side of youthful passion. The key to

Forster's depiction of all three may perhaps lie in an aside during his description of Lucy's interview with old Mr Emerson in Mr Beebe's study.

> She looked at the books again—black, brown, and that acrid, theological blue. They surrounded the visitors on every side; they were piled on the tables, they pressed against the very ceiling. To Lucy—who could not see that Mr Emerson was profoundly religious, and differed from Mr Beebe chiefly by his acknowledgment of passion—it seemed dreadful that the old man should crawl into such a sanctum, when he was unhappy, and be dependent on the bounty of a clergyman.[12]

Cecil, Mr Beebe and Miss Bartlett each display many estimable qualities. It is only their failure to acknowledge passion which marks them off and sets them in the 'armies of the benighted'. And beneath the darkness of their failure there remains in each of them some untouched point which enables them, on occasion, to pay tribute to human passions.

The various themes of the novel are given further play by the 'leitmotivs' which Forster uses throughout. The idea of the leitmotiv would be suggested, quite naturally, by his love of Wagner, but he also found it in contemporary writing. In *Aspects of the Novel*, he refers to the devices which George Meredith uses, such as the double-blossomed cherry tree which accompanies Clara Middleton and the yacht in smooth waters for Cecilia Halkett—but remarks that, graceful as they are, they only 'open the windows into poetry'.[13]

In *A Room with a View*, the strains of symbolism go rather deeper than Meredith's. There is, for example, Lucy Honeychurch's devotion to music, the one outlet for her undeveloped heart. When Mr Beebe hears her playing Beethoven in the pension, his mind goes back to an occasion when he heard her play one of the tragic Beethoven sonatas in Tunbridge Wells, and noticed how she accentuated the notes of triumph. He had remarked, 'If Miss Honeychurch ever takes to live as she plays, it will be very exciting—both for us and for her.'[14] After her playing, she decides to go out alone and Mr Beebe, watching her, says that he puts it down to too much Beethoven: Forster follows up the remark with the comment that Lucy never knew her desires so clearly as after music.

When, later, she plays for the Vyses, it is notable that she turns to Schumann's music, which is in tune with their witty weariness. 'The sadness of the incomplete—the sadness that is often Life, but should never be Art—throbbed in its disjected phrases, and made the nerves of the audience throb.'[15] Cecil asks for Beethoven, but she refuses, and continues to play Schumann. In so doing she passes a subconscious judgment on the atmosphere in which they have surrounded themselves.

There is another symbolic occasion when she plays again for the Vyses, having heard that George will be arriving.

> She had seen Gluck's 'Armide' that year, and played from memory the music of the enchanted garden—the music to which Renaud approaches, beneath the light of an eternal dawn, the music that never gains, never wanes, but ripples for ever like the tideless seas of fairyland.[16]

Cecil asks her to follow this with the garden music of *Parsifal*, but she refuses, and then turns to see that George has entered without interrupting. Again, the playing of Gluck and the refusal of the Parsifal music are significant. In the scene before her final encounter with Mr Emerson,[17] she is playing Mozart, with an excursion into Schumann, and ends by playing a song which Cecil has given her, ending with the words,

> Stop thine ear against the singer
> From the red gold keep thy finger;
> Vacant heart and hand and eye
> Easy live and quiet die.

The contrast between the romantic triumphing life offered by George and the weary turning away offered by Cecil is also presented in terms of painting. When Cecil meets her first in Italy, he is struck by the change from the suburban girl whom he has known into a woman who attracts him aesthetically.

But Italy worked some marvel in her. It gave her light, and—which he held more precious—it gave her shadow. Soon he detected in her a wonderful reticence. She was like a woman of Leonardo da Vinci's, whom we love not so much for herself as for the things that she will not tell us.

When he proposes to her a second time, in the Alps,

She reminded him of a Leonardo more than ever; her sunburnt features were shadowed by fantastic rocks; at his words she had turned and stood between him and the light with immeasurable plains behind her.[18]

Lucy in her turn, has an aesthetic vision, but it is a more vital one. When she sees George in Santa Croce, she thinks of Michelangelo.

She watched the singular creature pace up and down the chapel. For a young man his face was rugged, and—until the shadows fell upon it—hard. Enshadowed, it sprang into tenderness. She saw him once again at Rome, on the ceiling of the Sistine Chapel, carrying a burden of acorns. Healthy and muscular, he yet gave her the feeling of greyness, of tragedy that might only find solution in the night.[19]

In the bathing scene, likewise, George is described briefly as 'Michelangelesque on the flooded margin'.[20]

When Cecil mentions Mr Eager, Lucy remembers a lecture by him on Giotto which Mr Emerson interrupted, and becomes suddenly angry. Cecil's reaction brings together the two themes neatly:

He smiled. There was indeed something rather incongruous in Lucy's moral outburst over Mr Eager. It was as if one should see the Leonardo on the ceiling of the Sistine.[21]

But Cecil also finds approval for her outburst and goes on to pay tribute to this spring of Michelangelesque vitality within her:

He longed to hint to her that not here lay her vocation; that a woman's power and charm reside in mystery, not in muscular rant. But possibly rant is a sign of vitality: it mars the beautiful creature, but shows that she is alive. After a moment, he contemplated her flushed face and excited gestures with a certain approval. He forbore to repress the sources of youth.[22]

When he tells her that he is bringing the Emersons to the neighbourhood, she is again angry at his detachment. 'He stared at her, and felt again that she had failed to be Leonardesque.'[23]

Both music and art thus help, as underthemes, to express the forces which prevent Lucy from accepting Cecil's world and drive her into the more vital world of George Emerson. The central ministering theme, however, is the one that gives the novel its title—the theme of views and rooms. It is presented boldly in the first chapter, when Mr Emerson offers Lucy and Charlotte the two rooms with a view, and when Forster comments that Lucy 'had an odd feeling that whenever these ill-bred tourists spoke the contest widened and deepened till it dealt, not with rooms and views, but with—well with something quite different, whose existence she had not realized before'.

The symbolism of the 'view' is brought out still more strongly in a crucial, if somewhat contrived conversation between Lucy and Cecil. He has noticed that she never seems to walk away from the road to fields or woods when she is with him.

"I had got an idea—I dare say wrongly—that you feel more at home with me in a room."

"A room?" she echoed, hopelessly bewildered.

"Yes. Or at the most, in a garden, or on a road. Never in the real country like this."

"Oh, Cecil, whatever do you mean? I have never felt anything of the sort. You talk as if I was a kind of poetess sort of person."

"I don't know that you aren't. I connect you with a view—a certain type of view. Why shouldn't you connect me with a room?"

She reflected a moment, and then said, laughing:

"Do you know that you're right? I do. I must be a poetess after all. When I think of you it's always as in a room. How funny!"

To her surprise, he seemed annoyed.

"A drawing-room, pray? With no view?"

"Yes, with no view, I fancy. Why not?"[24]

The view with which Cecil associates Lucy is, of course, the Alpine view of rocks and sunlight and immeasurable plains against which she assumed Leonardesque qualities for him. But the first view, the view of Florence, has a more intimate place in her experience: for it is against this view that George Emerson embraced her. At the moment of the kiss, the view which the older Mr Emerson gave to her and Charlotte, the violets with which he filled the room of the Miss Alans, are the landscape around them. Words and actions echo beyond the immediate situation to take their place in a wider universe:

> Light and beauty enveloped her. She had fallen on to a little open terrace, which was covered with violets from end to end.
>
> "Courage!" cried her companion, now standing some six feet above. "Courage and love."
>
> She did not answer. From her feet the ground sloped sharply into the view, and violets ran down in rivulets and streams and cataracts, irrigating the hill-side with blue, eddying round the tree stems, collecting into pools in the hollows, covering the grass with spots of azure foam. But never again were they in such profusion; this terrace was the well-head, the primal source whence beauty gushed out to water the earth.
>
> Standing at its brink, like a swimmer who prepares, was the good man. But he was not the good man that she had expected, and he was alone.
>
> George had turned at the sound of her arrival. For a moment he contemplated her, as one who had fallen out of heaven. He saw radiant joy in her face, he saw the flowers beat against her dress in blue waves. The bushes above them closed. He stepped forward and kissed her.
>
> Before she could speak, almost before she could feel, a voice called, "Lucy! Lucy! Lucy!" The silence of life had been broken by Miss Bartlett, who stood brown against the view.[25]

The symbolism of 'life' and 'anti-life' which pervades the novel comes to a head here, when, at the moment of the embrace the 'silence of life' is broken by the 'brown' figure of Miss Bartlett. But there is also something more, a hint of further issues and subtler organization. 'This terrace was the well-head, the primal source whence beauty gushed out to water the earth.' The image is not just an extravagant way of describing an acute emotional experience. It suggests something more: that beauty is a primal reality, and that in this moment, therefore, Lucy is experiencing not simply heightened sensations, but reality itself.

Two people in the novel guide her to see this reality. The first is, of course, the elder Mr Emerson who, at the climax of his appeal to her, reminds her of the view from Fiesole:

> "Now it is all dark. Now Beauty and Passion seem never to have existed. I know. But remember the mountains over Florence and the view . . ."[26]

The other figure appears only briefly, but is interesting because he recalls Forster's devotion to Greek mythology. This interest is not so evident in the novels, but occasionally appears at significant moments. During the important description of the 'armies of the benighted' for instance, he remarks,

> They have sinned against Eros and against Pallas Athene, and not by any heavenly intervention, but by the ordinary course of nature, those allied deities will be avenged.[27]

The heart and the head are thus given their tutelary deities in Eros and Pallas Athene. But the third figure, the sun-like god of Love who reconciles head and heart in the moment of imaginative passion also makes a brief appearance in the novel, in the shape of the coachman who drives the party up to Fiesole.

> It was Phaethon who drove them to Fiesole that memorable day, a youth all irresponsibility and fire, recklessly urging his master's horses up the stony hill. Mr Beebe recognized him at once. Neither the Ages of Faith nor the Age of Doubt had touched him; he was Phaethon in Tuscany driving a cab.[28]

It is also 'Phaethon' who, later in the day, leads Lucy to George, as the result of a misunderstanding. Lucy, who is looking for the two clergymen of the party asks in her halting Italian for the 'good men'. The coachman understands her in his own way and leads her to George: and at the critical moment he cries out 'Courage! Courage and love.' When the party is finally driving away, Forster makes this comment on him:

> He alone had played skilfully, using the whole of his instinct, while the others had used scraps of their intelligence. He alone had divined what things were, and what he wished them to be.[29]

Forster's treatment of the coachman in these two passages provides a neat example of the virtues and defects of his methods in the novel as a whole. The symbolism of rooms and views is easy to grasp, for it lies on the surface and can act upon the reader's mind without his even being conscious of it. But it is a fairly obvious symbol. When the reader comes to the coachman, on the other hand, he would probably pass over Forster's description of him as Phaethon as being light-hearted—a swift classical reference with strictly local purpose. It is the same to a lesser extent with the other streams of symbolism: the references to Leonardo and Michelangelo are not readily connected by the reader, who is used to reading novels in which names and ideas of this sort are thrust at him in the guise of interesting chitchat.

It is thus that the novel is usually read as a light romance, employing the conventional symbols of outdoors against indoors, life against anti-life. Forster himself remarks that the novel appealed mainly to the young and to business men. It is only at a close look that the further pattern emerges, which throws the vague terms 'love' and 'life' into closer and subtler definition. Forster's use of the 'view' is straightforward: it takes its place in the plot and is fully realized at the point when Lucy experiences George against a background of the river, the golden plains and the hills. But because the other streams of symbolism fall away from the main current of the plot, the reader is liable not to see how organized they are, and how consistently they dam up behind the central idea to be released in old Mr Emerson's final plea for love as a creature both of body and of soul. Once this consistency is perceived, however, the novel gains in depth. The last chapter, for example, where so much time is spent in considering Miss Bartlett's part in bringing Lucy to George, ends with a brief paragraph which seems at first sight a rounding-off of the 'they all lived happily ever after' type. But the paragraph carries more weight than its length suggests. Phaethon has just reappeared, in the shape of a coachman who wants Lucy and George to go for a ride. When they refuse, he goes away singing. His song takes up the musical theme in the novel and then serves to introduce a different music, reaching below imaginative art to more basic instincts, which find their crown in youthful vitality and fertility. At this point, also, the 'view' finally comes into its own.

> Youth enwrapped them; the song of Phaethon announced passion requited, love attained. But they were conscious of a love more mysterious than this. The song died away; they heard the river, bearing down the snows of winter into the Mediterranean.

. . . .

Where Angels Fear to Tread may be regarded as a companion piece to *A Room with a View*. In the other novel, an English girl from a suburban town finds her true self by being exposed to the 'reality', physical and imaginative, of Italy. In the new one we see Sawston, the London suburb which is dismally representative of all London suburbs, drawn up in battle array against Italy.

The occasion of battle lies with a leading family in Sawston society, the Herritons: Mrs Herriton, the shrewd mother; her daughter Harriet, a starchy young woman who is a pillar of the local church; and her son Philip, a young man who has fallen in love with Italy—but with the Italy of art and romance. In the life of this conventional family there is an embarrassment. Lilia, the widow of another Herriton son, is brightly unconventional and constantly shocks the neighbourhood with her brashness. A temporary solution is being produced at the beginning of the novel, when Lilia sets out with Caroline Abbott, a family friend, for an extended tour of Italy: but this only leads to further trouble.

For news comes back that Lilia is engaged to an Italian. Philip Herriton is immediately sent out to stop the match.

Monteriano, the small town at which he arrives is, with its many towers and its Rocca, a thin disguise for the real town of San Gimignano. Santa Deodata, the satirized saint of the novel, corresponds to the Santa Fina of fact. Forster's descriptions of the town immediately remind us of his more straightforward runs of symbolism. The road to the town passes through a little wood which is to play some part in the novel and which stands in a sea of violets—like the terrace near Fiesole. In the town there is a tower, its head in sunlight and its base, covered with advertisements, in darkness, which is evidently intended to suggest the wide range of human experience in this small community.

In the opening chapters, Forster has been making full use of his gift for domestic comedy. When he turns to a description of life in this small Italian town, he has recourse to a different mode—a casual, drooping style with a touch of whimsical humour.

This house is bigger than it looks, for it slides for two storeys down the hill behind, and the wooden door, which is always locked, really leads into the attic. The knowing person prefers to follow the precipitous mule-track round the turn of the mud wall till he can take the edifice in the rear. Then—being now on a level with the cellars—he lifts up his head and shouts. If his voice sounds like something light—a letter, for example, or some vegetables, or a bunch of flowers—a basket is let out of the first-floor windows by a string, into which he puts his burden and departs. But if he sounds like something heavy, such as a log of wood, or a piece of meat, or a visitor, he is interrogated, and then bidden or forbidden to ascend. The ground floor and the upper floor of that battered house are alike deserted, and the inmates keep to the central portion, just as in a dying body all life retires to the heart.[30]

The presentation of the house as a labyrinth of decay with some life at the heart is cunningly achieved by describing the various approaches to it. The piece of humour in the middle is also related to Forster's moral purpose. The moral struggle between Sawston and Italy is between a society which thinks that people can be treated as business items and a community which makes many mistakes but never that one. The classification of visitors among 'heavy things' might seem at first sight to be Sawstonian: but the point of the whimsy is brought out in the emphasis on interrogating and ascending. This, together with the mood of the passage as a whole, reverses the effect, so that in the end the log and piece of meat themselves take on personal qualities. The absence of wit from the humour, like the absence of syntactical stringency from the style, is dangerous but deliberate. It expresses the slightly decadent but life-tenacious qualities of a society which knows nothing of the moral and intellectual stringencies of Sawston.

In the house described, Lilia lives with her husband. She made him buy it because it was there that she first saw him. As with Lucy Honeychurch, her love was the result of a momentary 'vision' but with a dangerous difference. The vision was sentimental, without basis in knowledge of the man, and therefore precarious. It would have been better left as a vision, but she was determined to bind to herself the joy:

> She made Gino buy it for her, because it was there she had first seen him sitting on the mud wall that faced the Volterra gate. She remembered how the evening sun had struck his hair, and how he had smiled down at her, and being both sentimental and unrefined, was determined to have the man and the place together.[31]

Her married life is brief and tragic. She is not prepared for the rigidity of Italian society, which leaves her alone for long periods, nor for her husband's infidelity. Quarrels and miseries ensue, and there is a moving passage in which Lilia suddenly finds herself longing for Sawston with its bicycle gymkhanas and Mrs Herriton's annual C.M.S. bazaar. 'It seemed impossible that such a free, happy life could exist.'[32] She comes to hope that her difficulties may still be solved if she gives Gino a child. Gino desires a son passionately—it is for him a form of personal immortality—and the son that is born to her might indeed have done something for the marriage. But she dies in giving birth to him.

Up to now, in spite of some ineptitude in handling the situation, Sawston has been right. The mingling of races has proved impossible.

No one realised that more than personalities were engaged; that the struggle was national; that generations of ancestors, good, bad, or indifferent, forbade the Latin man to be chivalrous to the northern woman, the northern woman to forgive the Latin man. All this might have been foreseen: Mrs Herriton foresaw it from the first.[33]

Even the staid Harriet is unexpectedly perceptive—'The whole thing is like one of these horrible modern plays where no one is in the right.'[34]

But now there is a new development. Lilia's small daughter by her first marriage, who lives with the Herritons, begins to receive picture-postcards from her 'littal brother' in Monteriano. After much discussion, it is generally agreed that the baby must be rescued from the clutches of his father, brought back, and educated in Sawston. Appeals by letter having failed, and Caroline Abbott having departed on her own initiative to adopt the child, the position becomes more desperate, and Mrs. Herriton swiftly plans a mission consisting of Philip and Harriet to fetch the baby.

In Italy, both Caroline and Philip find difficulty in not succumbing to the charm of the place as they had done before. Only Harriet remains inflexible, determined to retrieve the baby with a minimum of delay.

A visit to the theatre emphasizes the split between them. Harriet walks out in disgust at the vulgar behaviour of the audience, while Philip is caught and hauled up into a box by Gino and his companions, who hail him as a lost friend. Caroline Abbott returns home with her head full of music until she sleeps; in her troubled sleep she sees Sawston as a 'joyless, straggling place, full of people who pretended'.[35]

Next morning it is Miss Abbott who arrives at the house first. She is shown into a dusty, rakish, deserted reception-room which is sacred to the dead Lilia. From it she can see into Gino's room which is a complete mess. 'But it was the mess that comes of life, not of desolation.' Her sense of Gino moving about the house, unaware of her presence, brings on a hysterical state. Gino enters and, when she has recovered, takes her into the opposite room to see the baby. From any point of view, the passage that follows is the crux of the novel.

> She had thought so much about this baby, of its welfare, its soul, its morals, its probable defects. But, like most unmarried people, she had only thought of it as a word—just as the healthy man only thinks of the word death, not of death itself. The real thing, lying asleep on a dirty rug, disconcerted her. It did not stand for a principle any longer. It was so much flesh and blood, so many inches and ounces of life—a glorious, unquestionable fact, which a man and another woman had given to the world. You could talk to it; in time it would answer you; in time it would not answer you unless it chose, but would secrete, within the compass of its body, thoughts and wonderful passions of its own. And this was the machine on which she and Mrs Herriton and Philip and Harriet had for the last month been exercising their various ideals—had determined that in time it should move this way or that way, should accomplish this and not that. It was to be Low Church, it was to be high-principled, it was to be tactful, gentlemanly, artistic—excellent things all. Yet now that she saw this baby, lying asleep on a dirty rug, she had a great disposition not to dictate one of them, and to exert no more influence than there may be in a kiss or in the vaguest of the heartfelt prayers.[36]

That last sentence, with its combination of sentiment and realism, reminds one of George Eliot. A similar moral tone persists through the rest of the chapter, dominated as it is by the real, physical presence of the baby. Gino and Caroline discuss fiercely, they even quarrel, but in the end they find themselves washing the baby together.

From this point, Caroline begins to turn against the Herriton plan. In a fierce interview with Philip she urges him to make up his mind on a right course of action and then to pursue it. He says that he seems fated to pass through the world without colliding with it or moving it—that life to him is just a spectacle—and she replies, 'I wish something would happen to you, my dear friend; I wish something would happen to you.' Her arguments culminate in the contention that there is such a thing as the moment of moral choice:

". . . I feel you ought to fight it out with Harriet. Every little trifle, for some reason, does seem incalculably important today, and when you say of a thing that 'nothing hangs on it', it sounds like blasphemy. There's never any knowing—(how am I to put it?)—which of our actions, which of our idlenesses won't have things hanging on it for ever."[37]

For Philip the moment is crucial and he fails to respond existentially. 'He assented, but her remark had only an aesthetic value. He was not prepared to take it to his heart.' The result of his detachment follows swiftly. Harriet arranges that they shall catch the train for England that evening. Meanwhile, on her own initiative, she steals the baby. On the way to the station, the carriage overturns in the little wood and the baby is killed.

There follows a scene in which Philip goes to tell Gino what has happened and Gino responds by attacking and torturing him. He is rescued by the arrival of Miss Abbott, who intervenes and ministers to both men. The final scene takes place in the train bound for England. Philip brings Caroline to the point where he might propose marriage to her, only to elicit the confession that she is passionately in love with Gino, who is about to marry someone else.

As a straightforward narrative, the novel succeeds brilliantly in pitting Italian life against Sawston obtuseness without underestimating either the crudity and mess of the one or the hooded wisdom of the other. The burden of the attack on Sawston is not general but particular. At its worst it treats people as objects which it can trade in and use, and this is its unforgivable sin. That one moral point is in itself enough to sustain the narrative.

But once again the novel contains other elements. There is the character of Philip, for instance. In the beginning he believes that he has shaken off the trammels of Sawston in favour of Italy, but his 'Italy' is an aesthetic idea which cannot survive the blasts of contact with real Italian life. Even the idea of a dentist in Monteriano is enough to blow his vision sky high. The course of the novel is for him a progress from aesthetic detachment to involvement with life. When the process eventually culminates in his sight of Caroline Abbott ministering to Gino, Forster remarks, 'Quietly, without hysterical prayers or banging of drums, he underwent conversion. He was saved.'[38] The momentary indulgence in religious language reminds us of Forster's Evangelical background and suggests a slight residual preoccupation with the salvation of his characters. But of course Philip's salvation is in no way orthodox. It takes place as the result of several 'visionary moments'.

The moments pass quickly, and it is easy to take them in one's stride without grasping their full implications. It is an inevitable difficulty in writing narrative: the novelist feels the want of some device for slowing down events and impressing them with significance in the way that a film producer can rest his camera on a scene for several seconds. There is no equivalent technique in writing, but it is evidently the effect intended by Forster in his description of the first 'moment'—the moment when Philip enters to see Gino and Caroline with the newly-bathed baby.

> It shone now with health and beauty; it seemed to reflect light, like a copper vessel. Just such a baby Bellini sets languid on his mother's lap or Signorelli flings wriggling on pavements of marble, or Lorenzo di Credi, more reverent but less divine, lays carefully among flowers, with his head upon a wisp of golden straw. For a time Gino contemplated them standing. Then, to get a better view, he knelt by the side of the chair, with his hands clasped before him.
>
> So they were when Philip entered, and saw, to all intents and purposes, the Virgin and Child, with Donor.[39]

The casualness of the last sentence and its brevity—the 'to all intents and purposes'—invites fast reading, as though it were simply a clever observation. Yet its implications hang over the rest of the novel, to be reinforced later. Philip sees the scene, but sees it only aesthetically. Before he can grasp it properly he has to pass through a very different moment, one that owes little to the imagination. It is the moment in the carriage when Harriet shows him the stolen baby.

Philip winced. "His face, do you know, struck me as all wrong."

"All wrong?"

"All puckered queerly."

"Of course—with the shadows—you couldn't see him."

"Well, hold him up again." She did so. He lit another match. It went out quickly, but not before he had seen that the baby was crying.

"Nonsense," said Harriet sharply. "We should hear him if he cried."

"No, he's crying hard; I thought so before, and I'm certain now."

Harriet touched the child's face. It was bathed in tears. "Oh, the night air, I suppose," she said, "or perhaps the wet of the rain."

"I say, you haven't hurt it, or held it the wrong way, or anything; it is too uncanny—crying and no noise . . ."

. . . "Philip, don't talk. Must I say it again? Don't talk. The baby wants to sleep." She crooned harshly as they descended, and now and then she wiped up the tears which welled inexhaustibly from the little eyes. Philip looked away, winking at times himself. It was as if they were travelling with the whole world's sorrow, as if all the mystery, all the persistency of woe were gathered to a single fount.[40]

This episode is Forster's closest attempt to deal with the facts of evil and suffering in the early novels. The stupidity of Harriet and the unconcern of Philip have led to this moment, which seems while it lasts to symbolize all the misery in the world that is caused by stupidity and unconcern.

This moment of realism is the complement to the moment in which Caroline Abbott first saw the baby and saw it as a being in its own right, a subject as well as an object. It prepares Philip for the moment in which he sees Caroline Abbott in her true glory.

All through the day Miss Abbott had seemed to Philip like a goddess, and more than ever did she seem so now. Many people look younger and more intimate during great emotion. But some there are who look older, and remote, and he could not think that there was little difference in years, and none in composition, between her and the man whose head was laid upon her breast. Her eyes were open, full of infinite pity and full of majesty, as if they discerned the boundaries of sorrow, and saw unimaginable tracts beyond. Such eyes he had seen in great pictures but never in a mortal. Her hands were folded round the sufferer, stroking him lightly, for even a goddess can do no more than that. . . .

Philip looked away, as he sometimes looked away from the great pictures where visible forms suddenly became inadequate for the things they have shown to us.[41]

In Philip's two visions of Miss Abbott, the first purely aesthetic, the second passing through the aesthetic to the existential, Forster is using two of his favourite visionary modes—Italian renaissance painting and Greek mythology—to express his own form of humanism. His humanism includes the realism which works for social services and against social abuses, but regards this as unfulfilled unless it is led on to a point where it can see humanity as touched with glory—can see it neither statistically nor sentimentally, but with passion. This central point takes us, once again, beyond the straightforward values of 'truth and kindliness'. Forster suggests, here and elsewhere, that the two tend to get separated, that individual human beings swing towards one or the other and become preoccupied with it to their own destruction, unless they are backed by the more passionate vision, found for example in Italian painting or Greek mythology, that can bring together and organize the other values.

But it is only in the last chapter that one can see how vision has chimed against plot throughout. For in this novel, Forster has elected a different method—not to weave the visionary moments into the running plot as dynamic mechanisms, but to put them at one side as a running interpretation of what is happening, so that the full pattern is not seen until the end.

It is a subtle method, and one that is not readily apparent to the casual reader. It is easy to seize on Caroline Abbott's speech to Philip when she speaks of her physical love for Gino and to see in that the key to the novel as a whole:

> "Don't talk of 'faults'. You're my friend for ever, Mr Herriton, I think. Only don't be charitable and shift or take the blame. Get over supposing I'm refined. That's what puzzles you. Get over that."[42]

If the plot is regarded as a simple, consecutive unwinding, this statement rounds it off. Caroline has confessed to a coarse physical love for Gino which explains her own past conduct and means that any sort of love for Philip would now be out of the question. Philip's reactions then appear to be a slightly extravagant recognition of the fact

> As she spoke she seemed to be transfigured, and to have indeed no part with refinement or unrefinement any longer. Out of this wreck there was revealed to him something indestructible—something which she, who had given it, could never take away.
> "I say again, don't be charitable. If he had asked me, I might have given myself body and soul. That would have been the end of my rescue party. But all through he took me for a superior being—a goddess. I who was worshipping every inch of him, and every word he spoke. And that saved me."
> Philip's eyes were fixed on the Campanile of Airolo. But he saw instead the fair myth of Endymion. This woman was a goddess to the end. For her no love could be degrading: she stood outside all degradation. This episode, which she thought so sordid, and which was so tragic for him, remained supremely beautiful. To such a height was he lifted, that without regret he could now have told her that he was her worshipper too. . . .

At first sight this is high-flown emotion, and Forster's use of the word 'goddess' mere extravagance. But when one has followed the earlier clues it emerges differently. The relationship between Gino and Caroline is the apotheosis of humanity. What Caroline

75

herself sees as coarse passion is nothing of the sort. It is being revealed to Philip as passion transformed by imagination, which is in Forster's eyes the incarnation of the divine in the human. Gino, Caroline and the baby in the earlier scene are the true 'holy family'. What might appear at first to be a slightly cynical recall from ideals of spiritual and aesthetic love to material, physical realities turns out to be different. It is a reiteration of old Mr Emerson's plea, 'Love is of the body: not the body but of the body'.

Forster has in this novel made his basic philosophy so esoteric, so dependent on one or two key passages, that this further dimension is easily overlooked. On the other hand, he gains from this method, so far as the 'common reader' is concerned. This novel, as a device for making the reader turn the pages, is the best of them all. Moreover, it succeeds in combining an absorbing plot with a convincing moral point.

But when one looks deeper that moral point turns out not to be the central one. It is subordinate to another. The relationship between Caroline and Gino is the central fact, the moment of reality which condemns every other fact in the novel to varying degrees of unreality. In particular, it throws light on that other moment of moral choice when Harriet decided to rescue the baby and Philip stood back in detachment to observe. On the level of humanist reasoning this was a moral failure on Philip's part. One ought not to stand by in silence while others treat people as things. But when the other dimension opens out, it also emerges as a failure of vision. Had he been enrolled in the reality which enshrined Gino and Caroline, he could not have consented, either tacitly or otherwise, to the removal of the child, and the refusal would have come not from reason alone but from his whole self. True morality is dependent on vision.

This peculiar relationship between the 'moment' of vision and the 'moment' of moral choice is explored with still more subtlety in the next novel, *The Longest Journey*.

CHAPTER IV

Flame Boats on a Stream

*T*HE *LONGEST JOURNEY* marks a turning-point in Forster's development. It is also his most intense achievement. *Howards End* and *A Passage to India* are broader novels, worked on a larger canvas, but this novel is notable for its devotion to certain personal themes and for its subtlety and insight in dealing with those themes. Forster himself has described it as his 'preferred novel'.[1]

The novel opens with a group of undergraduates in Cambridge taking part in a philosophical discussion. This is not just a piece of local colouring, for the subject of their discussion turns out to touch the central theme of the novel. They are discussing the nature of reality. In their case, the discussion follows a well-worn path.

> They were discussing the existence of objects. Do they exist only when there is someone to look at them? Or have they a real existence of their own? It is all very interesting, but at the same time it is difficult. Hence the cow. She seemed to make things easier. She was so familiar, so solid, that surely the truths that she illustrated would in time become familiar and solid also. Is the cow there or not? This was better than deciding between objectivity and subjectivity. So at Oxford, just at the same time, one was asking, "What do our rooms look like in the vac.?"

One of the leading participants in the argument is Stewart Ansell, who stands throughout the novel as an embodiment of one virtue to be found at times in Cambridge—the disinterested pursuit of truth. When Forster wants to depict Ansell's personality, he pictures him drawing within a square a circle and within the circle a square, and inside that another circle, and inside that another square, and then explaining that the real figure is the one in the middle, that there's never room enough to draw.

In the background sits Rickie, owner of the room and hero of the novel, endeavouring to take part in the discussion, not finding it easy to do so. The elms beyond the window in the evening sky are Dryads, he is sure. And when he consciously recalls his attention from them to the problem of the cow, his imagination insists on painting her, too, in romantic colours.

> Either way it was attractive. If she was there, other cows were there, too. The darkness of Europe was dotted with them, and in the far East their flanks were shining in the rising sun. Great herds of them stood browsing in pastures where no man came nor need ever come, or splashed knee-deep by the brink of impassable rivers. And this, moreover, was the view of Ansell. Yet Tilliard's view had a good deal in it. One might do worse than follow Tilliard, and suppose the cow not to be there unless oneself was there to see her. A cowless world, then, stretched round him on every side. Yet he had only to peep into a field, and, click! it would at once become radiant with bovine life.

Then he realizes that something is wrong with all this. He has been overlaying philosophy with gross and senseless details. If the cow is not there, the world and the fields are not there either. He rebukes himself.

Yet, as we have said earlier, his reflections not only reveal a good deal of his own personality, but throw some light on the discussion itself. For the imagination *is* relevant to the problem of reality. It is an essential component in what we call our 'sense of reality', working with the world that is presented to our senses to create a world which will be at once true to itself and organized within our own minds. The danger for Rickie, however, is that his imagination may assume too powerful a place, until it dominates his perceptions and distorts the world outside to fit a more attractive pattern of its own.

A point of danger soon occurs. The party is broken up by the sudden entry of Agnes, who is visiting Rickie in Cambridge with her brother, Herbert Pembroke. Rickie, who invited them, has forgotten the invitation. At the moment when she enters the room, his susceptible imagination is impressed by her beauty. He is impressed at a deeper level when he visits her in Sawston later. He sees her in the arms of her lover, Gerald Dawes, and despite his knowledge of Gerald as a bully and a cad, the glimpse is a revelation of the glamour of mortal passion.

Gerald dies almost immediately afterwards, broken up in a rugby match. Everyone offers conventional comfort to Agnes except Rickie, who insists to her that she must care—' "In God's name, mind such a thing, and don't sit fencing with your soul." ' When he returns to Cambridge, he indulges in some of his usual artistic dreams, only to abandon them at a thought of the dead Gerald and the living Agnes: and when she visits Cambridge again in June, he becomes engaged to her.

The scene changes to Cadover, the Wiltshire home of Rickie's aunt Mrs Failing, a realistic woman who is inclined to reason in 'the facile vein of Ibsenism'.[2] She has lost her husband, who was an ardent socialist rather in the tradition of old Mr Emerson, and now looks after a pagan young man named Stephen Wonham. Rickie and Agnes are staying with her and all four make an expedition to Cadbury Rings. The symbolism of the place is stressed ('the fibres of England unite in Wiltshire')[3] and at the very heart of the Rings, Mrs Failing reveals casually to Rickie that Stephen is his half-brother. He faints.

The moment is of vital importance to Rickie and he recognizes the fact. Earlier in the story, Forster has commented on his lack of experience:

> . . . his friends are as young and as ignorant as himself. They are full of the wine of life. But they have not tasted the cup—let us call it the teacup—of experience, which has made men of Mr Pembroke's type what they are. Oh, that teacup! To be taken at prayers, at friendship, at love, till we are quite sane, quite efficient, quite experienced, and quite useless to God or man. We must drink it, or we shall die. But we need not drink it always. Here is our problem and our salvation. There comes a moment—God knows when—at which we can say, "I will experience no longer. I will create. I will be an experience." But to do this we must be both acute and heroic. For it is not

easy, after accepting six cups of tea, to throw the seventh in the face of the hostess. And to Rickie this moment has not, as yet, been offered.[4]

It is now offered in that moment of revelation from Mrs Failing, and Rickie sees its significance. When Mrs Failing tells Agnes, a little later, that she has no intention of telling Stephen the truth, she comes gladly to Rickie to tell him that there is no danger of the secret being let out. But Rickie, who is in the act of writing to Stewart Ansell to ask his advice, feels that Stephen ought to be told such a real thing.

> "It seems to me that here and there in life we meet with a person or incident that is symbolical. It's nothing in itself, yet for the moment it stands for some eternal principle. We accept it, at whatever cost, and we have accepted life. But if we are frightened and reject it, the moment, so to speak, passes; the symbol is never offered again."[5]

Yet in spite of his insistence, he still allows Agnes to talk him round, so that he does not reply when Stephen calls from outside the window, and finally tears up his letter to Ansell.

From this point Rickie begins to decline steadily. Despite his attempts to make a living by writing, he cannot find a publisher who will take his stories. As he drives away from an interview with one, he reflects on the flaw in his life: 'He loved, he was loved, he had seen death and other things; but the heart of all things was hidden. There was a password and he could not learn it, nor could the kind editor of the "Holborn" teach him. He sighed, and then sighed more piteously. For had he not known the password once —known it and forgotten it already?'[6]

He marries Agnes and accepts an offer from her brother to teach at Sawston School, the description of which contains some of Forster's best satirical writing. The school is a vehicle of snobbery and pettiness, where Mr Pembroke is able to inflict hurts and indignities unknown in the world outside, on the excuse that 'School is the world in miniature'. The effect of the school on Rickie is summed up in his reactions to the opening of a new term:

He resumed his duties with a feeling that he had never left them. Again he confronted the assembled house. This term was again *the* term; school still the world in miniature. The music of the four-part fugue entered into him more deeply, and he began to hum its little phrases. The same routine, the same diplomacies, the same old sense of only half knowing boys or men—he returned to it all; and all that changed was the cloud of unreality, which ever brooded a little more densely than before.[7]

Because he turned back at the symbolic moment, his sense of reality, the sense that binds romantic imagination to the outside world, has deserted him. Term after term he drifts through the unreal world of Sawston School, allowing worse things to happen around him, conscious of failure. He still feels dislike towards Stephen, in spite of an impulse to tell him the truth, because he can only associate him with his father, whom he hated.

A new crisis is precipitated when Ansell arrives one morning at the school, unheralded, and in the grounds meets Stephen, who has just learned the truth about himself from another source. Ansell rushes into the dining-hall and makes a speech to Rickie in front of the assembled school, in the course of which he reveals to him that Stephen is the son, not of his father but of his mother.

Rickie collapses again, but when he recovers his attitude has changed. Just as he had formerly disliked Stephen for being the son of his father, he now loves him because he is the son of his mother. In both cases, however, his interpretation is an imaginative construct: at no time is he seeing him as a man in himself. He decides to leave Herbert and Agnes and to go off with Stephen. Returning with him to Cadover, he has a long conversation with his aunt, who urges him to go back to his wife and to respect the conventions—for they are majestic in their way and will claim us in the end. Rickie disagrees, claiming that his path is right because it is restoring to him his sense of reality. ' "Because, as we used to say at Cambridge, the cow is there. The world is real again." '

She goes out, and while he is musing on their conversation, reflecting that he has now passed behind all things in his love for his mother's image in Stephen, that the conventions are not majestic and will not claim us in the end, there is a symbolic incident. A lump of chalk which stands on the mantelpiece falls from his hand as he is playing with it and smashes a fragile china cup. The solid earth has crushed the finer clay. Rickie goes out to look for Stephen and finds that, in spite of his promises, he is drunk. In the despair that follows the discovery, Rickie declares that once again he has made the mistake of supposing that people are real. The whole affair is a dream: in Stephen he will go on seeing his mother's image defiled, and soon his wife will claim him back. At this point he sees Stephen lying drunk across a level-crossing in the path of an approaching train. In saving him he is himself injured fatally, and he dies in Cadover, whispering to Mrs Failing that she has been right.

But a concluding chapter modifies this judgment. Stephen is shown established in Cadover, preparing Rickie's manuscripts for publication and remembering him in gratitude. 'The spirit had fled, in agony and loneliness, never to know that it bequeathed him salvation.'

. . . .

As before, the main run of the plot is clear. By means of it, Forster is making two points, the one moral, the other psychological. Both find their focus in the 'moment of moral choice', the symbolic moment in which a man either accepts or rejects life. The willingness to see clearly and to accept the symbolic moment when it is offered (in Ansell's language, the love of seriousness and the love of truthfulness) lie at the root of all morality.

The psychological point is linked with this. Philosophers argue endlessly about the nature of reality, but Forster finds that less is said about the inward 'sense of reality'. The sense of reality weds the earth to the human spirit, it combines imagination and a steady appraisal of 'things as they are'. The effect of rejecting life in the symbolic moment is to produce a small cloud of unreality which will, if unchecked, thicken until it takes complete possession.

These two interlinked ideas appear again as minor themes in later novels, but here they are central and dominant. Around them complexities ramify, for the idea of the symbolic moment as Forster uses it presupposes a constant dialectic between earth and the imagination. The true sense of reality acknowledges both and gives proper weight to each. In the present novel it is the imaginative values of Cambridge and the pagan values of Wiltshire that provide the dialectic. Sawston is the negation of both, but more likely to deceive Cambridge than Wiltshire (there is an excellent bargaining scene between Stephen and Herbert Pembroke in the last chapter which makes the point neatly). In the end Rickie's imagination transfigures the mortal passion of Stephen to crown the dialectic with a final synthesis.

It is a mistake to divide the characters of this novel into 'sheep' and 'goats',[8] for each character carries some weight, however small, in the dialectic. Herbert and Agnes Pembroke are nearest to being 'goats' because of their involvement with Sawston; but it is made clear towards the end of the novel that even they are devoted to convention and that convention also has its place—it is a way of paying respect to the earth, even if a negative way. With Herbert Pembroke, it is not difficult to display this modification of censure, for Forster depicts him throughout as a comic figure. If his desire for power in his house leads him to devise absurd bureaucratic methods, for example, he can also identify himself with his house and be ambitious for it. (And it has to be noted in passing that small boys are often Herbert Pembrokes in miniature.) He is no fool and on points of detail can show both intellectual and moral virtue. Mrs Orr's rejection of his marriage-proposal provides a scene of rich comedy—but it is later conceded in his favour that he finds more difficulty in offering himself to the church than to Mrs Orr. It is in his general outlook as a whole that he is muddled. He cannot face himself as he really is, he soon muddles the past: and so the root of the matter is not in him. Forster, in one of his glancing observations, treats him as kindly as he possibly can: Herbert, he says, was sometimes clear-sighted over details, though easily muddled in a general survey. These combinations of virtues and vices in Sawston man await a more detailed, less comic treatment in *Howards End*.

Agnes is more difficult to evaluate as a person. Although Forster insists by various means that there is something wrong with her, and although some of her actions are despicable, the reader may not find her immediately unsympathetic. Even Forster describes her later predicament with elements of sympathy.[9]

> Ansell was wrong in supposing she might ever leave Rickie. Spiritual apathy prevented her. Nor would she ever be tempted by a jollier man. Here criticism would willingly alter its tone. For Agnes also has her tragedy. She belonged to the type—not necessarily an elevated one—that loves once and once only. Her love for Gerald had not been a noble passion: no imagination transfigured it. But such as it was, it sprang to embrace him, and he carried it away with him when he died.

The following exchange with Forster, recorded by Angus Wilson, throws the problem into relief:

> I remarked that I could not help being fond of Agnes.
> E. M. F. (*sharply*). "Why are you?"
> A. W. (*trying to excuse himself.*) "There was something moving when she first came to Rickie's room. . . ."
> E. M. F. "I saw through her."[10]

Forster's reply suggests that he was (perhaps even deliberately) attempting something which Jane Austen had done before him in *Mansfield Park*. It is a common criticism of the latter novel that Miss Crawford is made too attractive compared with Fanny and enlists the reader's sympathies against her creator's evident intention. But Miss Crawford's conduct breaks down on further examination—there is always that telling split second between the spontaneous response which she might have made and the response which she does make. Professor Trilling has characterized her as one who 'impersonates the woman she thinks she ought to be', who 'cultivates the *style* of sensitivity, virtue and intelligence'.[11] From a straightforward point of view there is no doubt of Miss Crawford's attractiveness: it is only under close moral scrutiny that her inferiority is disclosed.

Agnes is rather the same. Her external behaviour never ceases to be attractive and socially acceptable. There are few tricks of the social trade with which she is unacquainted. She knows how to evaluate people and get the better of them if necessary. But, like her brother, she lacks imagination or true inner life of any sort. A minor character puts his finger on the spot when he describes the 'stoniness' of a meal at Sawston—' "No one stopped talking for a moment." '[12] An even more damning revelation of Agnes's spiritual poverty is Forster's account of her thoughts about Cadover:

> The first moment she set foot in Cadover she had thought, "Oh, here is money. We must try and get it." Being a lady, she never mentioned the thought to her husband, but she concluded that it would occur to him too.[13]

This account of her hidden motives (it is always in terms of money that the Sawston attitude crystallizes) can be set against Mr Failing's comments on human nature, as Ansell notes them in reading.

> Very notable was his distinction between coarseness and vulgarity (coarseness, revealing something; vulgarity, concealing something), and his avowed preference for coarseness. Vulgarity, to him, had been the primal curse, the shoddy reticence that prevents man opening his heart to man, the power that makes against equality.[14]

Agnes, for all her attractions, is a vulgar person by Mr Failing's standards.

The reasons for Rickie's attachment to her have not so far been made fully clear. Trilling, in his study of the novel, relates Rickie's error to an incident in the first chapter when Ansell puts his philosophical views into practice by refusing to acknowledge the existence of Agnes. On being taxed with rudeness by Rickie, he replies:

> "Did it never strike you that phenomena may be of two kinds: *one*, those which have a real existence, such as the cow; *two*, those which are the subjective product of a diseased imagination, and which, to our destruction, we invest with the semblance of reality? If this never struck you, let it strike you now."

Trilling argues that this gives us Rickie's essential error in the novel—that in loving Agnes, he had invested with the semblance of reality the subjective product of a diseased imagination.[15] If one disagrees with this analysis, it is to question the validity of the word 'diseased'. The Agnes whom Rickie invests with reality is the product not of a diseased imagination but of an unballasted one. It is a limitation on the part of Ansell that he cannot see this. Rickie falls in love with Agnes as the result of several 'visionary moments', the first of which occurs when she first enters his room:

> "And I thought she came into the room so beautifully. Do you know—oh, of course, you despise music—but Anderson was playing Wagner, and he'd just got to the part where they sing
>
> > 'Rheingold!
> > Rheingold!'
>
> and the sun strikes into the waters, and the music, which up to then has so often been in E flat. . . ."

The young man who sees the entry of Agnes in this light has a fine imagination, but morally he is in mortal danger. And the danger increases two chapters later when Agnes is kissed by her lover and her face shines like a star. For Rickie who sees it, inward vision and music rise to a crescendo.

> He thought, "Do such things actually happen?" and he seemed to be looking down coloured valleys. Brighter they glowed, till gods of pure flame were born in them, and then he was looking at pinnacles of virgin snow. While Mr Pembroke talked, the riot of fair images increased. They invaded his being and lit lamps at unsuspected shrines. Their orchestra commenced in that suburban house, where he had to stand aside for the maid to carry in the luncheon. Music flowed past him like a river. He stood at the springs of creation and heard the primeval monotony. Then an obscure instrument gave out a little phrase. The river continued unheeding. The phrase was repeated, and a listener might know it was a fragment of the Tune of tunes. Nobler instruments accepted it, the clarionet protected, the

brass encouraged, and it rose to the surface to the whisper of violins. In full unison was Love born, flame of the flame, flushing the dark river beneath him and the virgin snows above. His wings were infinite, his youth eternal; the sun was a jewel on his finger as he passed it in benediction over the world. Creation, no longer monotonous, acclaimed him, in widening melody, in brighter radiances. Was Love a column of fire? Was he a torrent of song? Was he greater than either—the touch of a man on a woman?[16]

In a discussion of the novel,[17] Mr W. J. Harvey has argued that although it is, or should be, one of the peaks of the novel, the style of the paragraph is that of a purple passage which would be more at home in a woman's weekly magazine than in the work of one of the great modern novelists. The judgment is tempting: few passages in Forster have dated so much. But Mr Harvey perhaps misses a certain Wagnerian magnificence in the passage.

And there are two further points to be made. Mr Harvey is right in saying that the passage marks one of the peaks of the novel, but the reader could be pardoned for passing it over altogether. For the next paragraph reads simply.

It was the merest accident that Rickie had not been disgusted. But this he could not know.

The reader who has been damped by Forster's ironic comedy and by the suburban setting of Rickie's experience might well take this laconic comment to clinch a view of the previous paragraph as recording no more than the extravagant emotions of a young man.

The other point to be made, however, is that this passage, unlike its women's magazine equivalents, displays a high degree of intellectual organization. The author is not simply pulling out high-flown phrases at random—he really believes that love can be a sublime and passionate experience. His description reminds one of Blake's paintings of love in the form of a young god. The closeness of organization emerges when one recalls the scene in *A Room with a View* where Lucy is first kissed by George Emerson. The same imagery of restoration to terrestrial paradise is there used to describe the profusion of violets at that spot—'this terrace was the well-head, the primal source whence beauty gushed out to water the earth.'[18]

There can be little doubt that so far as Rickie is concerned, the experience is intended as a true visionary moment—one of the rare moments when prose and passion are connected and love is seen at its height. The purpose of the little concluding paragraph is not to damp the vision of the preceding one, but to point the pervasive moral of the novel. Rickie was never wrong to treat his visionary experiences as a high form of reality—his fatal mistake lay in going on to identify his vision with the suburban girl who had called it forth and to think that he could gain permanent access to the vision by possessing the girl.

Forster makes very few direct comments on Agnes's failure. Stewart Ansell's objections to her are straightforward: '(1) She is not serious. (2) She is not truthful.'[19] Both objections are upheld in the novel, but Forster also hints at a deeper lack. He refers to a letter of hers as containing one of her few tributes to the imagination and he also says that her love for Gerald was one in which passion had not been transfigured by imagination.[20] Together, the two statements make a damning commentary. The tragic irony of the novel is that Rickie's imagination is stimulated by a girl who herself has none.

A similar distinction has to be made when considering the place of Cambridge as a symbol in the novel. Rose Macaulay is eloquent on the subject:

> Cambridge was the good life, the way of truth and salvation, outside it lay an alien world of false gods, of shoddy and sham, full of people not serious and not truthful. Cambridge was Eden, from whence, if one made the wrong choice, ate from the wrong tree, one's spirit was expelled with flaming swords, tow ander lost and half alive in the barren lands beyond. . . .[12]

Luckily, she makes it clear that Cambridge in this sense is a spirit as much as a place, but she is still in danger of suggesting that Forster regards the Cambridge of his youth as identifiable with paradise. Rickie makes a speech in the novel which might be quoted to support the same view:

"You see, the notion of good-fellowship develops late: you can just see its beginning here among the prefects: up at Cambridge it flourishes amazingly. That's why I pity people who don't go up to Cambridge: not because a University is smart, but because those are the magic years, and—with luck—you see up there what you couldn't see before and mayn't ever see again."[22]

Even the enthusiastic Rickie, however, does not say that the thing he is describing (the thing that he elsewhere calls the Holy Grail) actually exists in Cambridge, only that it may be seen from there. And there are enough references in the rest of the novel to make clear the failings of Cambridge as a society. A nearer approach to Forster's own view of the matter might be found in Ansell's remarks when Rickie has spoken of the contrast between Cambridge and 'the great world'.

"There is no great world at all, only a little earth, for ever isolated from the rest of the little solar system. The little earth is full of tiny societies, and Cambridge is one of them. . . . The good societies say, 'I tell you to do this because I am Cambridge.' The bad ones say, 'I tell you to do that because I am the great world'—not because I am 'Peckham', or 'Billingsgate', or 'Park Lane', but 'because I am the great world'. They lie."[23]

But Ansell's comments must in their turn be set against Forster's comments on his limitations as a person. He is confused and bewildered, for example, when he hears that Agnes is expecting a child—it is a point which has not entered his calculations. Elsewhere Forster remarks,

In many ways he was pedantic; but his pedantry lay close to the vineyards of life—far closer than that fetich Experience of the innumerable teacups. He had a great many facts to learn, and before he died he learnt a suitable quantity. But he never forgot that the holiness of the heart's imagination can alone classify these facts—can alone decide which is an exception, which an example.[24]

Ansell, too, represents a single element of Cambridge hypostatized: his devotion to truth needs to be counterweighted not only by Rickie s imaginative enthusiasm but by the wisdom of true experience. He writes his dissertation 'about things being real',[25] but when it comes to 'reality', Mrs Failing has as much to say in her way as Ansell in his. And if Ansell's virtues stand nearer to the virtues of the tangible Cambridge, the familiar Cambridge of mathematics and philosophy and science, it is Rickie's sense of the place as a town where natural beauty, civilized architecture and young people blend into one glamour that gives Cambridge its particular rôle in the novel, its peculiar distinction as an imaginative complement to the pagan, earthy virtues of Wiltshire.

So far we have only touched on Rickie s imagination, but it has a large part in the ultimate shape of the novel. Rickie himself stands in a peculiar relationship to his creator. The details of his academic career correspond roughly to those of Forster's, and the short stories which he writes can be identified in one or two instances with Forster's own. But it would be absurd to look for too close an identification. If Forster were Rickie he could not have written *The Longest Journey*. In one of the novels of Lawrence G. Durrell there is a character with the initials 'L. G. D.', but Durrell himself has explained, when questioned on the point, that in creating this character he was not attempting autobiography, simply playing a sort of hide-and-seek with himself.[26] Rickie seems to stand in the same category. He has Forster's imagination, his tendency to see trees as Dryads, his love of night and the stars, his enthusiasm for Wagner and Greek mythology. But Forster in creating him is imagining what might happen to a young man who followed those enthusiasms to the exclusion of all others. The result is not autobiography but imaginative self-caricature.

When this has been said, however, the fact remains that the personal relationship between Rickie and his creator sometimes operates with peculiar force in the novel. It is present, for example, in Rickie's preoccupation with the stars. Attention is drawn to this twice in the first chapter, when he sits looking out into the night while indulging his fantasies, and when he tells Agnes that he has no ideals.

> "The person who has no ideals," she exclaimed, "is to be pitied."
> "I think so too," said Mr Pembroke, sipping his coffee. "Life without an ideal would be like the sky without the sun."
> Rickie looked towards the night, wherein there now twinkled innumerable stars—gods and heroes, virgins and brides, to whom the Greeks have given their names.

The contrast between Mr Pembroke's conventional world of coffee-cups and Rickie's imaginative universe is neatly drawn in the imagery which they exchange. (Forster has elsewhere remarked on the impoverished imagination of the English, using as one illustration the fact that they have given names to only a handful of stars.)[27] Later in the narrative, a particular star symbol emerges at the point when Rickie's fortunes are at their lowest ebb, and when he passes a terrible night.

> Yet again did he awake, and from a more mysterious dream. He heard his mother crying. She was crying quite distinctly in the darkened room. He whispered, "Never mind, my darling, never mind," and a voice echoed, "Never mind—come away—let them die out—let them die out." He lit a candle, and the room was empty. Then, hurrying to the window, he saw above mean houses the frosty glories of Orion.[28]

Of the significance of the dream there can be no doubt, for Rickie himself remembers it again at a later crisis, the point when he has discovered that Stephen is the son, not of his father but of his mother. He has been tempted to curse her, until Ansell helps him to see things more clearly.

> He had journeyed—as on rare occasions a man must—till he stood behind right and wrong. On the banks of the grey torrent of life, love is the only flower. A little way up the stream and a little way down had Rickie glanced, and he knew that she whom he loved had risen from the dead, and might rise again. "Come away—let them die out—let them die out."

Surely that dream was a vision! To-night also he hurried to the window—to remember, with a smile, that Orion is not among the stars of June.[29]

At the end of the novel, Orion is introduced again. When Rickie discovers that Stephen has broken his promise to him, that the faith placed in him as a reincarnation of his mother has been in vain, he walks back in utter dejection with Leighton the butler.

> The shoulders of Orion rose behind them over the topmost boughs of the elm. From the bridge the whole constellation was visible, and Rickie said, "May God receive me and pardon me for trusting the earth."[30]

He stands on the bridge where he and Stephen had sailed a burning paper boat, but the visionary experience means nothing to him now.

> That mystic rose and the face it illumined meant nothing. The stream—he was above it now—meant nothing, though it burst from the pure turf and ran for ever to the sea. The bather, the shoulders of Orion—they all meant nothing, and were going nowhere. The whole affair was a ridiculous dream.

Orion is a mysterious symbol here. One could quite easily miss its presence altogether, since the references are scattered and look at first like natural description. Once noticed, however, they point to a symbolic significance. The symbolism is not explained in the novel and it seems clear that Forster is not concerned that it should be.

Yet its presence at these turning-points in the novel makes one look further: and one discovers the same symbol in some of the short stories. In 'The Point of It', for example, a story which has already been discussed,[31] the hero, having seen his best friend die at the oars of the boat in which they are rowing, becomes possessed of the love of mankind. Forster describes that love in the following terms:

> Love, the love of humanity, warmed him; and even when he was thinking of other matters, was looking at Orion perhaps

in the cold winter evenings, a pang of joy, too sweet for description, would thrill him, and he would feel sure that our highest impulses have some eternal value, and will be completed hereafter.[32]

But the love of humanity is not, in itself, enough. He has married a wife who, like Ansell, is devoted to truth: and when they die, he finds to his surprise that they are in different Hells. There is a Hell for those who have loved and gone soft, and a Hell for those who have been devoted to truth and gone hard. He begins talking to a man lying near by and in a heavily ironic conversation they agree on the superiority of their present state, where they can rest. Micky declares that he wasted too much of his life in the sun.

"In later years I did repent, and that is why I am admitted here where there is no sun; yes, and no wind and none of the stars that drove me almost mad at night once. It would be appalling, would it not, to see Orion again, the central star of whose sword is not a star but a nebula, the golden seed of worlds to be. How I dreaded the autumn on earth when Orion rises, for he recalled adventure and my youth. It was appalling. How thankful I am to see him no more."[33]

One begins to see in these two statements something of the significance of Orion. He is associated with the love of humanity as it is experienced in youth, splendidly, before a man 'goes soft' in benevolence. And the significance of this symbol is even more apparent when we turn to another short story entitled 'The Machine Stops'. In this story a state of affairs is pictured where humanity has come to be living in a complete machine underground, never experiencing the open air because all its travel is accomplished in closed vehicles. One man wants to break out because he suspects that there is some important reality outside the machine. He discusses the stars with his mother:

"Do you not know four big stars that form an oblong and three stars close together in the middle of the oblong, and hanging from these stars, three other stars?"

"No, I do not. I dislike the stars. But did they give you an idea? How interesting; tell me."

"I had an idea that they were like a man."

"I do not understand."

"The four big stars are the man's shoulders and his knees. The three stars in the middle are like the belts that men wore once, and the three stars hanging are like a sword."

"A sword?"

"Men carried swords about with them, to kill animals and other men."

"It does not strike me as a very good idea, but it is certainly original . . ."[34]

The constellation that he is describing is, of course, Orion. At the end of the story, when the machine runs down, and humanity faces destruction, the man and his mother meet again and weep for humanity:

> Ere silence was completed their hearts were opened, and they knew what had been important on the earth. Man, the flower of all flesh, the noblest of all creatures visible, man who had once made god in his image, and had mirrored his strength on the constellations, beautiful naked man was dying, strangled in the garments that he had woven.[35]

In the last quotation, the latent symbolism of Orion is finally made apparent. The highest glory of man is shown in the mythology of Orion, where man 'mirrored his strength on the constellations'.

This symbolism had evidently been indulged in by Rickie also —yet the significance of Orion is left unexplained in the pages of the novel, only to be discovered after a piece of detective work which cannot be expected of the average reader. It is a measure of Forster's reticence that he should underplay Rickie's imagination to this extent and leave it as something of an esoteric element in the story. Yet its importance in the total pattern of the novel cannot be disregarded. It finds its most permanent expression in a symbolic incident which has already been referred to in passing. Towards the end of the novel, before Rickie's final disillusionment concerning Stephen, the two of them are returning from Salisbury together one evening. There is a moment of harmony between them. Stephen offers to show Rickie a trick and pauses by a stream to light some paper. As he does so, Rickie looks at the face which is illumined by the burning paper and sees in it the lineaments of a different spirit, the legacy of their mother.

> The paper caught fire from the match, and spread into a rose of flame. "Now gently with me," said Stephen, and they laid it flower-like on the stream. Gravel and tremulous weeds leapt into sight, and then the flower sailed into deep water, and up leapt the two arches of a bridge. "It'll strike!" they cried; "no, it won't; it's chosen the left," and one arch became a fairy tunnel, dropping diamonds. Then it vanished for Rickie; but Stephen, who knelt in the water, declared that it was still afloat, far through the arch, burning as if it would burn for ever.[36]

This is the central 'visionary moment' of the novel. So far as Rickie is concerned, it seems as though his imaginative vision of Stephen has been realized. The 'rose of flame' expresses the spirit which he thinks has sprung up in Stephen, and the community of spirit between them. There is a prophetic touch at the end, where the flame is soon hidden from Rickie but goes on burning for Stephen. Even the bridge links with other symbols in the novel. Stephen is constantly asserting that the level-crossing near Cadover is dangerous and that a bridge is required. (Eventually one is built.) The level-crossing, the intrusion of modern civilization into old, of death into life, may here meet its contrary in the bridge that keeps different modes of life separate.

The passage is one of Forster's triumphs. The descriptive writing is at its highest level as he realizes the scene illuminated by the fragile flame of the paper rose. And although the vision slips from Rickie as he dies, it is to be perpetuated in Stephen. The figurative symbol of the paper flower will turn into the realistic symbol of the house where Stephen establishes his wife and child, keeping alive the values that he had learned from Rickie. And this symbol of the house, which comes into its own only in the last chapter, will in its turn dominate the next novel, *Howards End*.

The flaming, rose-shaped, paper boat on the stream is as fragile as the spirit which it represents. But, apart from the house, there is a recurring symbol in the novel which stands for imaginative reality in more permanent and solid form.[37] In Stephen's room at Cadover there is only one picture, the Demeter of Cnidus, which hangs suspended from the roof. She is never still, reflecting the various lights that enter the room. At one point, Rickie goes up to the room by night to look for a manuscript of his stories, and is startled to see the Demeter, 'shimmering and grey', swinging towards him.

The goddess appears again in the description of Ansell walking in the British Museum after he has heard that a child is to be born to Rickie and Agnes.

> He left the Parthenon to pass by the monuments of our more reticent beliefs—the temple of the Ephesian Artemis, the statue of the Cnidian Demeter. Honest, he knew that here were powers he could not cope with, nor, as yet, understand.

This brief incident helps to give fuller rounding to Ansell's character. In the novel as it stands, he is a somewhat monolithic figure. The same honesty that drives him ruthlessly in the pursuit of truth also impels a fearless appraisal of moral situations as he finds them: in consequence, his irruptions into the novel sometimes have a melodramatic touch. His personality is forceful but colourless. He distrusts Rickie's imagination and is even described at one point as pedantic. Yet Forster insists that his pedantry lies 'close to the vineyards of life' and that his devotion to the holiness of the heart's imagination will see him through in the end.[38] In the British Museum, again, his self-admitted inexperience in face of the more mysterious powers of earth is qualified by a hint that he will later come to terms with them.

Whereas Ansell honestly acknowledges an inability to deal with Demeter, however, Rickie finds her actively sinister. And although in the end he follows Ansell's honesty, his fear of the earth remains. Only once has it been intermitted. After the fainting-fit occasioned by the revelation at Cadbury Rings, he wakens to find Stephen massaging his blood back into circulation.

He woke up. The earth he had dreaded lay close to his eyes, and seemed beautiful. He saw the structure of the clods. A tiny beetle swung on the grass blade. On his own neck a human hand pressed, guiding the blood back to his brain.[39]

But his fear has re-emerged and persists. He must either be attracted or repelled by the earth. Mrs Failing's suggestion that he should respect it cannot touch him: and even though he dies murmuring 'You have been right' to her, these words, too, are an admission that he has failed to come to terms. His fear of Demeter epitomizes his tragedy.

Towards the end of the novel, the goddess is used again to point the sharpest contrast in the novel—that between Mr Pembroke and Stephen Wonham. Mr Pembroke stands in front of the picture of Demeter, thinking about Rickie's death. His chief reflection is cynical: death is merciful when it weeds out a failure. When, on the other hand, Stephen's daughter is being carried out to sleep under the stars she murmurs among her sleepy phrases, 'Good night, you pictures—long picture—stone lady. . . .'[40] The two reactions betray two attitudes to the earth. All Mr Pembroke's conventions in the end hark back to a distant fear of the earth; Stephen and his family are at peace with it. For Stephen, Pan never meant 'panic and emptiness': now, thanks to Rickie, imagination has supervened to transfigure his mortal clay and bring him into complete reconciliation with the universe.

. . . . .

The Longest Journey is a novel of complex origins. In his preface to the *Collected Short Stories*, Forster relates that it sprang from 'an encounter with the genius loci, but indirectly, complicatedly, not here to be considered'. More recently, he has considered its origins more fully, referring to notebooks which he kept at the time of composition.[41]

The first idea to come into his mind, he relates, was that of a man who discovers that he has an illegitimate brother. Significantly, this situation involves, first and foremost, the ethical theme of honesty: reality must be faced. But he recalls other themes which were revolving in his mind at the time, and which we have already noticed in our examination of the novel: the metaphysical question of the nature of reality; the idea, or ideal, of the British Public School; the doctrine of Shelley (reflected in the title) that love should not be devoted to one person alone; Cambridge; and Wiltshire.

He elaborates further on Wiltshire. In September 1904 he visited Figsbury Rings, a few miles east of Salisbury, and it was there that the 'encounter with the genius loci' took place. But whereas a previous encounter, the one that inspired 'The Story of a Panic', had been touched off mainly by a view, this one contained other elements:

> This time it wasn't just looking at a view, it was breathing the air and smelling the fields, and there was human reinforcement from the shepherds who grazed up there. They and I talked about nothing—still one of my favourite subjects; I offered a tip of sixpence which was declined, I was offered a pull at a pipe and had to decline. The whole experience was trivial in itself, but vital to the novel, for it fructified my meagre conception of the half-brothers. . . .

Among other recollections of themes and cancelled passages, he points out that it was an uncle (a 'meddlesome tease of a man', elsewhere identified as his Uncle Willie) who, 'though sedulously masculine, gave me hints for the character of Mrs Failing and whose house up in Northumberland provided the architecture and the atmosphere for Cadover'.

Comments such as these throw light on the nature and extent of Forster's involvement with the hero of his novel. As we have said, this self-involvement must not be overestimated: on the other hand it cannot be entirely ignored. Rather, the novel needs to be judged by the same unconventional canons that we apply to *Middlemarch*. George Eliot's involvement with Dorothea is equally evident, and although, as in Forster's novel, the author takes care to distance herself from her central character, the fact of her involvement must inevitably entail a certain distortion. Deliberately harsh judgments in some places will be matched by involuntary indulgence elsewhere. The novel will, in fact, owe some of its shape to the shape of the author's personality. There is no disadvantage in this: on the contrary, self-revelation is a necessary element in romantic literature. But if the novel is to achieve its total possible effect, a corresponding indulgence on the part of the reader is required.

A simple example of such a personal attitude can be found in the importance attached by Rickie to Stephen's failure to keep his promise. In his biography of Lowes Dickinson, Forster tries to describe his feelings on the outbreak of the First World War:

> Dickinson's feelings when the war broke out are best conveyed by an analogy: they resembled the feelings which arise when a promise has been broken by a person whom one loves. One knows all the time that the promise will not be kept, perhaps cannot be kept, yet the shock is none the less mortal. [42]

It is evidently a subject about which he feels exceptionally strongly, and the feeling has given a corresponding bias to the action of his novel.

The parallel with *Middlemarch* can be pressed further, moreover. Like George Eliot, Forster owes some elements in his values of seriousness, kindliness and truthfulness to that Christian tradition which, when presented as an organized body of doctrine, he rejects. He is a more pronounced Hellenist than she, more willing to acknowledge the force of the pagan in human behaviour (George Eliot's Hellenism is Apollonian rather than Dionysiac: Dorothea and Will Ladislaw meet in Rome near the statue of Apollo Belvedere); on the other hand, he shares her subconscious urge to introduce a redemptive force into his novels. In *Middlemarch* the point is thoroughly muffled, but the fact remains that when Rosamond is impelled by Dorothea's candour to reveal the truth about Ladislaw, she is described as 'taken hold of by an emotion stronger than her own—hurried along in a new movement which gave all things some new, awful, undefined aspect . . . urged by a mysterious necessity to free herself from something that oppressed her as if it were blood-guiltiness'. [43] Forster is equally reticent: his distinction between the 'saved' and the 'unsaved' in the earlier chapters is lighthearted. But in his crucial last words on Rickie he speaks of him as the spirit that had fled in agony and loneliness, 'never to know that it bequeathed salvation' to Stephen.

Most romantic artists find it necessary, at some point in their careers, to create a work of self-revelation and self-criticism. Having achieved this end with characteristic obliqueness, Forster could proceed to explore the same themes more impersonally and objectively in his last two novels. In spite of their greater success in communication, however, Forster himself still regards *The Longest Journey* as the novel which he is 'most glad to have written'. 'In it,' he remarks, 'I have managed to get nearer than elsewhere towards what was in my mind—or rather towards that junction of mind with heart where the creative impulse sparks.'[44]

CHAPTER V

In Country Sleep

IF *A Room with a View* is Forster's most lyrical novel, its success is strictly limited in compass. The main point, which concerns the holiness of the heart's affections, is fully made. But the peak of happiness finally reached by the chief characters makes it difficult to imagine them after the novel ends, for that sort of happiness, at least, could not be sustained. Forster's own attempt, fifty years later, to recount what subsequently happened to his characters makes rather sad reading.[1]

One reason for this is the importance given to visionary symbolism in that novel. Visionary moments may interpret the rest of time, they may be brought together in some large concluding symbol, but the realization in everyday life of the significance which they have revealed is a more difficult matter. The main physical symbol of the novel, the 'room with a view' itself, illustrates the point. The actual room of the pension in Florence where Lucy and George stay separately at the beginning, and together at the end of the novel, can be no more than a temporary resting-place. And all the other symbols of the novel have a similar transience. Most of them are concerned with springtime and youth: they serve the singleness of this novel but will not bear more lasting pressures.

In this respect, *Howards End* complements the earlier novels. Its visionary moments are important, but do not carry the same burden of significance. The important and overriding symbol of this novel is set firmly in space and time. It is the house, Howards End, which dominates the opening and close of the novel and is a presence throughout. Howards End is the main link between a realistic plot which can be grasped at one reading and a pattern of symbolism which throws the events against a wider background and makes them illuminate the modern world in general.

At a first reading, *Howards End* presents itself as a novel in which the reader is entertained, made to reflect, and from time to time surprised. It is the story of a long interaction between two families, the Schlegels and the Wilcoxes. The Schlegels consist of two sisters and a brother: Margaret, Helen and Tibby, who are descended from German stock. Their father, we learn, 'was not the aggressive German, so dear to the English journalist, nor the domestic German, so dear to the English wit. If one classed him at all it would be as the countryman of Hegel and Kant, as the idealist, inclined to be dreamy, whose Imperialism was the Imperialism of the air.' The daughters are figures which must have been familiar to Edwardian readers but are nowadays more rare—young women of independent means who are free to pursue a leisured life in the pursuit of culture and philanthropy. They attend concerts in the Queen's Hall, participate in elegant discussion groups and spend holidays exploring Germany and Italy.

It is a German holiday that first brings them into contact with the Wilcoxes. Between them, the members of this family represent a good deal of the England of 1910. Ruth Wilcox, the mother, is a countrywoman. Howards End, an old farmhouse dating back for generations, is in fact her property and she has a close affinity of spirit with it. Her husband and children, on the other hand, all belong to the 'new England' with which we have become familiar in Forster's accounts of Sawston. They are business people who think of houses in terms, not of the spirit of place but of the rights of property: in time of trouble their hand flies to the cheque-book.

The novel contains many references to their encroachment on England. Their loud and luxurious car, which in an early chapter sends dust on to the roses and gooseberries of wayside gardens and into the lungs of villagers, and which later kills the cat of a village girl, becomes hideously representative of them. London, the formless purposeless city devoted to their pursuit of wealth and power, is their great monument. Their influence goes back into history, moreover. Even when Henry and Margaret want to sit down by the Great North Road towards the end of the novel, the sad truth has to be reported:

The Great North Road should have been bordered all its
length with glebe. Henry's kind had filched most of it.[2]

Mentally, the Wilcoxes have one cardinal failing. They are
muddled. The reason is their constant devotion to action and the
practical, their unwillingness to be diverted from it by any
thoughts or considerations which might be 'soft' or 'unhealthy'.
Of Henry Wilcox, we learn,

> his mental states became obscure as soon as he had passed
> through them. He misliked the very word "interesting",
> connoting it with wasted energy and even with morbidity.
> Hard facts were enough for him.[3]

This attitude leads the Wilcoxes to suppress their emotions; it also
leads them ultimately to a sinister approval of impersonality.
Henry counters Helen's plea for poor people with just such an
argument:

> ". . . our civilization is moulded by great impersonal forces"
> (his voice grew complacent; it always did when he eliminated
> the personal), "and there always will be rich and poor".[4]

Muddle-mindedness retains its status as an index of error in this
novel and earns one of Forster's sternest and most explicit rebukes.
We have already quoted the passage in which, after recording to
Leonard Bast's credit that he never confused the past, he goes on
to quote a couplet of Meredith's:

> And if I drink oblivion of a day
> So shorten I the stature of my soul.

commenting,

> It is a hard saying, and a hard man wrote it, but it lies at the
> root of all character.[5]

One of the most successful sequences in the novel is that in
which Forster shows the Wilcoxes actually in the process of
muddling themselves, while they put on a superficial display of
clear thinking. It is the scene when the Wilcoxes discover the

existence of a note from Mrs Wilcox, who has just died, saying that she would like Margaret to have Howards End.[6] The note is a bombshell to the family.

> In silence they drew up to the breakfast-table. The events of yesterday—indeed of this morning—suddenly receded into a past so remote that they seemed scarcely to have lived in it. Heavy breathings were heard. They were calming themselves. Charles, to steady them further, read the enclosure out loud: "A note in my mother's handwriting, in an envelope addressed to my father, sealed. Inside: 'I should like Miss Schlegel (Margaret) to have Howards End.' No date, no signature. Forwarded through the matron of that nursing home. Now, the question is . . ."

Some discussion follows, and then Forster comments:

> The two men were gradually assuming the manner of the committee-room. They were both at their best when serving on committees. They did not make the mistake of handling human affairs in the bulk, but disposed of them item by item, sharply. Calligraphy was the item before them now, and on it they turned their well-trained brains. Charles, after a little demur, accepted the writing as genuine, and they passed on to the next point. It is the best—perhaps the only—way of dodging emotion. They were the average human article, and had they considered the note as a whole it would have driven them miserable or mad. Considered item by item, the emotional content was minimized, and all went forward smoothly.

In the end, by this simple expedient of considering the note point by point, they succeed in muddling themselves to the point where, with a clear conscience, they can throw the note on the fire. Forster, with characteristic irony, supports their action and then goes on to mention that there was perhaps one point in which they might be held reprehensible:

> For one hard fact remains. They did neglect a personal appeal. The woman who had died did say to them, "Do this," and they answered, "We will not."

The woman who had appealed to them never muddled things. 'She was not intellectual, nor even alert, and it was odd that, all the same, she should give the idea of greatness.'[7] And in spite of this judgment, she displays alertness of a rare order in an early scene, when a family quarrel is about to erupt.

"Yes or no, man; plain question, plain answer. Did or didn't Miss Schlegel—"

"Charles dear," said a voice from the garden. "Charles, dear Charles, one doesn't ask plain questions. There aren't such things."

They were all silent. It was Mrs Wilcox.

She approached just as Helen's letter had described her, trailing noiselessly over the lawn, and there was actually a wisp of hay in her hands. She seemed to belong not to the young people and their motor, but to the house, and to the tree that overshadowed it. One knew that she worshipped the past, and that the instinctive wisdom the past can alone bestow had descended upon her—that wisdom to which we give the clumsy name of aristocracy.[8]

The wisp of hay which Mrs Wilcox holds participates in a stream of symbolism that runs through the entire novel. She is first seen by Helen with her hands full of hay; and when Margaret begins to take her place, later, she also picks up the habit of playing with grass—at one point leaving a trail of it across the hall. The novel ends with a great hay harvest.[9]

Mr Wilcox and his children, on the other hand, are allergic to hay, and have to shut themselves away from it. Their allergy reflects a psychical limitation. Hay-fever, in fact, seems to correspond to the 'peevishness' of earlier novels—Margaret's brother Tibby, who also suffers from it, is described as losing some of his peevishness when he goes to Oxford.[10]

That the symbolism as a whole is deliberate is confirmed by a brief comment on Mrs Wilcox: 'Clever talk alarmed her, and withered her delicate imaginings; it was the social counterpart of a motor-car, all jerks, and she was a wisp of hay, a flower.'[11]

Ruth Wilcox resembles Mrs Moore in *A Passage to India* in that she is fighting a losing battle against impersonal forces and comes to lose interest in most human activities. Instead she falls back more and more upon her house. Her apathy is emphasized in a conversation with Margaret just before her death. Her voice 'suggested that pictures, concerts, and people are all of small and equal value. Only once had it quickened—when speaking of Howards End.'[12] And only in Margaret does she find anything of her own spirit, the spirit that can become devoted to a place. Hence her wish, incomprehensible to the rest of her family, that Margaret should have Howards End.

In spite of their impersonality, however, the Wilcoxes are treated more sympathetically in this novel than the Sawstonians of previous ones. Even Helen Schlegel has been impressed by their ideals, their firmness, their air of having hands on all the ropes. In the incident that begins the novel, however, their limitations stand revealed. She has fallen in love with Paul, the youngest son, and he has given her the impression of sharing her emotion. Yet he has felt nothing deeply, and has nothing to fall back on. At breakfast next morning she is horrified to see that he is frightened.

"When I saw all the others so placid, and Paul mad with terror in case I said the wrong thing, I felt for a moment that the whole Wilcox family was a fraud, just a wall of newspapers and motor-cars and golf-clubs, and that if it fell I should find nothing behind it but panic and emptiness."[13]

'Panic and emptiness': these words are to re-echo through the novel, and to dominate Helen's reactions to the Wilcoxes throughout. Margaret Schlegel takes a different attitude. She finds it more difficult to ignore the Wilcoxes and what they stand for.

"I've often thought about it, Helen. It's one of the most interesting things in the world. The truth is that there is a great outer life that you and I have never touched—a life in which telegrams and anger count. Personal relations, that we think supreme, are not supreme there. There love means marriage settlements, death, death duties. So far I'm clear. But here my difficulty. This outer life, though obviously horrid, often seems the real one—there's grit in it. It does breed character. Do personal relations lead to sloppiness in the end?"[14]

Much later in the novel, she is to declare, in a brief but telling sentence, "More and more do I refuse to draw my income and sneer at those who guarantee it."[15]

. . . . .

Margaret's concern with wholeness is her great quality: that and her sense of music, her harmonizing power. It is this which helps her to overcome the impersonal qualities of the Wilcoxes where Helen, who does battle with them impetuously from time to time, only succeeds in hardening them. But quite early in the novel Margaret and her qualities are caught up by another force— the gentle force of Ruth Wilcox and her instinctive wisdom, closely associated with the house, Howards End. When Mrs Wilcox dies, it is her wish that Margaret should have Howards End, and although her note is circumvented by the family, there is an inevitability in the rest of the novel which ensures that the dead woman's wishes will be fulfilled. Henry Wilcox later offers marriage to Margaret (it is no doubt a sub-conscious tribute to the memory of Mrs Wilcox that he should do so) and so the way is opened to the establishment of Margaret at the head of the Wilcox household in Mrs Wilcox's family home.

The device of setting the house, Howards End, at the centre helps to anchor the novel by a constant suggestion of permanence against the flux of events. Howards End is not the only important building, moreover. Throughout, there is a constant reference back to particular places, whether in the Hertfordshire countryside, in London, or in other parts of the country. It is interwoven skilfully with the events of the plot: and there is a constant suggestion that one chief difference between Schlegels and Wilcoxes lies in their respective attitudes to the spirit of place. The Wilcoxes and their kind are constantly insensitive to it: they are for ever pulling down the tasteful in order to put up the tasteless. Only the stubbornness of Mrs Wilcox stops her family from destroying the most beautiful elements in the setting of her house, when they introduce their various 'improvements'.

Another place which focuses respective attitudes is Oniton in Shropshire, a house which the Wilcoxes take for a short time after

Mrs Wilcox's death and from which Evie Wilcox is married. Twice brief comments are interposed.[16] Firstly, the wedding itself:

> In a few minutes the clergymen performed their duty, the register was signed, and they were back in their carriages, negotiating the dangerous curve by the lych-gate. Margaret was convinced that they had not been married at all, and that the Norman church had been intent all the time on other business.

And secondly, when they left it for ever:

> But the Wilcoxes have no part in the place, nor in any place. It is not their names that recur in the parish register. It is not their ghosts that sigh among the alders at evening. They have swept into the valley and swept out of it, leaving a little dust and a little money behind.

The idea of a spirit of place that preserves the older tradition of England is given its fullest expression in chapter nineteen, which is rounded at both ends by descriptions of the English downland, Poole Harbour and the Isle of Wight. Even in this chapter, however, a reference to Bournemouth reminds us that suburbia is encroaching everywhere. And the tentacles of suburbia reach back to an amorphous body, which is the new, formless London. Forster several times comments on that formlessness either directly or indirectly, through the narrative. The Schlegels lose their home in Wickham Place when it is bought to be pulled down by a speculative builder, and it is the news of this impending loss that prompts Mrs Wilcox's wish that Margaret should have Howards End. Of the actual demolition, Forster writes:

> The feudal ownership of land did bring dignity, whereas the modern ownership of movables is reducing us again to a nomadic horde. We are reverting to the civilization of luggage, and historians of the future will note how the middle classes accreted possessions without taking root in the earth, and may find in this the secret of their imaginative poverty. The Schlegels were certainly the poorer for the loss of Wickham Place. It had

helped to balance their lives, and almost to counsel them. Nor is their ground-landlord spiritually the richer. He has built flats on its site, his motor-cars grow swifter, his exposures of Socialism more trenchant. But he has spilt the precious distillation of the years, and no chemistry of his can give it back to society again.[17]

Wickham Place is pulled down, and shortly afterwards Henry Wilcox informs Margaret that Oniton is let. Margaret is oppressed by the sense of flux.

London was but a foretaste of this nomadic civilization which is altering human nature so profoundly, and throws upon personal relations a stress greater than they have ever borne before. Under cosmopolitanism, if it comes, we shall receive no help from the earth. Trees and meadows and mountains will only be a spectacle, and the binding force that they once exercised on character must be entrusted to Love alone. May Love be equal to the task![18]

Elsewhere Forster elaborates on the typicality of London in this respect.

Certainly London fascinates. One visualizes it as a tract of quivering grey, intelligent without purpose, and excitable without love; as a spirit that has altered before it can be chronicled; as a heart that certainly beats, but with no pulsation of humanity. It lies beyond everything: Nature, with all her cruelty, comes nearer to us than do these crowds of men. A friend explains himself: the earth is explicable—from her we came, and we must return to her. But who can explain Westminster Bridge Road or Liverpool Street in the morning—the city inhaling—or the same thoroughfares in the evening—the city exhaling her exhausted air? We reach in desperation beyond the fog, beyond the very stars, the voids of the universe are ransacked to justify the monster, and stamped with a human face. London is religion's opportunity—not the decorous religion of theologians, but anthropomorphic, crude. Yes, the continuous flow would be tolerable if a man of our own sort—not anyone pompous or tearful—were caring for us up in the sky.[19]

There is a Blakean note here—one is reminded of Los, the shaping spirit, who reads the stars, while his 'spectre' reads the voids between the stars.[20] And towards the end of the novel, at a moment when Margaret is depressed, this sinister aspect of London is crystallized into a single phrase. London is a 'caricature of infinity', expressing all that is formless, everything that is opposed to the spirit of love.

At such a point the inner philosophy of the novel is exposed to the bone. Man stands between infinity and infinity. He may accept the infinity that exists within the lineaments of love, and let this shaping spirit mould his civilization. But most men fear that infinity and, in running away from it, construct a different one—an infinity of formlessness in which no meaning can be found and from which no escape is possible because there is no containment. In this 'infinity', man is imprisoned not by the tangible, but by echoes and reflections.

For Margaret these moments when London is revealed as a place where the *genius loci* has no form induce a new feeling for the spirit of place where it does exist. At a time when the loss of Wickham Place is making her conscious of the new impersonalism abroad in the world, she values in Mrs Wilcox the spirit that associates itself personally with a house. It is the thought of Mrs Wilcox that stimulates an important exchange with Helen:

> "It is sad to suppose that places may ever be more important than people," continued Margaret.
> "Why, Meg? They're so much nicer generally. I'd rather think of that forester's house in Pomerania than of the fat Herr Förstmeister who lived in it."
> "I believe we shall come to care about people less and less, Helen. The more people one knows the easier it becomes to replace them. It's one of the curses of London. I quite expect to end my life caring most for a place."[21]

This thought, particularly as associated with Mrs Wilcox, revisits her from time to time, until a visit to Howards End on a summer day seizes her with visionary power.

All was not sadness. The sun was shining without. The thrush sang his two syllables on the budding guelder-rose. Some children were playing uproariously in heaps of golden straw. It was the presence of sadness at all that surprised Margaret, and ended by giving her a feeling of completeness. In these English farms, if anywhere, one might see life steadily and see it whole, group in one vision its transitoriness and its eternal youth, connect—connect without bitterness until all men are brothers.[22]

And in the end we see Margaret established in the house, in no way free from fears and anxieties, but contained by surroundings which give form and background to her whole life.

. . . .

Not the least virtue of *Howards End* is that it captures, as a running theme through the novel, a feeling for the house which is rare in English literature. It is a feeling that runs deep in the English character and has inhabited the minds of thousands who never succeeded in transmitting it into a lasting record. The link between a house and history has sometimes been expressed—for example in *Brideshead Revisited*—but that peculiarly warm association of sensibility between people and the house where they live is more difficult to achieve. Jane Austen expressed one side of it in *Mansfield Park*, Charles Lamb another in his essay, 'Mackery End in Hertfordshire'. Expression in general has not done justice to the intensity of the feeling, however, and with the disappearance of the civilization which was the seedbed of that feeling, it becomes steadily more difficult for a modern reader to feel that such emotions were ever strong. Forster not only conveys the intensity of the feeling, but gives it status and even philosophical significance.

In his biography of Marianne Thornton, Forster explains that the Howards End of the novel is based on the Hertfordshire home of his childhood ('which now stands just outside a twentieth century hub and almost within sound of a twentieth century hum'):

The garden, the overhanging wych-elm, the sloping meadow, the great view to the west, the cliff of fir trees to the north, the adjacent farm through the high tangled hedge of wild roses were all utilized by me in *Howards End*, and the interior is in the novel too.[23]

As we have seen, there is nothing fortuitous about its use in the novel. Forster (conscious that the belief is unfashionable) believes that a house such as the one he knew has a shaping influence upon its inhabitants of the indistinct, elusive sort that slips through the meshes of close analysis. The impressions gained from his home, he says,

> have given me a slant upon society and history. It is a middle-class slant, atavistic, derived from the Thorntons, and it has been corrected by contact with friends who have never had a home in the Thornton sense, and do not want one.

And when he describes the Thorntons losing their house, he writes:

> I understand many of their feelings: it has so happened that I have been deprived of a house myself. They will not be understood by the present generation.[24]

As Edwardian literature falls into perspective, one is impressed by the importance of the spirit of place in it. It is, for example, a point in common between Forster and Lawrence. But if Lawrence is the poet of place, Forster is its philosopher. The spirit of place is rooted not only in his work but also in the ideas about form and infinity that give shape to his thinking.

Howards End as a place is so vivid that it is easy to miss these additional philosophical currents, which give the novel its full significance. Of the Wilcoxes, Schlegels and Basts who interact constantly, only one family is in touch with them. The attitudes of the Wilcoxes and Basts are largely laid down for them by their environment: it is only the Schlegel sisters who order their conduct according to ideas. And they differ between themselves. Helen is constantly in pursuit of an absolute—she will give herself to any experience that promises spiritual intensity. Margaret, on the other hand, is looking for harmony. She surveys the field of human experience and tries to understand it all, looking for the key that will bring all into concord while giving each component its proper value. These varying philosophies are always implicit, seldom stated: but the statements are strategically placed. At the end of the novel, for example, when Margaret's state of turmoil and horror is relieved by the knowledge that Helen's child will give new opportunity and hope, her attitude is expressed philosophically at the very point when it is being transcended. 'To what ultimate harmony we tend she did not know, but there seemed great chance that a child would be born into the world, to take the great chances of beauty and adventure that the world offers.'[25]

In the case of Helen, there is a similar explicitness of statement at a low point in the novel. Margaret and Tibby, mystified and afraid because Helen is behaving strangely and keeping away from them, walk through London on a grey winter's afternoon. Everything that has previously been said about London as a nomadic city, headquarters of a new and impersonal civilization, now comes to a head:

> The mask fell off the city, and she saw it for what it really is—a caricature of infinity. The familiar barriers, the streets along which she moved, the houses between which she had made her little journeys for so many years, became negligible suddenly. Helen seemed one with grimy trees and the traffic and the slowly-flowing slabs of mud. She had accomplished a hideous act of renunciation and returned to the One. . . .
> . . . She went for a few moments into St Paul's, whose dome stands out of the welter so bravely, as if preaching the gospel of form. But within, St Paul's is as its surroundings—echoes and whispers, inaudible songs, invisible mosaics, wet footmarks crossing and recrossing the floor. Si monumentum requiris circumspice: it points us back to London.[26]

The moment of horror passes. Helen has indeed tried to make herself one with the absolute, but the impersonality of her action has a different source. Her reaching out to the absolute is informed by passion, not by greed, and the resulting issues are therefore precipitated also in human terms. Her action produces not formlessness and insanity but a death and a life—the death of Leonard Bast and the birth of his child.

But for a moment in St Paul's, Margaret has had a glimpse of that other absolute, that meaningless fabric of sights and sounds that stretches to infinity and returns only echoes and reflections to the questing human spirit. Margaret turns away from this sinister vision: she will look for a meaningful harmonious pattern within which she can live and give meaning to the lives of others. Helen, on the other hand, is not depressed but stimulated by such a negative vision—for her the goblin footfalls exist to be met by heroic action. The importance of these incidents lies in the light they throw on differences between Margaret and Helen—and also in their foreshadowing of a fuller treatment of the same theme. In the central incident of *A Passage to India*, echoes and reflections will again figure the shapeless absolute, in a cave where every sound turns into an echo and every sight is reflected from polished walls.

The contrast between Helen and Margaret reflects a contrast that intrigues Forster: the contrast between the hero and the man of civilization. The hero strives after some absolute ideal and is therefore liable to perish in youth, physically or spiritually: the man of civilization is intent on establishing a way of life. At one time Forster planned to develop the theme still further in a novel which would have explored the antithesis between 'the civilized man, who hopes for an Arctic Summer in which there is time to get things done, and the heroic man'. But the antithesis proved intractable when Forster tried to produce it into narrative, and *Arctic Summer* was never completed.[27]

In the event, therefore, Forster's main treatment of the contrast between the way of heroism and the way of civilization turns out to lie in his respective portrayals of Helen and Margaret. The existence in his mind of this contrast also helps to explain one of the most unexpected incidents of the novel, the scene in which Helen, in an attempt to atone for the injustices and wrongs of society, gives herself to the victim of the Wilcoxes, Leonard Bast. For Leonard too, in his limited fashion, has a touch of heroism. When the Schlegels first talk seriously to him, he tells them how he once walked through London during the night in order to see the dawn. And when, at the end of the novel he lies dead, killed through the impetuous action of Charles Wilcox, and Helen asks, ' ". . . what has Leonard got out of life?" ' Margaret replies, ' "Perhaps an adventure." '28

In spite of its philosophical subtlety, however, *Howards End* just misses greatness. Forster himself warns us against accepting the greatness of any novel too readily. 'Too many little mansions in English fiction,' he remarks, 'have been acclaimed to their own detriment as important edifices.' He cites as examples *Cranford*, *The Heart of Midlothian*, *Jane Eyre* and *Richard Feverel* and goes on: '. . . all four are little mansions, not mighty edifices, and we shall see and respect them for what they are if we stand them for an instant in the colonnades of *War and Peace*, or the vaults of *The Brothers Karamazov*'.29

Howards End comes off better than the novels he cites from such a comparison, but something is still lacking. The lack, as elsewhere in Forster, is implicit in the largeness of the aim. There is a singleness in the novel, yet it is not quite strong enough to take full control. The moral issues are too serious for the novel to be able completely to sustain the tight domestic comedy of Jane Austen, while the presence of domestic comedy prevents the moral issues from maturing into their full strength.

The clash of modes becomes explicit in the personality of Helen. In her central character she is an extremist, always striving after the absolute in some form or other. Yet we also see her playing the cosy cultural game with her brother and sister, enjoying fake quarrels with Margaret, indulging in family slang. This duplicity does not impair her effect upon the reader—it actually makes her more convincing as a person—but it means that she can never be the allegorical character which we look for in a great novel. Had she really yearned after the absolute with all her heart, she would have been impelled to struggle against the pleasant artificialities of life in Wickham Place. She did not. When, therefore, she does commit herself to a symbolic act in giving herself to Leonard Bast she is acting out of character—or rather acting the less familiar side of that character which has been established for her within the pages of the novel. The girl who gives herself to Leonard Bast is, as we know her, only an amateur of the absolute. As a result, we may even be forced into a certain sympathy with the Edwardian lady who said, on laying down the novel, that she did not think that Helen Schlegel 'would have forgotten herself so with that young Mr Bast'.[30]

We have noticed this flaw before. Domestic comedy and emotional seriousness are in danger of having a negating effect on each other, each impairing the effect which the other might have had in isolation. The effect of juxtaposing them is to impair the artistic singleness, even if there is a corresponding gain in realism.

There is a more blatant intrusion of 'realism' in this novel, moreover, which makes it still more adventurous as a work of art. Through the novel, affecting the plot at crucial moments, there walks the lugubrious figure of Leonard Bast, the clerk who stands 'at the extreme verge of gentility', 'one of the thousands who have lost the life of the body and failed to reach the life of the spirit',[31] and who exists in a limbo between the simple world of home and family which he has left behind him and the world of culture which beckons with its treacherous marsh-lights. He and his wife Jackie interrupt the ordered life of the Schlegels with intimations of squalor. Their intrusions are at first comic—Helen takes Leonard's umbrella by mistake—but become more serious when Leonard loses his post by taking Henry Wilcox's advice, Jackie is revealed as a former mistress to Henry Wilcox, Helen in a symbolic act gives herself to Leonard Bast and becomes the mother of his child, and Leonard finally perishes from a heart attack precipitated by a blow from Charles Wilcox.

Many readers feel uneasy about the Basts without being able to formulate their objections clearly. One reason is that Leonard is not altogether convincing in terms of the station in society assigned to him. Frank Swinnerton has put this objection succinctly:

> As for the uneducated Cockney clerk and his wife, I am an uneducated Cockney, and I have been a clerk. I was never learned enough to be employed in a bank; but my knowledge of clerks is very extensive. I have never met one who would be

overwhelmed by decent behaviour on the part of an under-graduate, or one to whom such decent behaviour would seem less than his due. A consciousness of condescension would seem rather to belong to the undergraduate. How can I possibly believe in a being so uncouth, when I am told that he springs from a class which I know to be above all others decent, well-behaved, and self-respecting?[32]

Leonard Bast does not quite ring true as a realistic figure, even if we grant that he is not intended to be representative of his class: and at the other extreme, his symbolical position means that he is caught between the contending modes of the novel. He first appears at a Beethoven concert attended by the Schlegels and their friends and is connected with Helen's reactions to the Fifth Symphony. For her the last movement begins with a goblin 'walking quietly over the universe, from end to end'.

They were not aggressive creatures; it was that that made them so terrible to Helen. They merely observed in passing that there was no such thing as splendour or heroism in the world.[33]

Whenever the Basts enter the scene we are reminded of that goblin footfall. Mrs Bast for Margaret rises 'out of the abyss, like a faint smell, a goblin footfall, telling of a life where love and hatred had both decayed'.[34] The Basts present both a general challenge to the Schlegels by their vulgarity and a particular one by reason of Leonard's aspirations to culture. Leonard's explanation of his ambitions to Jackie brings out this mixture of vulgarity and aspiration.

"I'll tell you another thing too. I care a good deal about improving myself by means of Literature and Art, and so getting a wider outlook. For instance, when you came in I was reading Ruskin's 'Stones of Venice'. I don't say this to boast, but just to show you the kind of man I am. I can tell you, I enjoyed that classical concert this afternoon."[35]

Leonard is one of those who are born to be impressed by high-sounding words, but Margaret is still drawn by the sincerity of his aspirations to feel that something ought to be done for him if 'culture' is not to be a vain hypocrisy. It ought to be able to reach out its hand and pull the aspirant to its shore. The effect of the novel is to suggest that there is a hopelessness in the venture. Leonard can read as much as he likes, can talk to cultured people, can go to concerts, but he will still only go through the motions of being a cultured man. The root of the matter will not be in him, for all his other virtues.

The effect of this is that Leonard's presence and speech cut right across the novel. One is reminded of the presence of Caliban in *The Tempest*—a being that actually represents all that is left when the work of art is created, the intractable surd that no artist can bring into his harmonic pattern. Leonard cannot figure in the novel's symphony because he himself contains no music. Every other character has some sort of style or note by which he or she is fitted into the action, but Leonard is a creature devoid of style.

In this respect, the presentation of him differs radically from Beethoven's goblin footfalls. The footfalls are themselves musical: they fit the harmonic pattern of the symphony; they do not fight against the artistic medium that contains them. Leonard does fight against the medium. In a novel which consists throughout of elegance and style he appears from time to time to put in an un-musical noise, to observe, as Beethoven's goblin footfalls never could, that there are such things as lack of music and uncultured living.

One can hardly imagine a foreign writer doing this. A French writer would find it impossible to introduce into a serious novel something which conflicted with and negated the prevailing style. Forster's insistence on doing so reflects that sense of morality which lies embedded in his outlook. It is the morality which possessed those Victorian thinkers who found their evangelical beliefs challenged and then responded to the truth in the challenge by transferring the uprightness with which they had learned to follow their faith to the faithless world which claimed them. With the intent earnestness that had characterized their efforts after moral perfection they now pursued a 'real' vision of the world—a vision which would not turn aside from fact. Novelists in this tradition were forced into one of two modes. They could either, like Thomas Hardy, indulge a persistent melancholia, which sprang from a full view of the unpleasant and inconvenient facts in the world and lived in their penumbra, or else, like George Eliot, write novels in a traditional pattern but bring about crises that were not artistic but moral, and during which sober daylight temporarily broke in upon the vision which had been playing on the action. Forster's method is nearer that of George Eliot: his moments of unilluminated 'reality' are not intended to give shape to the novel as a whole. But even George Eliot never cut across her own medium in the way that Forster cuts across his with the 'vulgarity' of Leonard Bast.

This paradox removes the novel temporarily from the canons of normal criticism. Criticism tries to deal with a total pattern, not with a pattern that from time to time undermines itself. Yet it is typical of Forster's unhesitating devotion to the fullness of reality that he should be prepared to do this. And in so far as the Basts participate in the novel's total effect, they act in the same way as the violences and sudden deaths. They undermine the artistic harmony of the novel and turn it into something else—into a work which tries to include the artistically impotent, a *Tempest* in which Caliban does not even speak poetry.

How is it then that the Basts do not in the end destroy the novel? We may begin to find an answer in Margaret's reflections after Leonard's death:

> To what ultimate harmony we tend she did not know, but there seemed great chance that a child would be born into the world, to take the great chances of beauty and adventure that the world offers. She moved through the sunlit garden, gathering narcissi, crimson-eyed and white. There was nothing else to be done; the time for telegrams and anger was over, and it seemed wisest that the hands of Leonard should be folded on his breast and be filled with flowers. Here was the father; leave it at that. Let Squalor be turned into Tragedy, whose eyes are the stars, and whose hands hold the sunset and the dawn.[36]

Margaret's thoughts are, in one sense, a betrayal of Leonard Bast. Basically, of course, they are not. She is looking behind the sordid exterior to the lineaments of the eternal man. But in terms of the novel this is unjust. The eternal man may have been there but it emerged only negatively, in Leonard's remorse and refusal to be muddled. So far as the novel is concerned he was never 'Tragedy' and to make him so is to rob him of his identity within that artistic framework. From this moment onwards, however, the novel is to be dominated not by past events but by Margaret's vision. She has a 'belief in the eternity of beauty' which cannot be shaken, and this belief will inevitably betray the sordid for the simple reason that the sordid will be outside its vision. Forster was to depict the sinister element in this betrayal after the First World War, when he had seen how artistic middle-class minds could turn even the obscenity of the trenches into 'Tragedy'.[37]

In this novel, untouched by that later darkness, he can treat Margaret as a value in herself. Her actions at the end of the novel finally establish as dominant the qualities for which she has stood throughout. And this means a significant advance in Forster's technique for expressing 'vision' in his work. In earlier novels the 'visionary moment' was a revelation of reality, by which other events in the novel were judged. In *Howards End*, there is stress not on the visionary moment but on the visionary person. Margaret has her moments of vision, but these will be drawn into a total outlook which is distinguished also by its ability to appraise facts as they are.

We have noticed before how Forster tends to protect the visionary elements of his novels by a screen of irony or comedy. It is so here: and this time it is an affinity with Jane Austen's style that provides the cover. The opening of *Pride and Prejudice* is well known:

> It is a truth universally acknowledged, that a single man in possession of a good fortune, must be in want of a wife.

The opening of the fifth chapter of *Howards End* is in similar vein:

> It will be generally admitted that Beethoven's Fifth Symphony is the most sublime noise that has ever penetrated into the ear of man.

This shares with Jane Austen's opening an air of leisurely elegance, coupled with an amused undertone—an awareness that we might disagree, but would find it very difficult to say so or to suggest alternative candidates if we did. The passage continues:

> Whether you are like Mrs Munt, and tap surreptitiously when the tunes come—of course, not so as to disturb the others —or like Helen, who can see heroes and shipwrecks in the music's flood; or like Margaret, who can see only the music; or like Tibby, who is profoundly versed in counterpoint, and holds the full score open on his knee; or like their cousin, Fraülein Mosebach, who remembers all the time that Beethoven is "echt Deutsch"; or like Fraülein Mosebach's young man, who can remember nothing but Fraülein Mosebach; in any case, the passion of your life becomes more vivid, and you are bound to admit that such a noise is cheap at two shillings. It is cheap, even if you hear it in the Queen's Hall, dreariest music-room in London, though not as dreary as the Free Trade Hall, Manchester; and even if you sit on the extreme left of that hall, so that the brass bumps at you before the rest of the orchestra arrives, it is still cheap.

The tone of light comedy which was set by the Jane Austen-like opening is sustained by the satiric references to Mrs Munt, to the solemn Tibby, to Fraülein Mosebach's young man and to the Queen's Hall. So dominant is this tone of quiet humorous charm that it is easy to miss other points in the description—the use of the word 'sublime', the picture of Helen seeing heroes and shipwrecks, and that vital statement, 'the passion of your life becomes more vivid'. When we recall the central statement of the book, 'Only connect the prose and passion . . .', however, we may suspect that there is a hard core of seriousness in the passage.

There is, for example, that reference to Margaret 'seeing only the music'. This turns out to be the key to her personality in the novel. One notices a tone, a note, which pervades and sounds through everything that she does and says. Because she is trying to connect across a gulf, the tone is sometimes muted: yet it persists. And at its most intense moments it becomes linked to the 'visionary' element in previous novels. At the heart of Margaret's vision is a faith that the key to human discords is the spirit of love, the true harmonizer, which is always waiting to become incarnate in human form. This is the faith which underlies her attempts to connect:

> Only connect the prose and the passion, and both will be exalted, and human love will be seen at its height.

The 'mythological' structure of that statement is evident, once one is familiar with Forster's other statements.

The other significant points are easy to miss because, like their predecessors, they occur in the course of heightened passages which modern taste dismisses as 'purple' and skims over without closer examination. Yet they are central to the novelist's purpose. Margaret's desire to 'connect' is seen as her major virtue, rivalled only by her determination not to be muddled. (She turns away even from Henry Wilcox when at a moment of crisis she sees him 'criminally muddled'[38]). The novelist endorses Margaret's view by placing the words 'Only connect' . . . on the title-page of his novel. And even connection is only the beginning of virtue. A particular sort of connection is required. It is not enough to build a bridge: the connection must take the form of a vital dialectic, from which something new will be born. Thus he writes, of Henry Wilcox and Margaret Schlegel:

> Mature as he was, she might yet be able to help him to the building of the rainbow bridge that should connect the prose in us with the passion. Without it we are meaningless fragments, half monks, half beasts, unconnected arches that have never joined into a man. With it love is born, and alights on the highest curve, glowing against the grey, sober against the fire. Happy the man who sees from either aspect the glory of these outspread wings. The roads of his soul lie clear, and he and his friends shall find easy-going.[39]

It is easy to see in the moralizing tone of the passage cover for an absence of thought: that is what we are nowadays encouraged to see in moralizing tones. The last sentence, in particular, is out of tune with modern taste. But there is in fact a degree of exact thought within the heightened style, and to ignore it is to miss an important element in the novel's structure.

Henry, deprived of the indwelling power of true love, exists as a dialectic between monk and beast. Margaret's idea is reiterated on the next page:

> Only connect! That was the whole of her sermon. Only connect the prose and the passion, and both will be exalted, and human love will be seen at its height. Live in fragments no longer. Only connect, and the beast and the monk, robbed of the isolation that is life to either, will die.

Henry cannot rise to her invitation. He does not achieve 'the tenderness that kills the Monk and the Beast at a single blow'.[40] Yet that vision of Love continues to haunt the novel, seen sometimes as a cosmic figure, sometimes as a precious jewel. (' "Men did produce one jewel," the gods will say, and, saying, will give us immortality.')[41]

Henry's failure gives the grit of realism to the novel, but Margaret's vision and music remain triumphant at the end. And Forster gives her 'music' further backing in the novel. It will be remembered that in *A Room with a View*, the musical element of the novel was constantly related to the natural imagery, until in the last paragraph the coachman's song died away to give place to the sound of the Arno, carrying away the snows of winter. The same theme is used more elaborately here. Margaret's constant sense of flux, though often oppressive to her, is at other times converted into music.

The sense of oppression comes, as we have seen, when she contemplates London and the so-called progress of civilization. The musical note comes in happier moments. It is there in the first description of Wickham Place on a peaceful morning:

> One had the sense of a backwater, or rather of an estuary, whose waters flowed in from the invisible sea, and ebbed into a profound silence while the waves without were still beating.[42]

Margaret's moment of decision, of pitting vision against reality by accepting the Wilcoxes, takes place by a real estuary—the estuary at Poole which corresponds to the Wiltshire of earlier stories. At Oniton, she goes to sleep 'tethered by affection, and lulled by the murmurs of the river that descended all the night from Wales'.[43] Towards the end of the novel, when she passes a peaceful evening with Helen,

> The present flowed by them like a stream. The tree rustled. It had made music before they were born, and would continue after their deaths, but its song was of the moment.[44]

Even at the moment when she sees Henry's failure to connect, the comment is 'At such moments the soul retires within, to float upon the bosom of a deeper stream. . . .'[45]

This image is bound in with others at the end, when the Six Hills near Howards End are used symbolically. They are 'tombs of warriors, breasts of the spring',[46] and when Margaret's moment comes at the end of the novel, in Henry's realization that his son will be sentenced for manslaughter, the 'new life' is born on the hill where he tells her the news.

> Margaret drove her fingers through the grass. The hill beneath her moved as if it were alive.[47]

But she could have achieved nothing in the novel without another power which stands in equally symbolic relationship to the forces of nature. Her state of inward happiness and reconciliation is like a stream, but it owes its existence to a 'central radiance' in her relationship with Henry which follows Forster's familiar mythological pattern by relating the god of Love to the sun-god:

> An immense joy came over her. It was indescribable. It had nothing to do with humanity, and most resembled the all-pervading happiness of fine weather. Fine weather is due to the sun, but Margaret could think of no central radiance here. She stood in his drawing-room happy, and longing to give happiness. On leaving him she realized that the central radiance had been love.[48]

The radiant, sun-like love which becomes incarnate at that moment in Henry Wilcox's drawing-room provides the necessary complement to Margaret's association with Ruth Wilcox, and through her with grass, streams and the earth. It completes her 'universe'. Sun and earth are wedded in that moment of human love when imagination transforms bodily passion.

Yet the symbolism of this novel shows a distinct advance from that of *A Room with a View*, where the central visionary scenes were associated with these moments of love. In spite of Margaret's love for Henry Wilcox, the most important visionary scene of the novel takes place without him, and in fact at a time when Margaret has temporarily rejected him for being 'criminally muddled'. The scene in question is the one in which Margaret and Helen spend a long evening together at Howards End against Henry's express commands.

A closer look at this chapter shows that it brings together several leitmotivs of the novel in a satisfying manner. In a recent discussion of the novel, Mr Cyrus Hoy has drawn attention to some themes of the novel, including two which are relevant to the 'space and time' motif. He points out that the sense of time is mentioned at intervals, as another means of distinguishing the Wilcox attitude from others:

> As is Man to the Universe, so was the mind of Mr Wilcox to the minds of some men—a concentrated light upon a tiny spot, a little Ten Minutes moving self-contained through its appointed years. No Pagan he, who lives for the Now, and may be wiser than all philosophers. He lived for the five minutes that have passed, and the five to come; he had the business mind.[49]

When Margaret visits Howards End for the first time, the sense of flux which has been haunting her all the year disappears, but she is hurried away by Henry, who has an engagement in London that evening. On the long evening that she spends with Helen, this sense of 'the present' comes to fruition. The present 'flows by them like a stream':

> The peace of the country was entering into her. It has no commerce with memory, and little with hope. Least of all is it concerned with the hopes of the next five minutes. It is the peace of the present, which passes understanding. Its murmur came "now", and "now" once more as they trod the gravel, and "now", as the moonlight fell upon their father's sword.[50]

As Leonard walks through the countryside towards Howards End, filled with remorse, the country 'was uttering her cry of "now"'.

Besides reducing time to a peaceful stream, the house creates a peaceful space in the midst of flux. This is the first thing that strikes Margaret when she first visits it, and she is also impressed by the wych-elm that Mrs Wilcox previously described to her. House and tree together come to have a supra-sexual significance:

> The wych-elm that she saw from the window was an English tree. No report had prepared her for its peculiar glory. It was neither warrior, nor lover, nor god; in none of these rôles do the English excel. It was a comrade, bending over the house, strength and adventure in its roots, but in its utmost fingers tenderness, and the girth, that a dozen men could not have spanned, became in the end evanescent, till pale bud clusters seemed to float in the air. It was a comrade. House and tree transcended any similes of sex.[51]

The long conversation with Helen takes place beneath the tree, and as they discuss everything that has happened, Margaret remarks on a feeling that all of them are only a part of Mrs Wilcox's mind:

> "She knows everything. She is everything. She is the house, and the tree that leans over it."[52]

And as Margaret herself becomes imbued with Mrs Wilcox's spirit, she too comes to have something of the same quality, transcending her sex in a complete, androgynous vision.

The central symbol of the novel, the house, by offering space and an enduring present, consolidates in physical terms the imaginative reality which has come into being in her love for Henry Wilcox. That which was a momentary revelation, an imaginative universe within herself alone, thus becomes established into an abiding way of life which can include other people.

Nevertheless, the world at large, the world of formless flux and 'the next ten minutes', continues to exist, and the consolidation of Margaret's vision in Howards End necessarily involves exclusion. From now on she will turn away from some elements in the world around her. She will have nothing to do with the tide of red-roofed houses which is gradually creeping nearer and nearer to her own, nor, as we have seen, can she do anything with Leonard's sordidness except turn it into Tragedy.

Her actions solve the artistic problem which we mentioned earlier. The unreality which has hovered round the Basts during the novel is finally confirmed, and the challenge which they offered to the novel's structure is finally drowned in a music which makes them as though they had never been. Margaret, meanwhile, has established her 'tone': and whether right or wrong, she is at least not muddled. She has looked steadily at the sordidness of the world, of which Leonard Bast is the most creditable representative, has done her best for it, and in the end chosen to concentrate on her own limited world, conscious that that in itself will provide problems and complexities enough for her powers. She has seen the 'caricature of infinity' which is London and her moment of negative vision in St Paul's has confirmed her in the desire to exercise herself within the finite and controllable, and to find infinity within the lineaments of love.

Helen also has retired, but from a more heroic struggle. Although her vision of the sordid frightened her, it impelled her in the first place not to retreat but to action and battle. As with Margaret, her attitude was exemplified in her response to Beethoven's Fifth Symphony. While Margaret was hearing only the music, she was seeing 'heroes and shipwrecks in the music's flood' and then a more sinister vision in the last movement:

... the music started with a goblin walking quietly over the universe, from end to end. Others followed him. They were not aggressive creatures; it was that that made them so terrible to Helen. They merely observed in passing that there was no such thing as splendour or heroism in the world. ... Helen could not contradict them, for, once at all events, she had felt the same, and had seen the reliable walls of youth collapse. Panic and emptiness! Panic and emptiness! The goblins were right.[53]

Once again, the whimsical tone is misleading, and makes it easy to miss the seriousness of the point here. One does not normally take goblins very seriously. They are fairy-tale stuff for most of us. We might regard the episode simply as light fantasy on Helen's part—unless we are well on our guard and remember the importance with which she invested 'panic and emptiness' when she saw it in the Wilcoxes.

And Helen, like Margaret, has her victory in the novel. It is suggested twice: first in a scene where Tibby walks with her through Oxford and questions her about the Basts.

> Her eyes, the hand laid on the mouth, quite haunted him, until they were absorbed into the figure of St Mary the Virgin, before whom he paused for a moment on the walk home.[54]

The theme recurs when Margaret finally runs Helen to earth and discovers that the reason for her strange behaviour is that she is pregnant:

> Only her head and shoulders were visible. She sat framed in the vine, and one of her hands played with the buds. The wind ruffled her hair, the sun glorified it; she was as she had always been.[55]

The madonna image is irresistible here and reminds us of that scene in *Where Angels Fear to Tread* where a man, a woman and a child become for a moment the 'holy' family.

Both sisters have their triumph in the novel, but it is Margaret's triumph that is central. And the fact that her value is, in the last analysis, a 'musical' value means that her triumph is aesthetic as much as moral. Her harmonious power is undeniable, but it was gained, as she herself acknowledges, because she had leisure, money and opportunities to cultivate herself. Leonard Bast had none of these. Aesthetically, it is perfectly in order that at the end of the novel her music should sound against his absence of music and reduce him to non-existence in the very act of elevating him to 'Tragedy'. But the aesthetic triumph induces a moral doubt. We are left reflecting that each human being has its own value, purely by being born to the human condition, and that Leonard has in this sense been deprived of his birthright.

Forster makes us aware of this dilemma in the novel, but offers no solution. He cannot, in fact. It is one thing to make a character sympathetic by identifying her with a musical quality, it is quite another to identify another character with the absence of music and yet try to render him equally sympathetic with the first. Any attempt to do so sets the work of art at war with its own medium in an impossible conflict.

Forster's local failures with Leonard Bast are a small price to pay for the undoubted success of the novel as a whole. It has a richness of conception and detail which has only been touched upon in the preceding pages. The symbols of house and tree exist triumphantly within the plot and also enable Forster to advance upon his earlier vision. The romantic union of hero and heroine is now superseded by an androgynous union of qualities within the heroine which overarches and includes all other unions, including her own marriage with Henry Wilcox. It is thus given a greater stability and wider relevance than that which would have resulted from a simple romantic marriage. All the threads of the novel are drawn together into the final, established household at Howards End, where the house and overarching elm represent the twin qualities of the chief character.

The failure, such as it is, provides the point of development for Forster's next novel. We have seen how the triumph of Margaret's vision does violence to Leonard's value purely as a human being: and Forster's attempt to counter such an effect by stressing Leonard's humanity only means that the darker theme of the novel, which Leonard from time to time represents, never assumes its proper significance. The echoes and reflections in St Paul's suggest it, but they only touch and horrify Margaret briefly: the Basts and Wilcoxes who represent that power at greater length, are too human to do justice to the full, impersonal horror of the goblin footfalls. The novel gains in roundness and completion from this constant subduing of the dull echoes and sinister footfalls, but that part of Forster's purpose remains, correspondingly, unfulfilled. The full extent of his 'realism' is not so far revealed.

The problem of giving roundness to a novel while still bringing vision and realism into full tension, one against the other, could not be achieved while Forster still compromised by identifying lack of vision with particular people. It was not in fact finally solved until he brought his characters to India. In the vastness of that setting, 'goblin footfalls' could achieve a final, impersonal horror by being revealed most fully in a place which had never been touched by any contact with humanity at all.

CHAPTER VI

The Undying Worm

FORSTER visited India twice, in 1912-13 and 1921. He has recalled some of his impressions, and included letters written at the time, in *The Hill of Devi*. But the seeds of *A Passage to India* lie scattered still further back. They were growing when Herbert Pembroke, addressing his house at Sawston School, pointed to portraits of empire-builders on the wall and quoted imperial poets.[1]

There is an inevitability in the choice of theme for this culminating novel. In the earlier ones, Sawston never quite found an antagonist worthy of its powers. In England, it was faced on one side by an aristocracy which patronized and used it, on the other by a working class with which it had long ago compromised. It existed only with the connivance of other classes of society which in their turn kept some check on it. Even when it set itself against the more spontaneous life of Italy, it was facing a society which in its treatment of women and relatives was even more rigid than itself.

But in India, Sawston could flourish with greater freedom. As a class it was single and distinct, not subject to checks from above or below: and the opposition to it came from a separate civilization which although more comprehensive, more venerable and more alive to the human condition than itself, was seen by its blinkered vision as naïve and primitive. The characteristics of Sawston were bound to become exaggerated in a situation where it lived both complacently assured of its own rightness and consciously embattled against forces which could easily, through some error or miscalculation, overwhelm it. A novel with such a setting is necessarily alive with dramatic tensions.

Into this precarious situation, as localized in the small station of Chandrapore, step Mrs Moore and Adela Quested, two visitors from England. Adela has come because a marriage is being arranged between her and Ronny Heaslop, the district magistrate; Mrs Moore in order to accompany her. Adela expresses a desire to see the 'real' India, and in order that she may do so Dr Aziz, a young doctor, arranges a trip to the famous Marabar caves. But during the expedition Adela enters a cave and on emerging has the impression that Aziz followed her in and assaulted her. Her accusations are made publicly, an explosive situation is created in the small town, and a trial is arranged at which she is to be called as a witness. Then, when the tension is at its height during the trial, Adela suddenly declares that no one followed her into the cave. The trial collapses; there is a temporary crisis during which there are fears for the breakdown of public order, and then life resumes its normal tenor. Adela, who has incurred universal dislike for her action, returns to England without marrying Ronny. The novel concludes with a long section devoted to an Indian festival which is attended by Mrs Moore's son and daughter. Mrs Moore herself, who stood throughout the novel as a reconciling power between English and Indians, has died on the voyage home after an illness which began, like Adela's crisis, with her experiences in a Marabar cave.

The dramatic situation of the novel, involving as it does an explosive human situation which can be ignited by the failure of a single individual, is finely conceived. If one regards plot as a means for manipulating the reader's expectations and responses, on the other hand, the novel is less successful. It is a major disappointment to readers who have been brought up on detective stories to find that there is no spectacular dénouement, no final revelation concerning the events in the cave, only Adela's denial that Dr Aziz followed her. And if this negation is all that is to be offered, the key events of the trial ought to come at the end of the novel. Why is there a long sequence dealing with irrelevancies such as the festival?

Forster has explained his introduction of the Hindu festival in an interview:

INTERVIEWERS: What was the exact function of the long description of the Hindu festival in *A Passage to India*?

FORSTER: It was architecturally necessary. I needed a lump, or a Hindu temple if you like—a mountain standing up. It is well placed; and it gathers up some strings. But there ought to be more after it. The lump sticks out a little too much.[2]

But this answers one question only to raise another. Why, when the climax of the book has been passed, should such a lump be 'architecturally necessary'? The answer can only be that it is there for some purpose other than the dramatic demands of the plot. In other words, we have to cope with the possibility that the structure of the novel does not consist simply of an arrangement of events. Behind that structure there is another, an arrangement of the novel's meaning.

   .   .   .   .

A reader who is looking for further meaning in the novel may well be attracted to the idea that it is intended as a piece of anti-imperialist propaganda, polemic against British rule in India. This interpretation was common at the time of publication, when the idea of Empire was a good deal more sacred than it is now. There are stories of civil servants, outward bound for India, who bought the novel as suitable reading for their voyage, only to throw their copies overboard angrily when they discovered the contents. If they did so, they were behaving more like the Indian civil servants of popular caricature than do Forster's own characters.

As a picture of British rule in India, the novel contains some distortions. Anyone who is so impressed by Forster's realism as to believe that it is universally accepted as a strictly documented record of modern India may read an article by Nirad Chaudhuri entitled 'Passage to and from India'.[3] Mr Chaudhuri does not necessarily speak for all Indians, but it is still interesting to observe the points in the novel with which he disagrees. He takes exception to an incident where officials are frightened and their wives and children take shelter in the club. 'Of this kind of cowardice no British official in India was to my mind ever guilty. . . .' He also finds Forster too charitable to Indians. 'Aziz would not have been allowed to cross my threshold, not to speak of being taken as an equal. Men of his type are a pest even in free India.' Some of the characters in the novel could be typical only of the sort of Princely State in which Forster spent most of his time, not of modern India. 'For instance, to those of us who are familiar with the teachings of the Hindu reformers of the 19th century, Godbole is not an exponent of Hinduism, he is a clown.'

Apart from these matters of detail, Mr Chaudhuri attacks the descriptions of personal relationships between British and Indians which are offered for our approval.

> The great Indians who brought about the Westernisation of their country and created its modern culture had none of the characteristic Indian foibles for which Mr Forster invokes British compassion. They were men of the stature of an Erasmus, Comenius, or Holberg, who could hold their own with the best in Europe. Yet some of them were assaulted, some insulted, and others slighted by the local British.

In making this point, however, Mr Chaudhuri is not attacking Forster's basic position. If Forster disapproves of patronizing those with 'characteristic Indian foibles', he would, *a fortiori*, argue still more vehemently against insulting India's true men of stature.

Mr Chaudhuri's further argument that it is misleading to see the Indian question in terms of human relationships, carries more weight. One is reminded of some remarks by George Orwell about the British in India:

> It may be that all that they did was evil, but they changed the face of the earth (it is instructive to look at a map of Asia and compare the railway system of India with that of the surrounding countries), whereas they could have achieved nothing, could not have maintained themselves in power for a single week, if the normal Anglo-Indian outlook had been that of, say, E. M. Forster.[4]

It is perfectly true that little attention is paid within the novel itself to the sheer vastness of the political and economic forces at work in India. But the novel ought never to have been read as an essay in *realpolitik*. It is at once too local and too universal. As a contribution to a 'practical' solution of the Indian problem as it existed at that time its value was limited, and the last chapter acknowledges the fact.

Beyond these immediate questions, the pettinesses of officials in a small Government station do have their relevance: for racial and economic questions are, ultimately, questions of human relations and it can never be out of place to say so.

Moreover, Mr Chaudhuri does not take sufficient account of the fact that Forster's satire is not directed only against the British. When he notices satire of Indians, it worries him: he does not seem to see that, as so often with Forster, we are being presented not with propaganda, but with a dialectic, of which the British and the Indians furnish respective limbs. The British may act badly in Forster's India, but so do the Indians. There is never any doubt that they need the justice and fair administration that the British give them. It is the hostility and lack of communication between the two sides that marks the failure—the old failure to 'connect'.

The gap between the two sides is, roughly speaking, the gap between head and heart. In his 'Notes on the English Character', Forster makes an observation which gives us the key to his view of the British in India:

(The English) go forth into a world that is not entirely composed of public-school men or even of Anglo-Saxons, but of men who are as various as the sands of the sea; into a world of whose richness and subtlety they have no conception. They go forth into it with well-developed bodies, fairly developed minds, and undeveloped hearts. And it is this undeveloped heart that is largely responsible for the difficulties of Englishmen abroad. An undeveloped heart—not a cold one. The difference is important. . . .[5]

Forster's Indians, on the other hand, make up for any failure in cold judicial reasoning by their highly developed hearts. Between the two groups there is a failure. But if the British are to be blamed for the failure, that is only because they were the group from which any initiative must necessarily have come.

Throughout his novel, Forster is at pains to stress the quality of achievement of the British and in particular their desire that justice be done. His central points both for and against the régime are made in his account of the work of Ronny as City Magistrate at Chandrapore:

> Every day he worked hard in the court trying to decide which of two untrue accounts was the less untrue, trying to dispense justice fearlessly, to protect the weak against the less weak, the incoherent against the plausible, surrounded by lies and flattery.

Adela, listening to his defence of his behaviour, is not satisfied however:

> His words without his voice might have impressed her, but when she heard the self-satisfied lilt of them, when she saw the mouth moving so complacently and competently beneath the little red nose, she felt, quite illogically, that this was not the last word on India. One touch of regret—not the canny substitute but the true regret from the heart—would have made him a different man, and the British Empire a different institution.[6]

Throughout the novel, this failure of connection between British and Indians is a running theme. There is no need to illustrate in detail what every reader can see for himself. Towards the end of the novel it is symbolized perhaps in the temple at Mau which has two shrines—the Shrine of the Head on the hill, the Shrine of the Body below. At all events, the separation is strongly emphasized in the last chapter, when the two characters who have tried hardest to come together, Fielding and Aziz, are out riding. The final passage, in which the whole landscape confirms Aziz's words about the impossibility of friendship between British and Indians, finely epitomizes this element in the novel:

> But the horses didn't want it—they swerved apart; the earth didn't want it, sending up rocks through which riders must pass single file; the temples, the tank, the jail, the palace, the birds, the carrion, the Guest House, that came into view as they issued

from the gap and saw Mau beneath: they didn't want it, they said in their hundred voices, "No, not yet," and the sky said, "No, not there."

For Fielding, a moderate man who is content with friendliness and sweet reasonableness in his dealings with other men, there can be no solution in India. He finds what he is looking for only when he visits Italy on his way home to England and rediscovers the beauty of its cities. 'He had forgotten the beauty of form among idol temples and lumpy hills.' The account of his visit concludes:

> The Mediterranean is the human norm. When men leave that exquisite lake, whether through the Bosphorus or the Pillars of Hercules, they approach the monstrous and extra-ordinary; and the southern exit leads to the strangest experience of all.[7]

This observation is sometimes taken to be Forster's final message in the novel: and it is true that in so far as it is a study of the conflict between two civilizations, at extreme poles from each other and separated by the Mediterranean, the passage offers the only hint of a solution. But it also has to be read in conjunction with another statement of Forster's: 'though proportion is the final secret, to espouse it at the outset is to insure sterility'.[8]

The point of the novel lies not in an assertion of normality, but in an exploration of extremes. And this exploration is not simply social and political. Further issues are involved, which reflect Forster's basic preoccupations as a thinker, and his own experiences in India.

The relationship between Forster's experiences and the final shape of his novel is a good deal more subtle than one might at first imagine. If one turns to *The Hill of Devi*, the later factual record of his visits, some points of contact with the novel stand out immediately. The details of the festival which he attended in 1921 correspond in some respects with those of the festival described in the last section of the novel: to mention a detailed example, the band strikes up incongruously with 'Nights of

Gladness' in both accounts.[9] But although Forster's whimsical humour and sense of the ridiculous is at work in both books, it is under a tighter rein in the novel. In *The Hill of Devi*, for example, he describes how on one occasion he had the task of setting up coconuts at certain points in the grounds:

> I must, however, see about those coconuts. I find that the motor-cars and the electric battery each want to worship one too. Hoping to have caught the spirit of Dassera, I then offered one to the Tennis Court, and another to the Guest House, but no, wrong again. The Tennis Court and the Guest House never pray to coconuts. . . .[10]

In the first chapter of *A Passage to India* humorous observation on this point is restricted to a single sentence. 'There are no bathing-steps on the river front, as the Ganges happens not to be holy here.' This strict control is exercised throughout, and where whimsical humour occurs it is usually in order to help with some other effect. The description of the civil station in the first chapter is a case in point. '. . . it provokes no emotion. It charms not, neither does it repel.' At first sight, the mannered style might seem unnecessary: but in fact the Biblical turn of phrase is helping to suggest the atmosphere of Sawston which pervades the station.

On a more intimate scale, events from his own friendships are sometimes introduced into the novel, as with an incident which he had already used to illustrate the difference between the British and Indian temperaments. The original account, in the essay 'Notes on the English Character', is lengthy. He had been on holiday with an Indian friend. At the end of the week his friend expressed overwhelming sorrow. 'He felt that because the holiday was over all happiness was over until the world ended.'

> . . . when we met the next month our conversation threw a good deal of light on the English character. I began by scolding my friend. I told him that he had been wrong to feel and display so much emotion upon so slight an occasion; that it was inappropriate. The word 'inappropriate' roused him to fury. "What?" he cried. "Do you measure out your emotions as if they were potatoes?" I did not like the simile of the potatoes,

but after a moment's reflection I said, "Yes, I do; and what's more, I think I ought to. A small occasion demands a little emotion, just as a large occasion demands a great one. I would like my emotions to be appropriate. This may be measuring them like potatoes, but it is better than slopping them about like water from a pail, which is what you did." He did not like the simile of the pail. "If those are your opinions, they part us forever," he cried, and left the room. Returning immediately, he added: "No—but your whole attitude toward emotion is wrong. Emotion has nothing to do with appropriateness. It matters only that it shall be sincere. I happened to feel deeply. I showed it. It doesn't matter whether I ought to have felt deeply or not."[11]

The conversation merits quotation at length because it throws light on that contrast between English and Indian character which is so important in the novel. In *A Passage to India*, the exchange reappears, condensed, in a conversation between Aziz and Fielding:

". . . Your emotions never seem in proportion to their objects, Aziz."

"Is emotion a sack of potatoes, so much the pound, to be measured out? Am I a machine? I shall be told I can use up my emotions by using them, next."

"I should have thought you would. It sounds common sense. You can't eat your cake and have it, even in the world of the spirit."

"If you are right, there is no point in any friendship; it all comes down to give and take, or give and return, which is disgusting, and we had better all leap over this parapet and kill ourselves. . . ."[12]

In the novel, once again, the humour is cut down and the pith extracted to make a witty exchange.

Sometimes whole phrases from descriptions in *The Hill of Devi* are taken over in *A Passage to India*—there is one, comparing the disk of the star Regulus to a tunnel, which is identical in the two accounts.[13] And longer incidents sometimes find their way into the novel, when some important purpose is to be served. There was, for example, his adventure during a walk:

> There we had an exciting and typical adventure. Our train of villagers stopped and pointed to the opposite bank with cries of a snake. At last I saw it—a black thing reared up to the height of three feet and motionless. I said, "It looks like a small dead tree", and was told "Oh no", and exact species and habits of snake were indicated—not a cobra, but very fierce and revengeful, and if we shot it would pursue us several days later all the way to Dewas. We then took stones and threw them across the Sipra . . . in order to make snake crawl away. Still he didn't move and when a stone hit his base still didn't move. He *was* a small dead tree. All the villagers shrieked with laughter.[14]

During the ascent to the caves in *A Passage to India*, there is a corresponding incident:

> Again, there was a confusion about a snake which was never cleared up. Miss Quested saw a thin, dark object reared on end at the farther side of a watercourse, and said, "A snake!" The villagers agreed, and Aziz explained: yes, a black cobra, very venomous, who had reared himself up to watch the passing of the elephant. But when she looked through Ronny's field-glasses, she found it wasn't a snake, but the withered and twisted stump of a toddy-palm. So she said, "It isn't a snake." The villagers contradicted her. She had put the word into their minds, and they refused to abandon it. Aziz admitted that it looked like a tree through the glasses, but insisted that it was a black cobra really, and improvised some rubbish about protective mimicry. Nothing was explained, and yet there was no romance.[15]

In *The Hill of Devi* there is also an account of an incident which puzzled Forster a good deal, and led him to wonder whether his Maharajah might possess super-normal faculties. A couple described how they had been motoring from Dewas to Indore, and how their car had been hit by some animal just as they crossed the Sipra so that it swerved and nearly hit the parapet of the bridge:

His Highness sat up keenly interested. "The animal came from the left?" he asked.

"Yes."

"It was a large animal? Larger than a pig but not as big as a buffalo?"

"Yes, but how did you know?"

"You couldn't be sure what animal it was?"

"No we couldn't."

He leant back again and said, "It is most unfortunate. Years ago I ran over a man there. I was not at all to blame—he was drunk and ran on to the road and I was cleared at the enquiry, and I gave money to his family. But ever since then he has been trying to kill me in the form you describe."[16]

Forster relates that he was left with the sense of 'an unexplained residuum'. In *A Passage to India* there is a similar incident, which takes place when Adela and Ronny are out driving.[17] An estrangement between them is just being resolved by their consciousness of physical attraction when the car is brought to a standstill by the impact of something against it. They get out and decide that a hyena has hit them. Shortly afterwards, Adela tells Ronny that she has no intention of breaking with him after all. When the incident is recounted to Mrs Moore, she shivers and says, 'A ghost!' No one can explain why she says this, least of all herself: but we later learn that the Nawab had hit a drunken man there some years before, just as Forster's Maharajah had done in real life.

An examination of the use of these incidents shows that Forster is not simply putting in useful local colour. A more subtle purpose is being served. Both help to suggest Adela's state of mind during the expedition to the Marabar caves.

In relating the actual incident of the snake and the tree, Forster remarks how it typified the difficulty of establishing the rights of a case in India. When he comes to use it in his novel, he brings this uncertainty to the fore so that it dominates the account. It thus helps to suggest Adela's sense of confusion during the expedition.

The second incident works more subtly in her mind. The

impact of the animal coincides with the point where physical attraction is healing the breach in her relationship with Ronny. It thus comes to remind her of, and even symbolize, the irruption of the physical into what is, essentially, a false relationship. On the morning of the expedition she is reminded of the incident when she passes the spot where it took place and again when, toiling up to the caves, she sees footholds in the rock which remind her of the dust-pattern created by the Nawab's car. Instantaneously, she realizes that she is not properly in love with Ronny. The realization contributes still more strongly to the muddle in her mind and has a crucial effect on her behaviour, as we shall see later.

A good deal of Forster's experience must have been used in producing the details which give the novel its deceptively casual appearance—its air that 'this is how things usually happen, one after another'. But the fact that some of the most important incidents appear, not at random but in order to subserve a particular effect, harmonizes with a statement by Forster in *The Hill of Devi*, in which he tries to explain the relationship between his Indian experiences and his Indian novel:

> I began this novel before my 1921 visit, and took out the opening chapters with me, with the intention of continuing them. But as soon as they were confronted with the country they purported to describe, they seemed to wilt and go dead and I could do nothing with them. I used to look at them of an evening in my room at Dewas, and felt only distaste and despair. The gap between India remembered and India experienced was too wide. When I got back to England the gap narrowed, and I was able to resume. But I still thought the book bad, and probably should not have completed it without the encouragement of Leonard Woolf.[18]

Only away from India could the patterns which were being woven to interpret his Indian experiences flourish without being swamped by the sheer mass of meaningless experience in everyday life there.

In the early part of the novel the 'pattern' consists mainly of a suggestive atmosphere. There is a constant emphasis upon the existence, side by side, of attractiveness and hostility in the Indian scene. The two interweave constantly. They are represented with particular strength in the tension between sky and earth—the sky benevolent, the earth hostile. The most important statement of this tension comes at the end of the first chapter:

> The sky settles everything—not only climates and seasons but when the earth shall be beautiful. By herself she can do little —only feeble outbursts of flowers. But when the sky chooses, glory can rain into the Chandrapore bazaars or a benediction pass from horizon to horizon. The sky can do this because it is so strong and so enormous. Strength comes from the sun, infused in it daily, size from the prostrate earth. No mountains infringe on the curve. League after league the earth lies flat, heaves a little, is flat again. Only in the south, where a group of fists and fingers are thrust up through the soil, is the endless expanse interrupted. These fists and fingers are the Marabar Hills, containing the extraordinary caves.

The juxtaposition of beauty and hostility continues. When Aziz is on his way to the beautiful mosque where he first meets Mrs Moore, Forster comments on the difficulty of walking in India. 'There is something hostile in that soil. It either yields, and the foot sinks into a depression, or else it is unexpectedly rigid and sharp, pressing stones or crystals against the tread.'[19] Mrs Moore notices the sky continually and feels a kinship with it. 'In England the moon had seemed dead and alien; here she was caught in the shawl of night together with earth and all the other stars.'[20] But at the end of the chapter, when she murmurs a vague endearment to a wasp which she finds sleeping on a clothes peg, it is against a sinister background. '. . . jackals in the plain bayed their desires and mingled with the percussion of drums.' Her voice floats out, 'to swell the night's uneasiness'. The double theme persists throughout the novel. At the climax, in the Hindu festival, there is a momentary reconciliation, symbolized when Aziz looks down on the tank from the road above. 'Reflecting the evening clouds, it filled the nether-world with an equal splendour, so that earth and sky leant toward one another, about to clash in ecstasy.'[21] But this is the nearest approach to fusion. In the last episode of the novel, earth and sky alike are made to agree in the impossibility of reconciliation between English and Indians here and now.

The discussion so far might suggest that the sky is only associated with benevolence, the earth only with hostility. This is not so, however. Forster's symbolism has to be referred back to his purposes in *Howards End*. Here, as there, Forster is concerned with the finite and the infinite. The earth represents the finite, the sky the infinite. But both are morally ambivalent. When the moonlight shines on the mosque, it offers 'acceptable hints of infinity'.[22] But when the sun beats down on a parched landscape, infinity becomes unbearable. In the same way, the finite earth can either harden to the hostility of rock, or relax to the benevolence of a fertile plain.

This moral ambivalence provides the warp and woof of the novel. But at its extreme points, the utmost of hostility is found in the finite intractability of rock, the utmost of benevolence in the infinite sun—not the unbearable sun which beats down on noonday India, but the gentler, more glorious sun which is seen for a moment at sunrise and which symbolizes the splendour of true love.

The two poles of the novel are narrowed and focused into more precise symbols. The hostility of rock is particularized in the Marabar caves. As Professor Frank Kermode has pointed out,[23] Forster achieves a good deal of his effect here by an insistent use of the word 'extraordinary'. The first sentence of the whole book reads, 'Except for the Marabar Caves—and they are twenty miles off—the city of Chandrapore presents nothing extraordinary.' The last sentence of the first chapter ends with a mention of 'the Marabar Hills, containing the extraordinary caves'. The innocent word recurs in a later dialogue, when Aziz tries to make Godbole explain why the Marabar caves are famous—but at each move in the conversation the listeners are further from discovering 'what, if anything, was extraordinary about the Marabar Caves'.[24] Even when the visitors are on their way, no one will tell them exactly why they are going or what they are going to see. In the meantime, however, there has intervened a description of the caves. Nothing, says Forster, distinguishes one cave from another:

> It is as if the surrounding plain or the passing birds have taken upon themselves to exclaim "extraordinary", and the word has taken root in the air, and been inhaled by mankind.[25]

This peculiar atmosphere, where all is ordinary to the point of being extraordinary, where nullity hardens into hostility, where lack of value turns dully malignant, is crystallized in another image. Elsewhere Forster has described the sinister atmosphere of the Grand Canyon, where the Colorado River 'rages like an infuriated maggot between precipices of granite, gnawing at them and cutting the Canyon deeper'.[26] In 'The Machine Stops', there is a horrifying scene where the hero, trying to escape, finds himself seized by hideous long white worms which overcome his struggles and suck him back from the surface of the earth into the Machine beneath.[27] This image-pattern is used by Forster to describe Mrs Moore's experience of the Marabar caves.[28] The echoes in the cave are little worms coiling, ascending and descending. What speaks to her there is 'something snub-nosed, incapable of generosity—the undying worm itself'. In this negative vision, the serpent of eternity is 'made of maggots'.

Against the nightmarish nullity of the caves there is to be set another voice which rings insistently in the novel. Professor Godbole represents the old Hindu tradition of love. At one point he sings a song expressing the earth's yearning for the heavens—the song of the milkmaid calling to Krishna, who refuses to come. In answer to a question from Mrs Moore, he explains that the god never comes in any of his songs. ' "I say to Him, Come, come, come, come, come, come. He neglects to come." '[29]

When Ronny and Adela pass through the countryside in the car, their estrangement unresolved, the landscape is described as too vast to admit of excellence. 'In vain did each item in it call out, "Come, come." There was not enough god to go round.'[30] The outward scene here expresses their own inward landscape, from which the visionary sun-god of love is absent. Again, when the train is steaming towards the Marabar caves, there is a long passage on India, culminating in the statement, 'She knows of the whole world's trouble, to its uttermost depth. She calls "Come" through her hundred mouths, through objects ridiculous and august. But come to what? She has never defined. She is not a promise, only an appeal.'[31]

Godbole's song may express the yearning of India, but the spirit of love which he also represents cannot cope with the intractability of the caves. As we have seen, he insistently refrains from specifying exactly what is 'extraordinary' about the caves: in particular, he does not mention the echo. Similarly, after the disastrous expedition, his lack of concern about it disconcerts Fielding. He explains that his unconcern is due to the fact that good and evil are 'both aspects of my Lord':

> "He is present in the one, absent in the other, and the difference between presence and absence is great, as great as my feeble mind can grasp. Yet absence implies presence, absence is not non-existence, and we are therefore entitled to repeat, 'Come, come, come, come.' "[32]

A similar limitation is apparent in his dance-ecstasy at the festival. As he dances his love, he brings more and more things into his vision, but when at last he imagines a stone, he finds that he cannot include it. Certain things always resist the harmonizing vision, which can only ignore them.

Yet, if the caves represent one extreme of India, its 'reality' in one sense, Godbole's spirit of love, rising to ecstasy, expresses its other extreme, its other 'reality'. And if the two extremes cannot quite meet, that does not mean that mankind ought to turn away from both and seek a compromise halfway between them. One is reminded again of that vehement assertion in *Howards End*:

> No; truth, being alive, was not halfway between anything. It was only to be found by continuous excursions into either realm, and though proportion is the final secret, to espouse it at the outset is to insure sterility.[33]

By this time, it will be observed, symbolic implications have transformed the pattern of the novel. What seemed at first sight to be only a conflict between British and Indians has broadened into a conflict between earth and sky—which in its turn veils the conflict between spirit and matter, between love and the intractable.

The title of the novel might have suggested these depths to us. Walt Whitman's poem, 'Passage to India', from which it is taken, begins as a poem about human voyaging. But as it proceeds, it turns into a poem about the voyage of the soul to God.

> O thou transcendant!
> Nameless—the fibre and the breath!
> Light of the light—shedding forth universes—thou centre of
> them!
> Thou mightier centre of the true, the good, the loving!
> Thou moral, spiritual fountain! affection's source!
> thou reservoir![34]

The poem continues with the reiterated cry, 'Passage to more than India!' Forster's use of Whitman's title has a distinctly ironical flavour, however, for if his two visitors are to find in India 'more than India', it will also be something very far removed from the transcendent or the Ideal: Mrs Moore will find herself confronted by the very negation of her values. The main events of Forster's novel are dominated not by the 'Light of light' but by an oppressive and hostile sun. Yet Whitman's ideal is not irrelevant. The symbolic events of Forster's first section, at least, are lit by a gentle moon, and throughout the novel there is suggestion of a greater power, a sun-like spirit of love which never quite manages to become incarnate. And Godbole's point becomes relevant: 'absence implies presence, absence is not non-existence. . . .'

Moreover, if Forster has not Whitman's full optimism, his central point is the same. Mrs Moore and Adela Quested, who think that they are making an ordinary tourist's trip to India, and that they know what they mean when they ask to see the 'real' India, are to find that they are making a spiritual passage, and that they will be brought face to face with 'reality' in a very different form. This confrontation reverberates throughout the novel, shedding light on and affecting everything else that happens in it.

It is here that the boldness of the novel becomes apparent. At the level of events, the plot which promises so much fizzles out in a negation. To find positiveness we have to move behind the simple action—first to the moral significance of the events and then, quite naturally, to a pattern of symbolism which rises behind the plot just as the Marabar caves rise silently against the sky behind the busy little station of Chandrapore.

We have already touched upon some of the symbolic themes. Their point of interaction with the plot, however, lies chiefly in the experiences of Mrs Moore and Adela Quested, and we cannot do justice to the subtlety of the interweaving without examining those experiences more closely.

There is one important respect in which an appreciation of what is going on at the symbolic and psychological level helps to unravel the plot itself. A point which troubles many readers is whether Aziz actually assaulted Adela or not. At first she declares that she was assaulted; then at the trial she says with equal conviction that Aziz did not follow her into the cave. Either or both statements as they stand might be the result of hysterical delusion. Which are we to believe? Even as close a friend as Goldsworthy Lowes Dickinson asked Forster, 'What did happen in the caves?'[35]

Confusion on this point has to do with a confusion concerning the place of 'reality' in this novel. Here, as in *The Longest Journey*, 'reality' is on the anvil. We are back with Forster's idea that its importance consists not only in its objective nature, but also in its psychological function. Whatever philosophical position they take up, men will normally agree that reality is one and unchanging. But a sense of reality can fluctuate: and according to Forster all men lose their sense of reality to a greater or lesser extent when they fail to connect head and heart.

This was what happened to Lucy Honeychurch when she entered the 'armies of the benighted', and to Rickie when he married Agnes and taught in Sawston School: it is also what happens to Adela Quested in this novel. She has arrived with the double intention of seeing the 'real' India and settling the question of her proposed marriage to Ronny Heaslop. Early in the novel, having observed the effect of India on Ronny, she has decided that she will not marry him after all. But the incidents just afterwards when they go out for a drive and are thrust together first by the jolting of the car then by the impact of collision with an animal, restore the relationship for the time being by reminding them of their physical attraction towards each other.

So the relationship stands until the day when Adela is climbing up towards the Marabar caves. We have described how two incidents affect her state of mind on this occasion: first the confusion over the snake, then, as she is thinking about her marriage, a reminder of the animal impact:

> But as she toiled over a rock that resembled an inverted saucer, she thought, "What about love?" The rock was nicked by a double row of footholds, and somehow the question was suggested by them. Where had she seen footholds before? Oh yes, they were the pattern traced in the dust by the wheels of the Nawab Bahadur's car. She and Ronny—no, they did not love each other.

She considers the position, pausing thoughtfully:

> Vexed rather than appalled, she stood still, her eyes on the sparkling rock. There was esteem and animal contact at dusk, but the emotion that links them was absent.[36]

Like Rickie at a corresponding moment, however, she fails to respond to the symbolic moment and decides to go through with the marriage. To break it off would cause too much trouble, and she is not at all sure that love is necessary to a successful union. She dismisses the thought and enters on a discussion of marriage with Aziz. Like Lucy Honeychurch, she is in the process of muddling herself: and it is in this state of muddle that she enters the cave.

The clue to her subsequent behaviour lies not in any outward event but in this muddled state of her mind at the crucial moment. It is still the vital clue when, after a long period of illness, she arrives at the trial to give her testimony. In the intervening period one important event has taken place. She has visited Mrs Moore, talking to her first about the persistent echo in her head, then about love and marriage. Afterwards, although in fact nothing has been said about the subject directly, she emerges with a conviction that Aziz is innocent and that Mrs Moore has said so. Questioned later, Mrs Moore denies having mentioned Aziz—but also says irritably, "Of course he's innocent."[37]

The remark does not deter Adela from going forward, but it has disturbed her. It has cracked, without breaking, the state of unreality in which she has been living since the day of the expedition. The state was created because she muddled herself about her relationship with Ronny, and Mrs Moore's ramblings have probed the muddle without exposing it. The exposure does not come until she is standing in the courtroom: and then, significantly, she thinks immediately of Mrs Moore:

> The Court was crowded and of course very hot, and the first person Adela noticed in it was the humblest of all who were present, a person who had no bearing officially upon the trial: the man who pulled the punkah. Almost naked, and splendidly formed, he sat on a raised platform near the back, in the middle of the central gangway, and he caught her attention as she came in, and he seemed to control the proceedings. He had the strength and beauty that sometimes come to flower in Indians of low birth. When that strange race nears the dust and is condemned as untouchable, then nature remembers the physical perfection that she accomplished elsewhere, and throws out a god—not many, but one here and there, to prove to society how little its categories impress her. This man would have been notable anywhere: among the thin-hammed, flat-chested mediocrities of Chandrapore he stood out as divine, yet he was of the city, its garbage had nourished him, he would end on its rubbish heaps. Pulling the rope towards him, relaxing it rhythmically, sending swirls of air over others, receiving none himself, he seemed apart from human destinies, a male fate, a winnower of souls. Opposite him, also on a platform, sat the little assistant magistrate, cultivated, self-conscious, and conscientious. The punkah

wallah was none of these things: he scarcely knew that he existed and did not understand why the Court was fuller than usual, indeed he did not know that it was fuller than usual, didn't even know he worked a fan, though he thought he pulled a rope. Something in his aloofness impressed the girl from middle-class England, and rebuked the narrowness of her sufferings. In virtue of what had she collected this roomful of people together? Her particular brand of opinions, and the suburban Jehovah who sanctified them—by what right did they claim so much importance in the world, and assume the title of civilization? Mrs Moore—she looked round, but Mrs Moore was far away on the sea; it was the kind of question they might have discussed on the voyage out before the old lady had turned disagreeable and queer.

While thinking of Mrs Moore she heard sounds, which gradually grew more distinct. The epoch-making trial had started. . . .[38]

At this, the crisis of the novel, there has been an irruption from an old world, the world of Forster's mythologies. The figure who catches Adela's attention is an incarnate god, an Indian Apollo. He is as real as the garbage-heaps of the city, yet he is also a visionary figure. His glory outshines the muddle which has made her confuse a mixture of desire and esteem with love, and releases a power which reminds her again and again of Mrs Moore, dissolving the cloud of unreality which has shrouded her since the day of her muddle, and restoring her sense of reality.

Looking at Aziz in the courtroom, she is once again wondering whether she has made a mistake, when the memory of Mrs Moore is unexpectedly reinforced. Her name is mentioned in court, and the defence suggests that she has been deliberately hidden in order that her witness may not clear Aziz. The grievance spreads to the crowd outside, who begin chanting

Esmiss Esmoor
Esmiss Esmoor
Esmiss Esmoor

in the way that at a festival they would chant 'Radakrishna Radakrishna'.

Just afterwards, Adela rises to give her evidence. She has always been shy of this moment, because in spite of her desire to tell the truth, she remembers that her entry into the cave was associated with thoughts about marriage, and thinks that her question to Aziz on the subject might have roused evil in him. Yet she would find it hard to recount a matter so intimate in open court. By the time that she rises, however, the 'naked god' and Mrs Moore have done their work.

> But as soon as she rose to reply, and heard the sound of her own voice, she feared not even that. A new and unknown sensation protected her, like magnificent armour. She didn't think what had happened, or even remember in the ordinary way of memory, but she returned to the Marabar hills, and spoke from them across a sort of darkness to Mr McBryde. The fatal day recurred, in every detail, but now she was of it and not of it at the same time, and this double relation gave it indescribable splendour. Why had she thought the expedition "dull"? Now the sun rose again, the elephant waited, the pale masses of the rock flowed round her and presented the first cave. . . .

Because her head has once again made contact with her heart (the 'Mrs Moore' in her) her sense of reality has been restored, and the memory of what happened is not only clear but magnificent. Imagination and perceptions have been reunited to make that state which is commonly acknowledged to be the true 'reality', where the universe of the heart and the universe presented to the senses form a single pattern. She is no longer separate from the scene—instead, the masses of the rock 'flow round her' in a symphony of experience.

The reality so presented to her governs her testimony, which brings the trial to its abrupt close. And at the close of the trial, the chief symbol in it is left in full possession of the scene.

> . . . before long no one remained on the scene of the fantasy but the beautiful naked god. Unaware that anything unusual had occurred, he continued to pull the cord of his punkah, to gaze at the empty dais and the overturned special chairs, and rhythmically to agitate the clouds of descending dust.

Once one has observed the symbolism of this figure, coupled with the train of mental development that has elapsed, it becomes clear that Adela's new state of mind is not and cannot be another hysterical state: it is a recovery from hysteria. The important thing is not what happened in the cave but what has been happening to Adela.

In the eyes of British India she is now finished. She has committed the unforgivable sin of betraying her fellow-countrymen and bringing about the possibility of rebellion. Certainly there can now be no question of her marrying Ronny Heaslop, even if she wanted to. She can only return to England, lucky that Dr Aziz does not press for heavy damages.

For her as an individual, however, the events have a decisive and formative effect. As Fielding talks to her later, he is impressed by her new attitude. 'Although her hard school-mistressy manner remained, she was no longer examining life, but being examined by it; she had become a real person.' Nevertheless, the progress has been made within strict limitations. She remains a creature dominated by her head, and so her behaviour cannot impress the Indians:

> For her behaviour rested on cold justice and honesty; she had felt, while she recanted, no passion of love for those whom she had wronged. Truth is not truth in that exacting land unless there go with it kindness and more kindness and kindness again, unless the Word that was with God also is God. And the girl's sacrifice—so creditable according to Western notions—was rightly rejected, because, though it came from her heart, it did not include her heart.[39]

We are reminded again of that husband and wife in 'The Point of It': the wife who loved truth and grew hard, and the husband who loved humanity and went soft.[40] The limitations of Adela's experience in the courtroom have now been exposed—her heart came into play in the service of truth but did not become engaged. The vision of the 'naked god' was a temporary stimulus, not a lasting revelation. The crisis of the novel over, Adela, now realized as a person but still a creature of the head, emerges in contrast to

Mrs Moore, whose heart is developed, but who cannot face the nakedness of truth.

This gives us the cue for an examination of Mrs Moore's experiences in India. In the early part of the novel, when the atmosphere is not oppressive and the two women are merely two travellers who are seeing the sights of the state, Mrs Moore figures in an incident which sets the tone of her character for the rest of the novel. Venturing into a mosque one evening she encounters Aziz, who is still smouldering under recent insults from the British. He speaks to her sharply, but she replies with friendliness, establishing a bond with him which is never afterwards broken. It is a peaceful, moonlit night as she returns to the club, but she is soon given to understand that she has behaved in an un-English way by speaking to Aziz. After an argument with her son Ronny she emerges from the club to find a small wasp on the peg where her cloak is hanging.

"Pretty dear," said Mrs Moore to the wasp. He did not wake, but her voice floated out, to swell the night's uneasiness.[41]

Mrs Moore's kindness to Aziz, and her treatment of the wasp, introduce one of the novel's main themes. Where is love to end? Mrs Moore has a developed heart and is kind to those whom she meets, but what is she in the face of India's teeming millions and manifold sufferings? Love in India: is it not like a snow-flake dropping into the ocean? It is not even simply a question of people, for India is shown to be a country which human beings have not quite dominated. In mentioning the wasp, Forster comments on the fact that no Indian animal has any sense of an interior. The animal and vegetable kingdoms have a prominence which they have lost in Western Europe: and behind them stretches something still more intractable—the hardness of rock itself.

At the moment, however, we are still at the more manageable level of animals and insects, and this theme is reinforced in the next chapter, where there is an account of Mr Graysford and Mr Sorley, the two missionaries of Chandrapore. Mr Sorley, who is more advanced than his older companion, considers that God's hospitality may extend to the animal kingdom, to monkeys for example. Even jackals might be included. But he is less sure about wasps.

He became uneasy during the descent to wasps, and was apt to change the conversation. And oranges, cactuses, crystals and mud? and the bacteria inside Mr Sorley? No, no, this is going too far. We must exclude someone from our gathering, or we shall be left with nothing.

The uneasiness about extending love to wasps foreshadows the more sinister atmosphere of the next section, which is dominated by the Marabar caves. The description of the caves at the beginning of the section is no mere chunk of local colour, but a statement of significance which 'places' the caves before they begin to act in the narrative. Their rockiness is not merely beyond the reach of civilization: there is a sense that they extend behind the time process itself, untouched by any human quality.

They are older than anything in the world. No water has ever covered them, and the sun who has watched them for countless æons may still discern in their outlines forms that were his before our globe was torn from his bosom. If flesh of the sun's flesh is to be touched anywhere, it is here, among the incredible antiquity of these hills.[42]

Hostility is a keynote of the whole section. The main scene of the first section took place in moonlight, a moonlight which helped to establish the atmosphere of human kindness. But even in that section the Marabar hills were always 'fists and fingers'. In this section, where they come into their own, the sun is the dominating presence, always hostile. This part of India is 'flesh of the sun's flesh'. On the morning of the ill-fated expedition to the Marabar caves, the sunrise which the visitors are looking forward to fails them.

They awaited the miracle. But at the supreme moment, when night should have died and day lived, nothing occurred. It was as if virtue had failed in the celestial fount. . . . Why, when the chamber was prepared, did the bridegroom not enter with trumpets and shawms, as humanity expects? The sun rose without splendour.[43]

Symbolic interpretations press hard here. Like Blake and Coleridge, Forster sees the moment of sunrise as the nearest approach in the universe at large to the splendid birth of love in human experience. For one moment an almost transcendent glory is revealed. But on this occasion, an unglamorous sunrise only serves to stress the hostility of a sun in which heat predominates. During the day the presence of the sun is mentioned again and again, always as a hostile presence. The experiences undergone by both Mrs Moore and Adela are ascribed partly to sunstroke and correspond to recorded case-histories of it.

The sun beats down on them as they toil up towards the caves and banks the oppressiveness that pervades the scene. It bars escape from the experiences that await them. Mrs Moore, entering a cave, finds the interior unpleasant and even horrifying. The cave is immediately filled by their retinue and begins to smell. Some 'vile naked thing' (which later turns out to have been a baby, astride its mothers hip) strikes her face and settles on her mouth. For an instant she goes mad, hitting and gasping like a fanatic, alarmed not merely by the crush and stench, but by the unexpected and terrifying echo.

The echo is the culminating horror of the novel. It reminds one directly of the echo that oppressed Margaret Schlegel in St Paul's and indirectly of the 'goblin footfalls' of the same novel.[44] It has the same nullity, the same ability to deny value: it is 'entirely devoid of distinction'.

Whatever is said, the same monotonous noise replies, and quivers up and down the walls until it is absorbed into the roof. "Boum" is the sound as far as the human alphabet can express it, or "bou-oum", or "ou-boum"—utterly dull. Hope, politeness, the blowing of a nose, the squeak of a boot, all produce "boum". Even the striking of a match starts a little worm coiling, which is too small to complete a circle but is eternally watchful. And if several people talk at once, an overlapping howling noise begins, echoes generate echoes, and the cave is stuffed with a snake composed of small snakes, which writhe independently.[45]

The echoes turn swiftly into worms and serpents, which reinforce the hint that their significance is reaching out beyond the cave. The worm and serpent have associations with an evil which is characterized more closely later, when Mrs Moore comes to reflect upon her experience:

> She minded it much more now than at the time. The crush and smells she could forget, but the echo began in some indescribable way to undermine her hold on life. Coming at a moment when she chanced to be fatigued, it had managed to murmur, "Pathos, piety, courage—they exist, but are identical, and so is filth. Everything exists, nothing has value." If one had spoken vileness in that place, or quoted lofty poetry, the comment would have been the same—"ou-boum". If one had spoken with the tongues of angels and pleaded for all the unhappiness and misunderstanding in the world, past, present, and to come, for all the misery men must undergo whatever their opinion and position, and however much they dodge or bluff—it would amount to the same, the serpent would descend and return to the ceiling. Devils are of the North, and poems can be written about them, but no one could romanticize the Marabar because it robbed infinity and eternity of their vastness, the only quality that accommodates them to mankind.
>
> She tried to go on with her letter, reminding herself that she was only an elderly woman who had got up too early in the morning and journeyed too far, that the despair creeping over her was merely her despair, her personal weakness, and that even if she got a sunstroke and went mad the rest of the world would go on. But suddenly, at the edge of her mind, Religion appeared, poor little talkative Christianity, and she knew that all its divine words from "Let there be Light" to "It is finished" only amounted to "boum".

The moment is a crucial one in Forster's writings, and Mrs Moore becomes here an allegorical figure. She possesses within herself all the virtues of the heart, only to find at this moment that her values are nullified by an echo.

There have been many visionary moments in the novel, but this is a moment of anti-vision—a vision of the horror of the universe which contrasts completely with Adela's moment of vision in the court-house. Mrs Moore passes into what Forster describes as 'that state where the horror of the universe and its smallness are both visible at the same time—the twilight of the double vision in which so many elderly people are involved'. And he goes on to work out the significance of the echo:

> What had spoken to her in that scoured-out cavity of the granite? what dwelt in the first of the caves? Something very old and very small. Before time, it was before space also. Something snub-nosed, incapable of generosity—the undying worm itself. Since hearing its voice, she had not entertained one large thought, she was actually envious of Adela. All this fuss over a frightened girl! Nothing had happened, "and if it had", she found herself thinking with the cynicism of a withered priestess, "if it had, there are worse evils than love". The unspeakable attempt presented itself to her as love: in a cave, in a church— Boum, it amounts to the same. Visions are supposed to entail profundity, but—Wait till you get one, dear reader! The abyss may also be petty, the serpent of eternity made of maggots. . . . [46]

It would be easy to see this moment of nightmare vision as the core of the novel. For many readers, it leaves a deeper impression than anything else, and it is not therefore surprising that they should invest it with central significance. Such centrality, however, is not assigned by Forster, who has called it 'a moment of negation . . . the vision with its back turned'.[47] Nor is it assigned in the novel itself, for as Mrs Moore leaves India, other voices speak to her. The train passes a place called Asirgarh, which consists of bastions and a mosque. Ten minutes later, Asirgarh reappears, the mosque now on the other side of the bastions. The train has described a complete semicircle round it. She has nothing with which to connect it: 'But it had looked at her twice and seemed to say: "I do not vanish." ' It evidently reminds her of the moonlit mosque of the first section, which had offered a more agreeable India, a less hostile infinity. Similarly, the hostility of the caves is contrasted with the scene where her boat moves out of the harbour and thousands of coconut palms wave her farewell. ' "So you thought an echo was India; you took the Marabar caves as final?" they laughed. "What have we in common with them, or they with Asirgarh? Good-bye!" '48

The echo, after all, does not undermine Adela, who also experiences it. It enters her only for a time, echoing and re-echoing in her head during her illness, but disappears during her conversation with Mrs Moore. Mrs Moore's failure, on the other hand, is the physical enforcement of a psychical lack. She is old, and after a lifetime of developing her heart rather than her head, she cannot stand against a re-orientation of reality. When this basis is gone, the cave becomes the universe, her values are destroyed and she dies. Nevertheless, even then her spirit is not extinguished. It can still, even when she is rambling, suggest to Adela that Aziz is innocent. And it survives in the memories of those who have known her. As with Rickie and Mrs Wilcox, her vicarious survival is a form of redemptive immortality. She is resurrected in the mind of Adela during the trial and the crowd outside chant her name. She is resurrected again towards the end of the novel, when Professor Godbole is dancing himself into an ecstasy of love at the Hindu festival. The image of Mrs Moore then comes into his mind:

Chance brought her into his mind while it was in this heated state, he did not select her, she happened to occur among the throng of soliciting images, a tiny splinter, and he impelled her by his spiritual force to that place where completeness can be found. Completeness, not reconstruction. His senses grew thinner, he remembered a wasp seen he forgot where, perhaps on a stone. He loved the wasp equally, he impelled it likewise, he was imitating God. And the stone where the wasp clung— could he . . . no, he could not, he had been wrong to attempt the stone, logic and conscious effort had seduced, he came back to the strip of red carpet and discovered that he was dancing upon it.49

Later, the ecstasy over, he steps out of the temple into the grey of a pouring wet morning, thinking, "One old Englishwoman and one little, little wasp. It does not seem much, still it is more than I am myself."

The images that occurred in his ecstasy reiterate themes of the novel. Unlike the two missionaries, but like Mrs Moore, Godbole can extend his love to include the wasp. His failure to include the stone is equally significant. There is always something that resists and denies love, and the stone is reminiscent of the intractable Marabar caves.

Forster's inclusion of this intractable element even in Godbole's ecstatic dance is another indication of its importance in the novel as a whole. Once again, he insists on having a Caliban on his island. But the Marabar caves, which make no pretensions at all to humanity, are better than Caliban or Leonard Bast for his purpose. As symbols, their excellence can be measured by the number of significances which critics have found in them. They have been respectively described as 'bare, dark, echoing', echoing 'eternity, infinity, the Absolute'; 'the very voice of that union which is the opposite of divine; the voice of evil and negation'; 'wombs'; and 'it may be, the soul of India'.[50]

Forster's own account of them in an interview helps to point their significance:

> When I began A Passage to India I knew that something important happened in the Marabar Caves, and that it would have a central place in the novel—but I didn't know what it would be.
> . . . The Marabar Caves represented an area in which concentration can take place. A cavity. They were something to focus everything up: they were to engender an event like an egg.[51]

Everything in the novel has to be confronted by the caves. The head of Adela and the heart of Mrs Moore are equally challenged by the negation of a cave which can only reflect sights and sounds. For them it is a confrontation with 'reality' in the worst sense of the word: matter without mind, substance devoid of imaginative appeal. But this is not full reality even if it is an element without which reality cannot exist. The attempt to love a stone breaks into Professor Godbole's ecstasy and brings him back to the strip of red carpet where he is dancing, but it does not stop him dancing. Similarly the existence of the Marabar caves in India does not prevent thousands of palm-trees from waving farewell to Mrs Moore, nor does the hostility of the sun invalidate the hints of a more benevolent infinity offered in the first section of the novel.

The Marabar caves are not a revelation of reality, but a touch-stone by which reality is tested. They are a 'vortex', in the sense in which Blake used the word.[52] The forces of the novel are attracted towards the experience which they offer, and in passing through it are transformed. They are drawn in and englobed, to emerge with form and new life. Adela becomes a person. Mrs Moore is destroyed in the body but, as we have seen, her spirit lives on in the lives and spirits of others: and in the last section of the novel it is actually reincarnate in physical form, when her children Ralph and Stella visit India.

At this point, moreover, the spirit of Mrs Moore is absorbed into the total spirit of Love which is shadowed, however un-certainly, by the Hindu festival of the same section. We have already mentioned Forster's reference to this as 'architecturally necessary', meeting the need for 'a lump, or a Hindu temple if you like—a mountain standing up'.[53] The image which he is here using may well derive from a wartime experience which he described in a broadcast talk and later in a book review. Writing of an exhibition of Indian temples which Stella Kramrisch (together with Dr Saxl) devised in London in 1940, he says:

Briefly she showed me the temple as the World Mountain on whose exterior is displayed life in all its forms, life human and superhuman and subhuman and animal, life tragic and cheerful, cruel and kind, seemly and obscene, all crowned at the mountain's summit by the sun. And in the interior of the mountain she revealed a tiny cavity, a central cell, where, in the heart of the world complexity, the individual could be alone with his god. Hinduism, unlike Buddhism, Islam and Christianity—is not a congregational religion: it by-passes the community and despite its entanglement with caste it by-passes

class. Its main concern is the individual and his relation t
reality, and however much it wanders over the surface of th
world mountain it returns at last to the mountain's heart. Th
happens to appeal to me.[54]

In retrospect, the Hindu festival evidently seems to him t
possess some of the same qualities. It is a final image of all
inclusive reality, through which some of the chief characters mu
pass before his novel can be concluded.

Together with Fielding, to whom Stella is now married, Mi
Moore's children come to take part in the festival. They take
boat on the water when the festival is at its height and are joine
grudgingly by Aziz, who has been moved by Ralph's resemblanc
to his mother to set aside, at least for an evening, the hatred fo
English people which has possessed him since his trial.

Unfortunately, a slight gale is running on the tank, heralding
storm: and the result is that they lose control of the boat, which
having collided with another boat, drifts towards the servito
with his tray and strikes it. Stella, by shrinking first towards he
husband, then flinging herself against Aziz, capsizes the boat an
plunges them all into the warm shallow water. Meanwhile ther
is a crescendo of noise from artillery, drums and elephant
culminating in an immense peal of thunder. The climax, 'as far a
India admits of one', has been reached, and rain sets in steadily t
wet everything and everybody.[55]

Symbolic meaning surges again at this point. It is significan
that the capsizing is caused by Stella throwing herself at botl
Fielding and Aziz in quick succession; it is significant that after
wards letters from Ronny and Adela float on the water. Thi
mêlée at the feast of Krishna, prince of love, is the nearest approach
to a birth of brotherly love in the novel—it at least marks th
release of Aziz from the hatred which has confined him since hi
trial. It is equally typical of Forster's firm realism in this nove
that the approach should only be made in the middle of th
upsetting of a boat, and that the accompanying climax of th
festival should immediately dissolve in rainy confusion. If ther
is a mystery of love in India, it subsists only at the heart of a hug
muddle.

Unlike the civilization of Sawston, which has gradually selected a manageable segment of human experience to be its world, India represents the whole of human experience. It contains at one extreme the ecstasy of human and divine love, at the other the sort of basic stony 'reality' which baffles an undeveloped head and challenges an undeveloped heart. When someone remarked earlier in the novel that India was a muddle, Mrs Moore recoiled. Her 'undeveloped head' could not deal with muddles:

"I like mysteries but I rather dislike muddles," said Mrs Moore.
"A mystery is a muddle."
"Oh, do you think so, Mr Fielding?"
"A mystery is only a high-sounding term for a muddle. No advantage in stirring it up, in either case. Aziz and I know well that India's a muddle."
"India's—Oh, what an alarming idea!"[56]

Fielding represents the British attitude which has done so much for India in clearing away administrative inefficiencies and giving her improved communications, but which is dead to other perceptions. Yet he, too, can still recognize other possibilities. When he is saying good-bye to Adela later, they sense a certain similarity in their outlooks and gain satisfaction from it.

Perhaps life is a mystery, not a muddle; they could not tell. Perhaps the hundred Indias which fuss and squabble so tiresomely are one, and the universe they mirror is one. They had not the apparatus for judging.[57]

After that it is fitting that when they part, 'A friendliness, as of dwarfs shaking hands, was in the air.' They seem for a moment to see their own gestures from a great height—there is a wistfulness, the shadow of a shadow of a dream.

Adela and Fielding for their part have missed something great: and so, for her part, has Mrs Moore. The familiar broken dialectic between head and heart is still operative. The final events of the novel confirm the impression that Fielding has failed by his disregard of mystery, Mrs Moore by her dislike of muddles. In this way, they have each shown that they are still half in touch with the Sawston which tries to evade both muddles and mysteries at one and the same time. India, on the other hand, because it contains the extremes of human experience, is both a vast muddle and a concealed mystery.

In his culminating view of India, Forster thus achieves his greatest fusion of vision and realism, for each quality has its objective correlative in this great panorama. India's muddle needs all the efficiency which British administrators brought to it: at the same time its mystery asks for the reverence of a fully developed heart. In presenting the situation, moreover, Forster is able to present the 'muddle' with a completeness which Virginia Woolf, like most readers, finds highly attractive:

> We notice things, about the country especially, spontaneously, accidentally almost, as if we were actually there; and now it was the sparrows flying about the pictures that caught our eyes, now the elephant with the painted forehead, now the enormous but badly designed ranges of hills. The people too, particularly the Indians, have something of the same casual, inevitable quality. . . .[58]

D. A. Traversi has commented on the fact that this casualness becomes an essential part of the novel's meaning: Godbole declares that Krishna 'neglects to come'; the echo comes upon Mrs Moore when she 'chanced to be fatigued'; 'chance' brings Mrs Moore into Godbole's mind while he is dancing, and so on.[59] The casualness is an essential part of the Indian mind, as compared with the English. And so the 'reality' which is so broad and casual and attractive can also be refined to the point where echoes and reflections in a cave mirror the terrifying, casual, incomprehensibility of the entire universe: the 'Pan' of Forster's early short stories, the 'earth' of The Longest Journey, which is best avoided unless it can be met with a fully developed head and heart. In the same way, 'vision' can be presented broadly in the spirit that informs the actions of Fielding and Mrs Moore, but it can also be intensified to the ecstatic love which is still to be found in the old Hindu traditions of Forster's India.

Vision and reality are not at one, even in India, and Forster is at pains to emphasize the fact. But his last words on the festival are a way of suggesting that somehow, somewhere, India, at least, manages to preserve a connection between them:

> Looking back at the great blur of the last twenty-four hours, no man could say where was the emotional centre of it, any more than he could locate the heart of a cloud.[60]

CHAPTER VII

Serving the World

IN style and subject-matter, *A Passage to India* represents a considerable advance on the previous novels. The use of high-flown language, which had still been acceptable to the Edwardians, drops away considerably. There is also a greater toughness, particularly in the conversations, where sexual and sadistic themes play a greater part. The cynical realism against which its human values are presented has made the novel popular to a generation which would be less ready to accept Forster's previous work.

The prime factor in this changing attitude was, of course, the First World War. That war could not have been fought as it was without the full weight of Edwardian sensibility and idealism behind it, and in the harsh reality of the battlefields those qualities received a blow from which they have never recovered. Scott Fitzgerald expresses this double fact vividly in the thoughts of an American visiting the trenches after the war.

> This western-front business couldn't be done again, not for a long time. The young men think they could do it but they couldn't. They could fight the first Marne again but not this. This took religion and years of plenty and tremendous sureties and the exact relation that existed between the classes. The Russians and Italians weren't any good on this front. You had to have a whole-souled sentimental equipment going back further than you could remember.[1]

The blow which the war dealt to European sensibilities corresponds to the impact of India on Forster's characters. As the train presses towards the Marabar hills, Adela asks, 'Do you remember Grasmere?'

> 'Ah, dearest Grasmere!' Its little lakes and mountains were beloved by them all. Romantic yet manageable, it sprang from

a kindlier planet. Here an untidy plain stretched to the knees of the Marabar.

Similarly, when Ronny decides that she must release him, he sees her as belonging to the callow academic period of his life: 'Grasmere, serious talks and walks, that sort of thing.'[2]

Sensibility is not finally extinguished by these events. When Fielding returns to England, 'tender romantic fancies that he thought were dead for ever, flowered when he saw the buttercups and daises of June'.[3] But the episodes connected with the Marabar caves stick obstinately in the reader's memory because the attrition of sensibility which they describe has been a feature of our time.

Moreover, the two world wars have only been hastening an inevitable process. The literary history of the period shows that a profound change in the orientation of literary art was in any case beginning before 1914. The movements associated with Hulme, Pound and Eliot represent a revulsion against the cult of 'sensibility' which had possessed literature for more than two centuries. And they in their turn reflect a further intellectual movement. The cult of the absolute was giving way to a cult of the relative. Einstein's scientific theories have their counterpart in other fields of thought. Forster himself has remarked that the most important shift in artistic thought in recent times has been the one from the world of Wagner to the world of Proust. In the one, men are still reaching out to an ideal; in the other, these strivings are contained by a sense that human feelings are limited, existing in a returning orbit.

This shift in taste corresponded with the middle period of Forster's life. His own shift in the direction of a tougher style may also have been prompted by hostile criticism of his earlier work. (Edmund Gosse, for example, had written that he was forced to read Mrs Gaskell in order to take the taste of the last chapters of *Howards End* out of his mouth.[4])

Among the various feelings of the post-war world, however, the most immediate was a disgust at what had happened and a determination to prevent, if possible, a repetition. This revulsion was often matched by a new sympathy for socialist feelings. In some of his political essays of the time, Forster gives vent to indignation with a virulence that might startle those who had been accustomed to his subtler satire. He fiercely attacks the Dean of Durham, who had censured the 'vulgar profanity' of the language used by the Labour Party, and pours bitter scorn on an Academy picture of the trenches which he finds hanging amid conventional portraits of 'important people':

You had been plentiful enough in the snow outside (your proper place), but I had not expected to find You here in the place of honour, too. Yours was by far the largest picture in the show. You were hung between Lady Cowdray and the Hon. Mrs Langman, and You were entitled 'Gassed'. You were of godlike beauty—for the upper classes only allow the lower classes to appear in art on condition that they wash themselves and have classical features. These conditions you fulfilled. A line of golden-haired Apollos moved along a duck-board from left to right with bandages over their eyes. They had been blinded by mustard gas. Others sat peacefully in the foreground, others approached through the middle distance. The battlefield was sad but tidy. No one complained, no one looked lousy or over-tired, and the aeroplanes overhead struck the necessary note of the majesty of England. It was all that a great war picture should be, and it was modern because it managed to tell a new sort of lie. Many ladies and gentlemen fear that Romance is passing out of war with the sabres and the chargers. Sargent's masterpiece reassures them. He shows that it is possible to suffer with a quiet grace under the new conditions, and Lady Cowdray and the Hon. Mrs Langman, as they looked over the twenty feet of canvas that divided them, were still able to say, 'How touching', instead of 'How obscene'.[5]

Other works of the period employ Forster's more familiar tone. He himself had spent the latter years of the war in Alexandria, where he was close to the war but escaped the horror of the trenches. Apart from a few scattered impressions in later essays, the chief memorial of those years is to be found in two Alexandrian volumes: the guide-book to the city and *Pharos and Pharillon*. The guide-book is a model of its kind, approaching its subject first historically then topographically. As a result, the visitor can either read the history of the city, studying the relevant antiquities in chronological order, or make his tour of the city, referring back to historical details as he wishes. Throughout, Forster's style is that of his more graceful historical essays: history is recalled simply and straightforwardly but with an occasional quiet humour, as when an account of Plotinus' regret for the descent of his soul into this world is followed by the description of a disastrous expedition in which he 'was very nearly relieved of the disgrace of having a body'.[6] *Pharos and Pharillon* elaborates on some Alexandrian topics and includes an account of C. P. Cavafy, the Greek poet, of whom Forster says (perhaps with a side-glance at his own character), that he 'has the strength (and of course the limitations) of the recluse, who, though not afraid of the world, always stands at a slight angle to it'.[7]

Throughout the troubled years of the 'twenties and 'thirties, Forster's position within the literary scene remained unobtrusive but firm. His essays of the time show a marked leaning towards literary subjects—with customary side-thrusts against the foibles of the middle-class from time to time. He continued to have a notable effect upon the young, partly from the uncluttered straightforwardness of his writing and thinking, partly by his direct encouragement of young writers.

During the Second World War he came into new prominence. His broadcasts of the time struck a new note in wartime apologetic. In a war where heroics counted for less than ever before, a war which was won by people who wore shabby clothes and ate shoddy foods and endured, his type of unassuming firmness had a symbolic value. In 1944, William Plomer wrote a description of him which brings out these qualities to the full:

> To a superficial eye, his appearance is inconspicuous. He is the reverse of a dandy, and his fellow-passengers in a train, if incurious, might dismiss him, in his old water-proof and accompanied by a piece of anachronistic hand-luggage, as some provincial of settled habits. They would be astonished (if capable of astonishment) to know of his experience, learning, vivacity, and openness to new impressions. Those who know

him best are impressed by the timelessness of his appearance (one never thinks of him in terms of age); by certain quick darting movements and bird-like inclinations of the head; by the intense blueness of his eye in certain lights—it seems actually to change colour; by the sweetness of the smile; by the little puffs of satirical laughter through the not neat moustache; and by a real and not officious politeness, a winning considerateness, to the shyest and least self-important persons in mixed gatherings. As for his private life, it is perhaps permissible to say that it has strong roots in the country, in Cambridge, and in London, and that while he often varies his surroundings and his company, no man could be more tenacious of associations once cherished. 'Only connect' is a phrase familiar to readers of *Howards End*: its author has a unique capacity for establishing and maintaining the most various connexions with his fellow-beings.[8]

After the war, he was made an honorary fellow of King's College, Cambridge, and offered a set of rooms, which he gratefully accepted. In this way, the Cambridge which had been a value in all his novels became his home in old age. 'Cambridge', he has said, 'is a place for the very young and the very old,' and he proceeded to enter the life of the college, making friends with old and young alike. Recent interviewers have described his rooms, furnished, in Edwardian style, with portrait-drawings of his Thornton ancestors, books of all sorts in English and French, and an elaborate carved wooden mantelpiece with blue china in its niches. Angus Wilson has also contributed an impression of Forster's conversational manner:

E. M. F. speaks in quick, little bursts of words, which end, as it seems, inconclusively, and then he usually adds one or two words more, which though they seem tangential, nevertheless are often the real core of what he is saying. It is as though a firework did its stuff adequately but not excitingly, never fizzling but hardly illuminating, and then just as the onlookers are about to give a polite smile and say "very pretty" in a slightly disappointed tone, there shoot up one or two very bright lights that in turn fade away, making one wish for more. But E.M.F.'s indecisive, spasmodic manner seemed to me to contain ("to mask" would imply all sorts of intention of which I saw no sign) firm decision.[9]

His status as a figure representing the mass of quiet, peace-loving human beings has thus continued in the post-war world. His signature has constantly been found supporting progressive causes, popular and unpopular. In particular, his gift for under-statement has appealed to a generation tired of braggery and bluster. He began a speech on nuclear weapons with the words, 'Nuclear weapons are not in my line. Unfortunately, I am in theirs. . . .'

In 1958 he commemorated the fiftieth anniversary of *A Room with a View* by writing an article in which he recounted the fortunes of his chief characters in subsequent years.[10] The six years after their marriage were the happiest for Lucy and George: they settled comfortably in Highgate with a modest income and a servant. During the First World War George was a conscientious objector and Lucy annoyed susceptible patriots by continuing to play Beethoven. Old Mr Emerson died shortly afterwards, 'still confident that Love and Truth would see humanity through in the end'.

When the Second World War broke out, George enlisted, for he could recognize in Hitlerism an enemy of the heart as well as of the head and the arts. Meanwhile the small flat at Watford, where Lucy was trying to keep things together was bombed, and George, now a prisoner in Mussolini's Italy, discovered that the Florence of their honeymoon had also been heavily damaged. So that when, after the war, the couple are reunited, they still have a View, but no longer a Room. In this, they symbolize their generation.

In such a situation, Forster, too, is an allegorical figure. One understands his growing devotion to his household gods—the devotion that made him write his last two books on his early impressions of India and on the great-aunt, Marianne Thornton, whose timely legacy had given him independence and room to manœuvre in his literary career.

But in spite of the fact that events have deprived him of the

THE ACHIEVEMENT OF E. M. FORSTER

world in which he grew up, Forster remains outstanding for hi
insight into the human condition. Exalted as a figurehead, h
constantly shows himself greater than the image which is projected of him. When, for example, he appeared for the defence
in the trial of *Lady Chatterley's Lover* in 1960, his brief evidence
stood out, among a good deal of muddled thinking on both sides,
for the clarity of mind and attitude which it showed. Questioned
about the word 'puritan', which had already been used to describe
Lawrence, Forster replied that he was aware that the usage was
paradoxical and then proceeded to defend it:

> 'I would say, if I may speak of antecedents, of great names,
> Bunyan on the one hand and Blake on the other, Lawrence too
> had this passionate opinion of the world and what it ought to
> be but is not.'[11]

One notices the subtlety and precision of this brief analysis—the
quick placing of Lawrence's 'puritanism' by reference to figures
who represent, respectively, high seriousness and high imagination.
Once again one is made aware that words which are often used
slackly by modern writers have in his writings and speech a background of close thought.

This point becomes relevant whenever Forster is made into a
figurehead of humanism. The image which is projected by
enthusiasts becomes slightly unfocussed as soon as one compares
it with the man himself. In spite of his admiration for Voltaire,
for example, he cannot be identified with the pure rationalists of
his acquaintance. At one point, indeed, he describes how he once
tested the 'magic' of Wiltshire by staying there with Lytton
Strachey—and how the magic won.[12] He praises Strachey's
urbanity and delightfulness, but a point of difference is no less
implied.

Again, he owes a good deal of his standing in the post-war
world to the fact that he was not closely involved with any of the
major political movements of the 'thirties. His individuality of
position was due to a persistent awareness of the weakness of
human nature, a tempering of his idealism by unwillingness to
idealize human beings in the mass.

With most of his contemporaries, therefore, he has marked points of difference. They themselves comment on the fact. Leonard Woolf's account is both detailed and typical:

> . . . Morgan, I suppose, was still up at King's when I first knew him, though not in my last two years. We did not see very much of him, but he was a fascinating character and what I knew of him I liked immensely. He was strange, elusive, evasive. You could be talking to him easily and intimately one moment, and suddenly he would seem to withdraw into himself; though he still was physically there, you had faded out of his mental vision, and so with a pang you found that he had faded out of yours. He was already beginning to write his early Pan-ridden short stories and *A Room with a View*. You always felt in him and his conversation the subtlety and sensibility together with the streak of queer humour which you always also feel in his books. Lytton nicknamed him the Taupe, partly because of his faint physical resemblance to a mole, but principally because he seemed intellectually and emotionally to travel unseen underground and every now and again pop up unexpectedly with some subtle observation or delicate quip which somehow or other he had found in the depths of the earth or of his own soul.

Many of his friends characterize this elusive quality in Forster as 'occultism' or 'mysticism'. Thus Lowes Dickinson's puzzlement about the caves incident in *A Passage to India* is matched by the comments of other friends. Edward Marsh wrote:

> *A Passage to India* . . . is certainly a masterpiece, tho' rather spoilt for me by my being completely mystified about the main incident in the story, and there has been a strain of occultism in his books which has baffled me—but he's a great and charming artist. . . .[13]

Roger Fry wrote, of the same novel:

> I think it's a marvellous texture—really beautiful writing. But Oh Lord I wish he weren't a mystic, or that he would keep his mysticism out of his books . . . I'm certain that the only meanings that are worth anything in a work of art are those

that the artist himself knows nothing about. The moment he tries to explain *his* ideas and *his* emotions he misses the great thing.[14]

Whether one can dismiss the esoteric element in Forster so easily is open to doubt, however. That his vision is individual is a necessary, if unfortunate, result of the age in which he lives, where there is no longer a shared vision of the meaning of life. But that vision, as we have seen, is woven into the very fabric and structure of his novels.

And if one simplifies his basic philosophy to the single, ramified point that Love is the ideal, it will be found also to pervade his more serious essays, which only make sense when read with the full weight of the novels behind them. Writing on the 'Raison d'Être of Criticism in the Arts', he concludes that the establishment of such a raison d'être is prohibited by the gulf between creative and critical states.[15] He adds, 'The only activity which can establish such a raison d'être is love.' Or again, he compares Hayek's assertion that freedom is the supreme political value with Laski's assertion that socialism should have pride of place: and then goes on to mention that he himself is 'a sentimentalist who believes in the importance of love'—a value which, he finds, is little regarded by either thinker.[16] And there is that well-known phrase 'two cheers for democracy' which furnishes the title for a collection of his essays. It is a dangerously whimsical phrase, redolent of that humorous understatement which one associates with certain tiresome forms of humour. But in its original context, it represents a closeness of thought which might surprise those who have merely noticed it as an eye-catching title:

> So Two cheers for Democracy: one because it admits variety and two because it permits criticism. Two cheers are quite enough: there is no occasion to give three. Only Love the Beloved Republic deserves that.[17]

The word 'love' has been so overworked in this century that Forster's various references to it might, at a casual reading, savour of cant. But the detailed exploration in the novels gives the necessary backing to his use of the word. In them, love is disciplined by an insistence on the necessary conditions within which it operates, and given full substance by descriptions which stress both the physical ground and the visionary power which co-exist in true love.

To Love, so interpreted, the reader is at liberty to ascribe metaphysical validity or not, according to his own view of the matter. But there is every evidence that Forster himself sees it as the supreme value, the supreme reality. He even goes so far as to reinterpret Christian statements in the light of it. Thus Love the Beloved Republic becomes a synonym for the 'City of God'. In the same essay, Love is the key to freedom, because it leads, in Christian terms, to 'the service that is perfect freedom'.[18] Or again, he can find use for another famous text in discussing post-war reconstruction: 'I only feel certain that unless the Lord builds the house, they will labour in vain who build it. Perhaps, when the house is completed, love will enter it, and the greatest force in our private lives will also rule in public life.'[19] He would agree, no doubt, that 'where there is no vision, the people perish'. His essential difference from the dogmas of organized Christianity, on the other hand, is epitomized in his well-known affirmation, 'Lord, I disbelieve—help thou my unbelief'.[20]

In the same way, while Love is made actual in the plot of his novels, its nature is revealed more esoterically in the symbolic patterns that can be traced behind them. It is there revealed, not simply as a heightened mode of sensibility, but as a revelation of reality, the incarnation of God in human beings.

In this apotheosis of the Imagination, as the mode by which Love, the final interpretative reality in the universe, is made manifest in human beings, Forster shows that he is at one with the first Romantics: with the Blake who created a complete religious position upon the assumption that the Jesus of the Gospels was to be seen as protagonist of the human Imagination, and with the Coleridge who affirmed that the primary imagination was 'a repetition in the finite mind of the eternal act of creation in the infinite I AM'.[21] One does not have to share this view in order to enjoy the novels, for their author has been at pains to give prominence to the external workings of love rather than its inward nature. The novels, like all novels, are primarily intended to be read from without; but, as we have seen, they gain in depth and sometimes in intelligibility if they are also read from within.

As to the nature of love as it emerges in the total pattern of the novels, Forster's distinctive contribution lies less in the idea that love is an affair both of the body and of the imagination (although this idea was not as common when he wrote as it is today) than in his exploration of what happens when body and imagination are both active in love, and of the relation between this 'glorious' effect and the sense of reality. But even when he goes on to create a complete metaphysical position on his assumptions, he is not without his predecessors in the field. A good deal of Romantic thinking follows a similar pattern. The novels can, in fact, be read as successive commentaries upon a single sentence of Shelley's which he himself once quoted in an essay to voice his own beliefs: 'Imagination is as the immortal God which should assume flesh for the redemption of mortal passion.'[22]

CHAPTER VIII

In and out of Time

INTERVIEWING Forster in 1957, Angus Wilson asked him whether his ceasing to write novels was in any way connected with the collapse of Mrs Moore in *A Passage to India*. Forster replied that it was not. His final answer was, 'I just drifted out of it.'[1]

Our examination of the developing achievement in the novels has presented us with materials for an explanation of that 'drift'. It is difficult to see what could have followed the masterly array of all Forster's previous themes in *A Passage to India*, where they were finally presented in a complete universe, physical and imaginative. A new novel could hardly have been achieved without a firm and difficult departure from all that had gone before.

Changes in the world since 1914 have made the possibility of such a departure still more difficult. In a recent letter to Jonathan Spence, Forster wrote:

> The point that I have blessed progressive movements from a convenient distance is a fair one. As for the ends of *The Longest Journey* and *Howards End* they are certainly unsatisfactory, but perhaps were less so at the time. Then the English countryside, its reality and creative retreat into it, were more plausible than they are today. Events have damaged my stock-in-trade as a novelist in this direction as they have in another: the existence, in an established home, of the family. I don't fret over the changes in the world I grew up in. But I can't handle them. I would write atomically if I could.[2]

Elsewhere he remarks that the England which Stephen Wonham had seemed destined to inherit is done for. 'The growth of the population and the applications of science have destroyed her between them. There was a freshness and an out-of-door wildness in those days which the present generation cannot imagine.'[3]

But if further creation has been made difficult, what is the position of Forster's achieved work in such a world? What for example is the fate of his humour and wit now that the middle-class society which was its proper target has given place to a society where values are propagated by mass communication and where kindliness and charm have themselves a strong commercial value?

Consideration of the point raises a crucial issue. Forster himself has a gift for whimsy which has always been his most dangerous asset: because it can too easily minister to the taste for 'charm'. Evelyn Waugh has said somewhere that charm is the English vice. It certainly has a good deal to do with that well-known phenomenon, the English sense of humour. And like that sense of humour it is a powerful social weapon. It has shaped the English attitude to religion, for example. In England, the agnostic or atheist who comes sailing in to the attack, arms flailing, eyes flashing, is liable to find himself facing, not a waspish orthodoxy, but a drawing-room filled with well-bred laughter.

To some extent, this behaviour was originally shaped by religious people as a fortification against disruption from within. It was the most powerful weapon available to the womenfolk of Evangelical households, for example. When religious questions led to family discord, when uncle was pitted against uncle in religious controversy, when doubt arose as to whether the daughter of the house was 'saved', what more important than the presence of an aunt who, with quiet grace and pointed wit that did not wound, could save the situation? One is reminded again of Jane Austen.

Forster, himself a self-confessed Jane Austenite ('and therefore slightly imbecile about Jane Austen'[4]) knows all this well. Indeed, he has given us a full account of such an aunt in his biography of Marianne Thornton. During the course of the book, her comic gifts are brought to life. Here, for example, she is describing a religious meeting:

Lord Gambier, who is the best friend in the world, is for that reason the worst Chairman. His friendly feelings so got the better of his decorum that he took to tacking the oddest resolutions together, such as that Missions should be sent to Otaheite and that the Meeting returned their warmest thanks to his very dear very much esteemed very excellent much beloved friend William Wilberforce; the next time he stuck the poor Bishop to some other, and so he went on to the no small annoyance of the poor suffering praised.[5]

But Forster also comments on the ruthlessness which can be veiled by the silken glove of charm and good humour. What, for example, could be more good-humoured than Miss Thornton's letter to Forster's mother, asking for details of her forthcoming accouchement? As Forster points out, it avoided all the obvious vices. It was not snobbish, it was not patronizing, it was full of sweet reasonableness. The only thing wrong with it was that it had a palpable design on the recipient. It somehow failed to recognize that Mrs Forster might want to lead her own life in peace.[6]

The difficulty with charm is that there is no defence against it. All arguments blunt their edge on it, all passions are crude at its side. Forster knows this well, as he shows in his essay on Mrs Miniver:

What answer can the villagers make to a lady who is so amusing, clever, observant, broad-minded, shrewd, demure, Bohemian, happily-married, triply-childrened, public-spirited and at all times such a lady? No answer, no answer at all. They listen to her saying the right things, and are dumb. They watch her doing the right things in the right way, and are paralysed. Even if they disgrace themselves by spluttering smut in her hearing, she is not put out, for the class to which she and the parson belong has grown an extra thickness of skin in the last thirty years. 'Touchée!' she would exclaim, with her little ringing laugh, and pass on untouched. She is too wonderful with the villagers, she has them completely taped. Taximen, too. One day she overhears two ridiculous fat bottle-nosed taximen talking about the subconscious self. She takes the absurdity back to her husband, whose sense of humour coincides with her own, and if the taximen had turned the tables and ridiculed *her* she would have taken that back, too. She has learnt the defensive value of honesty, which was unknown to her immediate forebears, and consequently nothing short of physical violence can ever do her in. Even when the Highlanders take off their trousers at the Games she is not disconcerted; it is the governess who looks the other way. And she writes so well, knowing just where to place each word. And she has delighted thousands upon thousands of readers of *The Times* and been the subject of two *Times* leaders and of innumerable letters to *The Times* calling her charming, and she has been a clue in *Times* crossword puzzles. Why do a few of us stand glum by the roadside as the gallant little pageant passes? Is it not just our own silly jealousy that prevents us from following in her train?[7]

Forster proceeds to a piece of analysis in which by examining the sociological status of the Mrs Minivers of the modern world, he demonstrates the falsity of their position: but the main point of his argument has already been made. The passage is, indeed, one of his best pieces of moral persuasion through irony. As with Marianne Thornton, one cannot fault Mrs Miniver. Analyse her behaviour, and no item fails beneath the scrutiny. It is only the whole that is disquieting, because behind it one sees Mrs Miniver's design upon society. Her charm has great defensive potentialities against any encroachment upon her economic position, and it is also a protecting factor. It shields her from any true intercourse with men and women, the sort of intercourse where human beings act face to face, and not obliquely by way of social niceties. The moral weapon of Jane Austen has been turned into a defence mechanism for the middle-class escapist.

Forster suggests all this and more. His carefully reiterated references to *The Times* contrive to relate Mrs Miniver to a complete stratum of society which not only reads *The Times* but looks upon it with protective jealousy. It consists of people who if that paper is criticized in their presence, will refer affectionately to 'Auntie Times' by way of reply. We are back in the carefully cultivated charm of the domestic circle.

Forster can see through the 'charm game' more keenly and devastatingly than any other writer. He has attached the fetish which is made of the 'sense of humour' nowadays.[8] Why, then, do some critics feel that certain works of his show too much of this very same quality? The collection of essays in *Abinger Harvest* has been particularly criticized from this point of view.

The answer seems to be twofold. Charm does have a place in the Forsterian universe. Again and again he stresses the importance of personal relationships, of affection between men and women. And charm is a way of expressing affection without necessarily implying approval. So that when he writes about Coleridge or Keats in whimsical fashion, his whimsy is both friendly and barbed. He can describe the 'Difficulties' of Mr and Mrs Abbey and then reveal, to those who are not in the secret, that their chief difficulty, their young ward, was no other than that prophet of imagination and the holiness of the heart's affections, John Keats.[9]

But at the same time one has to acknowledge that this sort of writing, though not logically dissociated from Forster's main position, is lacking in intellectual astringency. It is a way of free-wheeling. And when the intellectual backing is so far removed, there is a strong danger that readers will bask in the prevailing atmosphere of charm and not notice the barbs which are woven into the cotton-wool. There is justice in Lionel Trilling's assertion that some of these essays could not have been written by a lesser man, but ought not to have been written by Forster.[10]

At the other extreme from Trilling one finds a critic as sensitive as Rose Macaulay praising some of these essays for the very same quality. Discussing an essay of 1903 entitled 'Macolnia Shops', she says, 'In this exquisite brief essay you will find all the charm, the humour, the gay, gentle, mocking flexibility of rhythm, almost every characteristic turn of style, that you will find in essays on Jane Austen and Hannah More thirty years later. That is odd and unusual. Most of us experiment, begin clumsily, blunder and tumble leggily about like young colts, beat out our style little by little. Mr Forster seems to have slipped into his early, as into a suit made for him.'[11]

This is true, but not the whole truth. The qualities which Miss

Macaulay finds in Forster have always been a part of his endowment, but it has been a further characteristic of his to reach beyond their limitations. The danger comes when Miss Macaulay's standards are used to condemn other parts of his work. For example, she praises 'The Machine Stops' but finds it, in manner and matter the least 'Forsterian' of his writings. 'It has a Forster moral, but lacks charm, humour and style; it might have been written by someone else. Not so the *Story of the Siren*. . . .'[12]

To call one story 'Forsterian', the other not, is dangerously misleading. 'The Machine Stops' is a bare story but it has power, and its moments of poignancy are enhanced by the fact that they do not have to contend with a charming or humorous context.

The reason that Professor Trilling and Miss Macaulay can take up such extreme positions, however, is that there is a real conflict involved within Forster himself. Miss Macaulay sees him in the context of his society, Professor Trilling in the context of his intellectual achievement: and the two are at variance.

So far as style is concerned, Forster writes most easily when he is dealing with the society he knows best. His ear for middle-class conversation is acute, as may be illustrated by this snippet from *Howards End*.

"... Did you ever know anyone living at Stettin?"
"Never," said Mrs Wilcox gravely, while her neighbour, a young man low down in the Education Office, began to discuss what people who lived at Stettin ought to look like. Was there such a thing as Stettininity? Margaret swept on.[13]

Again, one can point to a series of exchanges between Margaret Schlegel and Henry Wilcox, each exchange making a different point about their relationship (their semi-seriousness; Henry's social dominance; Margaret's acute woolly-mindedness compared with Henry's obtuse clear-mindedness, and so on).

"Tell me, though, Miss Schlegel, do you really believe in the supernatural and all that?"
"Too difficult a question."
"Why's that? Gruyère or Stilton?"
"Gruyère, please."

"Better have Stilton."

"Stilton. Because, though I don't believe in auras, and think Theosophy's only a half-way house—"

"—Yet there may be something in it all the same," he concluded, with a frown.

"Not even that. It may be halfway in the wrong direction. I can't explain. I don't believe in all these fads, and yet I don't like saying that I don't believe in them."[14]

In this sort of situation, Forster shows a complete mastery which he derives from his background. It is the same with his characters. Readers will differ as to which they find unconvincing, but it would be surprising if their list included any of those whom Forster admits to having based on real people:

> E. M. F.: ". . . Miss Bartlett was my Aunt Emily—they all read the book but they none of them saw it. Uncle Willie turned into Mrs Failing. He was a bluff and simple character (*correcting himself*)—bluff without being simple. Miss Lavish was actually a Miss Spender. Mrs Honeychurch was my grandmother. The three Miss Dickinsons condensed into two Miss Schlegels. Philip Herriton I modelled on Professor Dent. He knew this, and took an interest in his own progress . . ."[15]

In the same way, some of the less realistic episodes in the novels are those where there is a strong undercurrent of symbolism. For example, Rose Macaulay has objected that no Edwardian young lady would have behaved quite like Lucy Honeychurch after being kissed by a young man[16]; Lord David Cecil has objected to the conversation and actions of Stephen Wonham in *The Longest Journey*[17]; and the portrayal of Leonard Bast, together with Helen's actions in relation to him, have come under heavy fire. I am not as convinced as some critics about the impossibility of these actions: but their uneasiness is, indisputably, an indication that Forster has here moved away from his normal portrayal of what is immediately convincing to every reader. And the reason for that departure lies in the demands of his symbolism and the intellectual structure of the novels.

In the case of many novelists, there would be no need to bother

further at such points. We could simply follow D. H. Lawrence'
advice: 'Never trust the teller, trust the tale.' But such a cours
would be manifestly wrong with Forster. His novels depend to
much on their intellectual content for us to be able to ignore i
If we do, we miss some of the point of the plot, and the fulle
point of those scattered observations which need to be read in th
light of his central beliefs. To take only one instance out of many
the farewell scene between Fielding and Adela Quested in *A
Passage to India* is almost impossible to understand without a gras
of the symbolic issues involved.[18] Instead, we need to look bot
at Forster's native gifts and at those which he has acquired in th
course of his intellectual quest, and to see how the two interact.

As we have seen, many of the peculiarities of his writing sprin
from his desire to work between domestic comedy and a romanti
intensity of vision. Between the two, sometimes linking them
sometimes autonomous, lies that firm morality which has dis
carded the dogmas of Evangelical Christianity while preservin
its underlying earnestness and even, sometimes, its tendency t
dogmatize. Thus at one point we actually find Forster 'preaching
against the most debased form of the Evangelical attitude:

> Ronny's religion was of the sterilized Public School brand
> which never goes bad, even in the tropics.[19]

His more usual habit is to suggest by understatement. This habi
also operates at moments of important action, helping to sugges
the way in which the important event may seem ordinary unti
we grasp its significance. So, in *Howards End*, there is a recurren
deceptive casualness. Our first intimation of Mrs Wilcox's death
is a chapter which begins, 'The funeral was over.' Mr Wilcox'
proposal to Margaret interrupts a train of thought ('Just as thi
thought entered Margaret's brain, Mr Wilcox did ask her to be
his wife . . .'). We are made aware of Leonard's body before we
are made aware of his death ('They laid Leonard, who was dead,
on the gravel . . .').[20]

Forster will in like manner introduce, hesitatingly and subtly, a
quiet-voiced suggestion which cuts through the sophistical argu
ments of his characters. A good example can be found in the

episode, already touched upon in an earlier chapter, where the Wilcoxes settle down to deal with Mrs Wilcox's startling request that Margaret should have Howards End. In his description of the way in which they handle the matter, gradually breaking down the request until, having taken it point by point, they can end by rejecting it altogether, Forster is modelling himself upon a similar situation in Jane Austen's *Sense and Sensibility*, which he has described with admiration in his essay, 'Notes on the English Character':

> ... the classical example of two English people muddling themselves before they embark upon a wrong course of action is to be found in the opening chapters of *Sense and Sensibility*. Old Mr Dashwood has just died. He has been twice married. By his first marriage he has a son, John; by his second marriage three daughters. The son is well off; the young ladies and their mother—for Mr Dashwood's second wife survives him—are badly off. He has called his son to his death-bed and has solemnly adjured him to provide for the second family. Much moved, the young man promises, and mentally decides to give each of his sisters a thousand pounds; and then the comedy begins. For he announces his generous intention to his wife, and Mrs John Dashwood by no means approves of depriving their own little boy of so large a sum. The thousand pounds are accordingly reduced to five hundred. But even this seems rather much. Might not an annuity to the stepmother be less of a wrench? Yes—but though less of a wrench it might be more of a drain, for 'she is very stout and healthy, and scarcely forty.' An occasional present of fifty pounds will be better, 'and will, I think, be amply discharging my promise to my father.' Or, better still, an occasional present of fish. And in the end nothing is done, nothing; the four impecunious ladies are not even helped in the moving of their furniture.[21]

Forster goes on to comment that the peculiar hypocrisy of the Dashwoods is that they muddle themselves. It is a typically English trait—it accounts for the fact that where other nations do wrong quickly, the English take time to do evil. His own account of the Wilcoxes is of a similar step-by-step muddling, but with the

difference that he himself intervenes, mildly and damningly, at
the end:

> . . . To follow [the discussion] is unnecessary. It is rather a
> moment when the commentator should step forward. Ought
> the Wilcoxes to have offered their home to Margaret? I think
> not. The appeal was too flimsy. It was not legal; it had been
> written in illness, and under the spell of a sudden friendship; it
> was contrary to the dead woman's intentions in the past,
> contrary to her very nature, so far as that nature was understood
> by them. To them Howards End was a house: they could not
> know that to her it had been a spirit, for which she sought a
> spiritual heir. And—pushing one step further in these mists—
> may they not have decided even better than they supposed?
> Is it credible that the possessions of the spirit can be bequeathed
> at all? Has the soul offspring? A wych-elm tree, a vine, a wisp
> of hay with dew on it—can passion for such things be trans-
> mitted where there is no bond of blood? No; the Wilcoxes are
> not to be blamed. The problem is too terrific, and they could
> not even perceive a problem. No; it is natural and fitting that
> after due debate they should tear the note up and throw it on to
> their dining-room fire. The practical moralist may acquit them
> absolutely. He who strives to look deeper may acquit them—
> almost. For one hard fact remains. They did neglect a personal
> appeal. The woman who had died did say to them, "Do this,"
> and they answered, "We will not".[22]

Jane Austen would have handled the situation differently. She
would not have put in those last sentences, with their distinction
between practical morality and the deeper sort. It is only very
rarely that she puts in a direct moral judgment, and then it is
usually a conventional one. But when Forster, who is equally
loath to show his hand, comes through with an open judgment, it
normally has a directness and unconventionality that cuts across
the prevailing tone.

The trait reminds us once again that between Jane Austen and
Forster there has intervened the figure of George Eliot, a novelist
naturally sympathetic to him by reason of her early pietistic up-
bringing and her later revolt: Forster has the same austerity in the

face of moral issues. His attitude is at once laxer and starker than hers, however. He can excuse much more readily the weakness of the flesh: what he cannot excuse is the failure to face the existence and results of that weakness. Even here, however, his attitude is not rigid. In *Howards End*, Mrs Munt shows herself as muddled as Mr Wilcox: after she has brought disaster in her attempts to help Helen in an early chapter we are told that in the end she will come to believe that this was the one time when she really *did* help the sisters. But her muddledom is comic: it results mainly from the fact that she is acting outside the sphere that she knows well. When she is visited by the sisters in Poole there is little hint of criticism.

Forster's moral standards can, in fact, only be properly stated by relating them to his basic philosophy. Both his indulgence and his severity are related to his assertion that if human beings do not succeed in being true to both head and heart they will not be living in the 'real' world. It is against such standards that the Wilcoxes fail totally, while Mrs Munt, who lives in a limited world at best, can be regarded comically and with affection.

By invoking this further standard, however, we make both social comedy and moral purpose subordinate to Forster's visionary philosophy. There is a peculiarly complicated effect involved in the passage we have been examining. At the end we are faced by a savage stroke of indignation which is made to fall obliquely across the line of an ironic agreement: and this indignation owes some of its force to Forster's vision, which is thus at this point doubly masked.

At other times, his vision is masked in a different way. We have already seen how the humorous elegance with which he introduces the scene in the Queen's Hall, and the ensuing satirical descriptions of several listeners might cause an unwary reader to miss the seriousness of the descriptions of Helen and Margaret, which are central to the novel. Forster's reticence in these later novels, his unwillingness to expose visionary statements unprotected, also helps to explain the effect of another passage, the one in which Margaret Schlegel sits above Poole Harbour, considering her proposed marriage to Henry Wilcox. Helen regards it as a betrayal; she herself as an opportunity to effect a fruitful synthesis between Wilcoxes and Schlegels.

> There was a long silence, during which the tide returned into Poole Harbour. "One would lose something," murmured Helen, apparently to herself. The water crept over the mud-flats towards the gorse and the blackened heather. Branksea Island lost its immense foreshores, and became a sombre episode of trees. Frome was forced inwards towards Dorchester, Stour against Wimborne, Avon towards Salisbury, and over the immense displacement the sun presided, leading it to triumph ere he sank to rest. England was alive, throbbing through all her estuaries, crying for joy through the mouths of all her gulls, and the north wind, with contrary motion, blew stronger against her rising seas. What did it mean? For what end are her fair complexities, her changes of soil, her sinuous coast? Does she belong to those who have moulded her and made her feared by other lands, or to those who have added nothing to her power, but have somehow seen her, seen the whole island at once, lying as a jewel in a silver sea, sailing as a ship of souls, with all the brave world's fleet accompanying her towards eternity?[23]

Dr Leavis, with his customary acuteness, has singled out this passage to illustrate what he believes to be an inherent weakness of the novel:

> Mr Forster's 'poetic' communication isn't all at this level of poeticality (which, had there been real grasp behind his intention, Mr Forster would have seen to be Wilcox rather than Schlegel), but it nevertheless lapses into such exaltations quite easily. And the 'somehow' in that last sentence may fairly be seized on: the intention that can thus innocently take vagueness of vision in these matters for a virtue proclaims its inadequacy and immaturity there.[24]

One has to grant that the final sentence of the passage, with its rhetorical flourishes, is not happy. But one might not guess from Dr Leavis's analysis that the passage is not a statement but a question—a question which, moreover, is evidently left open. And of course Forster recognizes the 'Wilcox' element in the 'vision' of England, the way in which such sentiments can be dangerously misused. Was it not Mr Pembroke himself who quoted Shakespeare's 'jewel set in a silver sea' in his opening address to his pupils?[25] The 'somehow' to which Dr Leavis takes exception may be regarded not as a concession to the Wilcoxes but as a defence against them. There is an affirmation that in spite of all the misuses of such sentiments they contain something permanently valuable: that because some people play upon a visionary conception of England for debased ends, those others who genuinely possess a unifying vision of their country are not thereby disqualified.

Dr Leavis's criticism rather serves to point out something that has constantly been emphasized in these pages—that despite Forster's natural feeling for imaginative vision, he is often diffident in actually presenting it. But whereas his diffidence often wraps the visionary statement in some form of distancing irony, he has here adopted an alternative method, stating the vision with unaccustomed rhetoric, yet acknowledging also the 'realists', the Wilcoxes who actually create the riches of England. If there is a failure in the final flourishes, then, it is neither as deep or as typical as Dr Leavis would seem to suggest.

His comments, however, remind us once again of the problems of style which are constantly raised by this juxtaposition of the three elements, comedy, moral purpose and vision. They emerge again in connection with another passage which Dr Leavis has selected for detailed criticism: the reactions of Hamidullah and Fielding to the news of Mrs Moore's death, in *A Passage to India*:

> The other smiled and looked at his watch. They both regretted the death, but they were middle-aged men, who had invested their emotions elsewhere, and outbursts of grief could not be expected from them over a slight acquaintance. It's only one's own dead who matter. If for a moment the sense of communion in sorrow came to them, it passed. How indeed is it possible for one human being to be sorry for all the sadness that meets him on the face of the earth, for the pain that is endured not only by men, but by animals and plants, and perhaps by the stones? The soul is tired in a moment, and in fear of losing the

little she does understand, she retreats to the permanent lines which habit or chance have dictated, and suffers there.[26]

Dr Leavis, who has elsewhere offered high praise for the novel, calling it 'a classic: not only a most significant document of our age, but a truly memorable work of literature', comments on the present passage as follows:

> The touch seems sure in the first sentences—in fact, but for one phrase, in the whole passage. Consider, for instance, how different an effect the second sentence would have out of its context: one would suppose it to be in satiric tone. Here, however, it is a means to the precise definition of a very different tone, one fatigued and depressed but sympathetic. The lapse, it seems to me, comes in that close of the penultimate sentence: '. . . plants, and perhaps by the stones.' Once one's critical notice has fastened on it (for, significantly too, these things tend to slip by), can one do anything but reflect how extraordinary it is that so fine a writer should be able, in such a place, to be so little certain just how serious he is? For surely that run-out of the sentence cannot be justified in terms of the dramatic mood that Mr Forster is offering to render? I suppose the show of a case might be made out for it as an appropriate irony, or appropriate dramatically in some way, but it wouldn't be a convincing case to anyone who had observed Mr Forster's habit. Such a reader sees merely the easy, natural lapse of the very personal writer whose hand is 'in'.[27]

Forster has more than one habit, however, and the reader may feel some dissatisfaction with this judgment. It is not just that the impossibility of sympathizing with stones is endowed with seriousness by the novel's constant preoccupation with rocks, stones and caves as symbols of the basic matter, the intractability that opposes human values: the reader who has observed Forster's irony in the matter of Mrs Wilcox's will may suspect that the second sentence is after all satirical and that the reference to stones indicates an irony as well as a symbolism. Perhaps in this passage, as in the former, generalized sympathy is masking a specific moral condemnation.

'They were middle-aged men who had invested their emotions elsewhere.' To the reader who is familiar with Sawston and its pervading devotion to business values, there can be little doubt that the use of 'invested' has satirical point. The only question is whether it is simply a single sniping shot, a concession to Forster's permanent values, or whether it is intended to reverberate in the rest of the paragraph. The reference to stones suggests the latter. Forster, having begun a reasonable argument, is taking it to the point of absurd exaggeration in order to suggest that it is an argument which protests too much. No one was asking Fielding or Hamidullah for such an effort of sympathy as that: but they might still have responded to Mrs Moore's death without impoverishing other emotional commitments.

The difficulty for the reader springs from the fact that Forster's sympathy here is as genuine as his irony. His other statements make that quite clear. We go badly wrong if we expect to find in Forster's irony the carefully placed minefield of a Swift, which at a prearranged signal will blow the accumulated structure of a paragraph sky-high. Forster's effect is more muffled. His irony is intended to explode as a depth-charge, to do its damage somewhere below the surface. His sympathy is genuine, because he can perceive the logic and kindliness of the attitude which he is examining. Wives and children do come first: and the fate of Mrs Moore might in itself suggest the danger of trying to love too much.

But his irony remains, to remind us that two questions might still be asked. Are emotions intended to be 'invested', as though they were gilt-edged securities? And if they are so invested, can we never allow our hearts the adventure of a single emotion without being in danger of exhausting their resources?

Forster does not attempt to answer the questions or even to formulate them. He merely suggests them by introducing two rather strange images into a lengthy paragraph. But elsewhere he has quoted with approval Shelley's lines,

> True love in this differs from gold or clay,
> That to divide is not to take away.[28]

And in *A Room with a View*, George Emerson, evidently a disciple of Shelley, incurred Miss Alan's disapproval by arguing that liking one person was an extra reason for liking another.[29] If one takes Forster's thinking as a whole, the point is unmistakable.

It must still be acknowledged, nevertheless, that in terms of style a combination of genuine sympathy with genuine satire may lead to a muffled effect. It is a part of the price that Forster pays for his subtlety of attitude.

If the 'muffling' effect is sometimes present, there is a further omission in Forster's writing which we may also regard as a necessary defect. A writer's limitations sometimes appear most in his criticism of other writers: and this particular limitation is suggested by some remarks in *Aspects of the Novel*. In one of the lectures, Forster compares two funeral scenes without first disclosing the authors of the novels concerned:

(i) "All the preparations for the funeral ran easily and happily under Mrs Johnson's skilful hands. On the eve of the sad occasion she produced a reserve of black sateen, the kitchen steps, and a box of tintacks, and decorated the house with festoons and bows of black in the best possible taste. She tied up the knocker with black crape, and put a large bow over the corner of the steel engraving of Garibaldi, and swathed the bust of Mr Gladstone that had belonged to the deceased with inky swathings. She turned the two vases that had views of Tivoli and the Bay of Naples round, so that these rather brilliant landscapes were hidden and only the plain blue enamel showed, and she anticipated the long contemplated purchase of a tablecloth for the front room, and substituted a violet purple cover for the now very worn and faded raptures and roses in plushette that had hitherto done duty there. Everything that loving consideration could do to impart a dignified solemnity to her little home was done."

(ii) "The air of the parlour being faint with the smell of sweet cake, I looked about for the table of refreshments; it was scarcely visible until one had got accustomed to the gloom, but there was a cut-up plum cake upon it, and there were cut-up oranges, and sandwiches, and biscuits, and two decanters that I knew very well as ornaments, but had never seen used in all my life; one full of port, and one of sherry. Standing at this table, I became conscious of the servile Pumblechook in a black cloak and several yards of hat-band, who was alternately stuffing himself, and making obsequious movements to catch my attention. The moment he succeeded, he came over to me (breathing sherry and crumbs) and said in a subdued voice, 'May I, dear sir?' and did."[30]

After revealing that the passages are by Wells and Dickens respectively, and enumerating various qualities which they have in common, Forster continues,

And perhaps the main difference between them is the difference of opportunity offered to an obscure boy of genius a hundred years ago and forty years ago. The difference is in Wells' favour. He is better educated than his predecessor; in particular the addition of science has strengthened his mind and subdued his hysteria. He registers an improvement in society: Dotheboys Hall has been superseded by the Polytechnic—not any change in the novelist's art.

The analysis is acute; the conclusion drawn from it, to one reader at least, astonishing. The first description is good: it is closely observed: but it could have been achieved by any good satirical novelist of the time who had an eye for the detail of small homes. The second shows an entirely personal touch. The first is a detached, visualizing satire: the second has an uncanny gift of penetrating the scene, to evoke a sensuous and imaginative response from within it. It is a complex response: the gloom of the parlour, the richness of the provisions and the lugubriousness of Pumblechook fuse to evoke a sickly-sweet, choking atmosphere which yet contrives to hang somewhere near real richness and real sorrow, and to draw strength from the resources of both.

Linguistically, too, the passages differ strongly. The syntax of the first is tame and monotonous. 'She ... and ... She ... and ... and ... She ... so that ... and ... and ...' One may also compare Wells's careful formality with the way in which Dickens first evokes the refreshment table out of the gloom and then uses it as a stepping stone to the picturing of Pumblechook. Wells looks at his scene but never touches it; Dickens is in his scene all the time.

But it has to be acknowledged that the second type of writing does not appear in Forster's work, either. He has all Wells's gifts and many more: he is more acute, more sensitive, more skilled in satire than Dickens: but his work is deprived, by its very intelligence and polish, of the blunter tools which might penetrate to a warmth behind cultural impoverishment.

The point can be made by looking back at the opening of the sixth chapter of *Howards End*.

> We are not concerned with the very poor. They are unthinkable, and only to be approached by the statistician or the poet. This story deals with gentlefolk, or with those who are obliged to pretend that they are gentlefolk.
>
> The boy, Leonard Bast, stood at the extreme verge of gentility. . . .

There is here, behind Forster's ironic touch, a certain sleight of hand. By the time that we reach the second paragraph, the gap between extreme poverty and the beginning of pretensions to gentility has been wiped out altogether. But, as we all know, even in Forster's day a large section of mankind lived their lives between the two—there was a great English working class who had enough to eat, but for whom all the business of gentility and culture was meaningless.

Unfortunately, something has happened to that life since the middle of the nineteenth century, so that the Falstaffian element in it, the zest which provided a ground-bass for Dickens's writing has largely disappeared. In a technological society which cuts men off from the earth, coarseness is replaced by vulgarity and an active hostility to culture. As a result, a novel which is about 'culture' is automatically debarred from any serious dealings with working-class life. The English novel is the poorer for the loss, but it is inevitable.

Forster, whether he likes it or not, is committed by his birth, his gifts, most of all by the place of culture in modern society, to being an intellectual novelist. His novels aspire to the condition of music, and are governed by that end in every part. He is aware of the other side of humanity, the side that is mediated by the blood rather than the nerves and that can best be evoked by a more basic rhythm and intuitive imagery, but it is not a world in which he is properly at home. His novels are shaped not by unconscious forces but by conscious. Experience is brought to consciousness and produces certain interpretative themes, which are then worked out in a novel. Each novel follows naturally from the previous one, in the sense that each time fresh themes are brought into play and the previous ones dealt with more subtly than before. This complexity of organization makes the novels highly satisfying. But in the end interpretation has completely mastered experience.

There is not, therefore, the sense of renewing springs which one has with some writers—the sense that points of experience in one novel will spontaneously recombine to furnish the basic pattern of the next. So far as the process does occur, it occurs indirectly, with powerful mediation by the intellect. The distinction can best be made by comparing Forster with Lawrence at his best. In many respects, Forster is the subtler writer and the more reliable moralist of the two: but he lacks Lawrence's singleness of vision.

And, paradoxically, it sometimes seems as though it is Lawrence who has developed Forster's themes. A good deal of his thinking about sex leads directly on from Mr Emerson's remarks in *A Room with a View*: and there may have been a more detailed influence. *A Room with a View* was first published in 1908. In the following year, Lawrence completed *The White Peacock*. When he first began this novel several years before, it had concerned a noble young farmer, George, 'who married a socially unattainable Lettie after she had been seduced by a young man of still higher social status'. By the time of its completion, this had changed into the less conventional theme of a Lettie who rejects the nobler George in favour of a rich young man, Leslie Tempest, thus precipitating the spiritual decay of both herself and George.[31] The theme is strangely complementary to Forster's. One does not want to make too much of what, after all, were common themes of the time: but a second coincidence may be mentioned. In 1922, Lawrence wrote to Forster, recalling how, many years before, Forster had said to him on top of the downs in Sussex, 'How do you know I m not dead?'

> Well, you can't be dead, since here's your script. But think you *did* make a nearly deadly mistake glorifying those *business* people in *Howards End*. Business is no good.[32]

In spite of that, there may well be a connection between Margaret, trying to help Henry Wilcox to 'the building of the rainbow bridge that should connect the prose in us with the passion' and Ursula's vision of the rainbow at the end of Lawrence's later novel. The closing scenes of the two novels, with harsh new houses engulfing the countryside in each, have a strange similarity. But if there has been an influence, it is one that illustrates Lawrence's ability to take and transform. He has extrapolated one element from Forster's novel and made it a living organism in its own right. Forster's connecting rainbow, which brings into unity the 'meaningless fragments, half monks, half beasts, unconnected arches that have never joined into a man', is transformed into Lawrence's rainbow which 'arches itself in the blood' and rears over man and woman.[33]

Forster in his turn has praised Lawrence highly. In a tribute broadcast soon after his death, he recalls that he met him three or four times in the spring of 1915 and discusses what he regards as his essential qualities: 'the poetry that broods and flashes, the power to convey to the reader the colour and weight of objects.' He finds special praise for *The Plumed Serpent* and declares that Lawrence's philosophy was justified because it liberated his imagination, possessing a quality that is sometimes missed by those who judge it too hastily:

> Tenderness is waiting behind the pseudo-scientific jargon of his solar plexuses and the savagery of his blood-tests. It is his concession to the civilization he would destroy and the flaw in the primitive myths he would recreate. It is the Morning Star, the Lord of Both Ways, the star between day and the dark.[34]

In *Aspects of the Novel*, published some years before, he had offered a more radical judgment:

> (Lawrence) is, as far as I know, the only prophetic novelist writing today—all the rest are fantasists or preachers: the only living novelist in whom the song predominates, who has the rapt bardic quality, and whom it is idle to criticize.

After turning to comment on Lawrence's preaching, his 'bullying', he had continued,

> This bullying, and the honeyed sweetness which is a bully's reaction, occupy between them the foreground of Lawrence's work; his greatness lies far, far back, and rests, not like Dostoevsky's upon Christianity, nor like Melville's upon a contest, but upon something aesthetic. The voice is Balder's voice, though the hands are the hands of Esau. The prophet is irradiating nature from within, so that every colour has a glow and every form a distinctness which could not otherwise be obtained.[35]

The sort of element which Forster is here describing has a place in his own novels, but with a difference. His greater novels possess the visionary experience, but are not possessed by it. In the choice that faces every Romantic writer, between the way of Wordsworth and the way of Keats, he has elected to compromise. The compromise is of great relevance to life, for it corresponds to the compromise that most human beings are forced to make at some time, when it becomes necessary for their inward vision to conform to the realities of marriage or business or ordinary social relationships. And because Forster, unlike most of us, does not reject what has gone before, or laugh at the vision of the young as immature, but sees the loss of it as a tragic fact, his contribution is particularly valuable. Yet because his novels deal with the struggle and the compromise between vision and physical fact, there is an effect within the style. The bardic powers of rhythm and tone exist only occasionally, appearing almost as a side-effect.

Lawrence himself evidently regarded Forster's failure to

achieve singleness of vision as a basic defect. 'There is more in him than ever comes out,' he wrote. 'But he is not dead yet. I hope to see him pregnant with his own soul.'[36] What Forster loses in power, on the other hand, he makes up in total consistency and truth to the whole. While Lawrence is rapt in his bardic vision he is necessarily ignoring some parts of the human scene and some awkward questions that might be asked. The point could be illustrated over and over again; it stands out strongly in an incident recorded by Dorothy Brett:

> A group are talking in Taos one evening, and Lawrence starts passionately declaiming against divorce: "very intense, very evangelic", as he sometimes becomes when a subject moves him deeply, says Miss Brett. At last one of them observes: "Isn't that funny, coming from you." Lawrence looks surprised and asks "Why?" "Well," she replies, "you are staying in the house of one divorcee; you are visiting another; and you are married to another." Lawrence looks at her for a moment; then suddenly drops his head. "Yes, you are right," he says, sadly and heavily.[37]

A man who had spent more of his time in academic pursuits would hardly have let slip such an inconsistent remark in the first place. Nor, on the other hand, would he have been a prophet. It is one of the things that Forster means when he says elsewhere, 'To have a philosophy—even a poetic and emotional philosophy like Hardy's and Conrad's—leads to reflections on life and things. A prophet does not reflect.'[38]

To this extent, and this extent only, we may allow the claim that Forster is an academic novelist. He has the Coleridgean urge to include everything, to see every side of every question, to allow every viewpoint. It is sometimes a dangerously disintegrating agent in his writing: but his firm grasp of plot, characterization and satirical comedy avert disaster.

We have seen again and again, however, that his double aim of being true to both visionary and realistic elements leads to a peculiar duality of effect. The novels may be read in two ways at once. One can trust either the teller or the tale.

If one trusts the tale, the final 'meaning' of it often lies with a single character who has been partly involved in the events, partly detached from them. Forster has acknowledged that there is a good deal of himself in Cecil Vyse (*A Room with a View*), Philip Herriton (*Where Angels Fear to Tread*) and Rickie Elliot (*The Longest Journey*).[39] He could presumably have added Fielding in *A Passage to India*. And it is notable that in each case these are the characters who acquire wisdom in the course of the narrative. The impression which they leave at the end of the story is one of detachment: they emerge unattached to any creed, but with a new wisdom about humanity, and in some cases, a new involvement with life.

These characters may not represent the author, but they are impressive simply as dramatized minds in touch with the actual events of the story. For this reason, the reader may well share their detachment at the end of the novel. (For example, Fielding's marriage to Mrs Moore's daughter has symbolic value, but it is not made real within the novel itself and therefore does not impress at the level of events.) This detachment, which is satisfactory in terms of the presented plot, is, however, unsatisfactory in other respects. The reader who relies on plot alone will be left with nothing concrete to grasp when he lays down the novel. Even in *Howards End*, where something more is achieved in the establishment of the main characters in a house which will shelter them and nurture their values, Forster is swift to bring his sense of realism into play and to emphasize that Margaret Schlegel's achievement is only a temporary structure, reared against an encroaching tide of suburban houses which may soon engulf it. The detachment here belongs not to an individual but to a group: the house is an isolated fortress against forces which are always in danger of swamping the values which it protects.

Nevertheless, in *Howards End* it is at least true to say that something more than loneliness has been established. In *The Longest Journey*, likewise, there is a final glimpse of Stephen in a house which not only protects his family but nurtures the values which he learnt from Rickie. And in *A Passage to India*, the figure of the Hindu temple is reared in the last section with similar effect.

With these symbols, however, we are beginning to pass from the plot, dominated by time, to a spatial dimension which, since it stands behind the plot, makes more demands on the imagination. These spatial symbols echo the more temporary 'room with a view' that dominates the earlier novel: they straddle the closing events to impress some permanency upon the flux of time. From them, the next step is to 'visionary moments' which, although in time, have a significance removed from time and stand away from the tightly bound sequence of events in the novel, interpreting them.

But it has to be acknowledged that these two 'timeless' elements, though present within the plot, are reaching out to something which is not contained within the plot at all. Behind the events, affecting them only obliquely, stands Forster's fuller philosophy, which has to be expressed mainly through such spatial symbols and visionary moments, and which needs to be grasped itself as a separate organism, with its own structuring, before its relevance to the events can be seen. At this point, in other words, we need to trust the teller, not the tale.

Virginia Woolf, whose essay on Forster is one of the most sensitive to have appeared, comments amusingly upon the conflicts of mode which we have been noticing:

> . . . we have the sense that there is some perversity in Mr Forster's endowment so that his gifts in their variety and number tend to trip each other up. If he were less scrupulous, less just, less sensitively aware of the different aspects of every case, he could, we feel, come down with greater force on one precise point. As it is, the strength of the blow is dissipated. He is like a light sleeper who is always being woken by something in the room. The poet is twitched away by the satirist; the comedian is tapped on the shoulder by the moralist; he never loses himself or forgets himself for long in sheer delight in the beauty or the interest of things as they are.[40]

This criticism well represents the exasperation of the reader who wants Forster to write in a particular mode, and not to keep moving from one to another. But Mrs Woolf's comments also reflect a lack of sympathy with the thinker behind the tale. She complains that we are made to 'step from the enchanted world of imagination . . . to the twilight world of theory'. The contrast seems less justified as one grasps the full effect of the novels. Gradually one becomes more aware of the unity of Forster's processes: what at first appeared to be intellectual observation turns out to be touched by imaginative vision, and imaginative passages are found to be serving an intellectual purpose. One comes to read the novels less from without, more from within. And the modes jar against each other less and less, as one becomes steadily more aware of the personality behind, which reconciles them.

.   .   .   .

The gap between Forster's realism and his vision, between the society he knows well and the imaginative universe of his symbolism, has thus defined itself as a conflict of styles in what is presented to 'the common reader'. So far we have concentrated attention on the gap and emphasized the challenge which it presents—the challenge of becoming the 'uncommon reader' who will understand Forster himself. But we have hardly mentioned another factor which works towards such an appreciation within the novels themselves, and makes the task of synthesizing a good deal less formidable than it might at first appear.

Towards the end of *Aspects of the Novel*, Forster discusses at length a quality in the novel which he finds most important— namely, 'rhythm'. Rhythm, he says, can be quite easy—the rhythm, for example, which begins Beethoven's fifth symphony and which the audience can beat out physically if it wishes. But the same symphony has another rhythm, associated with the relation between its movements, 'which some people can hear but no one can tap to.'[41]

He proceeds to trace equivalents of these two types of rhythm in fiction. The first, 'easy' type of rhythm he finds in the *leitmotivs* employed by some novelists, such as Proust or Galsworthy or Meredith, in order to keep alive a particular theme or point a particular character. The second type is more difficult to achieve— it is the equivalent of the effect of the Fifth Symphony as a whole where, 'when the orchestra stops we hear something that has never been played. The opening movement, the andante, and the trio-scherzo-trio-finale-trio-finale that composes the third block, all enter the mind at once, and extend one another into a common entity'. For this effect he can find no obvious analogy in fiction, although he thinks it may exist, and finds something of the sort in *War and Peace.* '. . . As we read it, do not great chords begin to sound behind us, and when we have finished, does not every item—even the catalogue of strategies—lead a larger existence than was possible at the time?'

If Forster finds no strict analogy in fiction to the second type of rhythm, the fact that both *The Longest Journey* and *A Passage to India* exist in three large, designated blocks suggests that he may have been trying for some such effect in his own writing. In the last novel particularly, large themes expand in each section, giving a separate colouring and a developed symbolism (for example Forster himself relates them to the three seasons of the Indian year[42]: we might add to this the moon and the mosque of the first, the harsh sun and caves of the second and the love-god and Hindu festival of the third). These themes are undoubtedly effective, though it is doubtful whether they quite resound against each other in a symphonic manner. They are perceived intellectually rather than harmonically.

Nevertheless, there is a strong musical element elsewhere in the novels, which helps to bind visionary and realistic elements into a single pattern. At first sight, indeed, there seems to be no reason why characters and events should not be completely presented within a 'musical' framework: one has the parallel example of opera. But there are reasons which make such a straightforward solution difficult: the unmusical nature of the English character, for example, and the tradition of the English novel, which normally allows little room for the play of symbolic factors.

This problem of the relation between music and character is touched upon by Forster in discussing Virginia Woolf's novel, *The Waves*, which he describes as 'an extraordinary achievement'. The main qualification of his enthusiasm comes when he describes her characterization:

Life on the page she could give. . . . Life eternal she could seldom give; she could seldom so portray a character that it was remembered afterwards on its own account, as Emma is remembered, for instance, or Dorothea Casaubon, or Sophia and Constance in *The Old Wives' Tale*. What wraiths, apart from their context, are the wind-sextet from *The Waves*, or Jacob away from *Jacob's Room*![43]

The criticism is fair, but does not quite do justice to one fact. Virginia Woolf was facing precisely the problem which we have been discussing. Forster tries to give 'life eternal' to his characters and at the same time to suggest in the background an intellectual music, a wider pattern in which they have a place. Virginia Woolf, in a similar attempt to reconcile the music of art with the chaos of character, was trying a different method. In *The Waves*, each of the 'characters' is more like a strong 'personality tone', with light constantly playing on the one consistent trait. For this reason they do not live as *people* away from the page. But, as Forster and others have pointed out, it is possible to see the various 'characters' as different facets of a single personality. In that case, the novel possesses a fullness of personality which is denied to its individual characters—and its musical qualities have been assisting that effect. Some human characteristics may have been omitted, but at least omissions do not jar. If Forster insists on putting in these qualities, on the other hand, the music of his novels will be impaired by some jarring notes. We shall have been reminded that our own human existences tend to break the bonds of any patterns that may be imposed upon them: but to that extent the moral will have been emphasized at the expense of the aesthetic.

A musical effect comes through the novels in another way, moreover. Harder to define than as a tone or quality, to the ear that has caught it it is unmistakable. It is a tone existing within the speech and actions of some of the characters. Lucy Honeychurch, an early example of such a character, was herself a musician. In later novels, the reference is made more subtly, as in the description of the Schlegels listening to music: Helen sees heroes and shipwrecks in the music's flood, where Margaret sees only the music. Rickie in *The Longest Journey*, Margaret Schlegel in *Howards End*,

Mrs Moore in *A Passage to India*, each expresses a particular tone in everything that he or she does and says, so that at the end of the novel, we are aware of a strain that is still sounding. To return to an imagery which has sometimes appeared in the novels, we are aware of a moonlight that reflects and keeps alive the lost sun of Love.

More than any other factor, these 'tonal' characters link together the visionary and realistic elements in the novels, providing a constant bridge between the steady working out of a plot dominated by the cause and effect of events in time, and the looming presence of another universe of meaning, existent in timeless moments and spatial symbols. One of the chief impressions which remain with the reader is the vividness of the personal relationships which Forster introduces into his work. It is in such relationships that 'connection' is seen at its best: the characters are working out the meaning of love in actual human relationships, while the presentation of their thoughts and feelings relates them to the inward structure of Forster's own thought.

. . . .

A revival of interest in Forster's work began early in the 1940s. The date is perhaps significant, for it was at that time that Great Britain moved into the defensive position which she still occupies in the world. After the war, the polarization of power into two vast nation-groups dominated by the U.S.A. and the U.S.S.R. respectively, and the growth of movements towards national independence in other countries, meant that the shrinkage of British economic and political power must continue.

The present demands for physical and moral endurance in no way match those which were made in the war years, of course. It is only in isolated incidents that the conflicting demands for maintenance of prestige and recognition of new political facts come to a point of crisis. But the fact remains that the expansive mood of the nineteenth century cannot flourish now. In the immediate future, the imagination of humanity will continue to be held chiefly by the technicians, and the urge to conquer nature by technological progress will continue to be a supreme driving force. What is true of civilization is true of literature. The initiative is likely to lie with writers who evolve a dynamic style of writing in which narrative comes first and other factors are held in strict subordination.

In such a context, Forster's novels must appear slow and digressive to many critics. He is not carried by the strongest currents. He accepts technological advances without sneering but also without enthusiasm, for technology is at war with inward vision. In the mass-movements which technological organization encourages, Forster sees a menace to individuality and, to intelligence; and in industrial development he sees a threat to the spirit of place. His values remain unchanged, however. Recently Mr K. W. Gransden, in an interview, asked him whether he now personally agreed with Margaret Schlegel, whom he had made to say, 'I quite expect to end my life caring most for a place.' He replied that he did not. His order is the same as it has always been: first people, then books, then places.[44]

This statement might be said to represent the minimal content of the novels: it gives the key to Forster's position for the common reader of the present day. The First and Second World Wars have destroyed two great pillars of his art as it was developing in the novels. The social revolution which they brought have destroyed that stable social scene which is the bulwark of his comedy, while subsequent disillusionment and cynicism have sapped assurance from the romanticism which has been a mainstay of his vision. Only his moral position is left untouched. The life which was exercising itself in broader fields has been forced to work within a more limited compass. Essays and comments have replaced the fuller creative achievement of the novels.

In one essay, he comments on the new situation in writing and analyzes some characteristics of the prose and fiction which came forward between the wars. He draws attention, in particular, to the great amount of psychological analysis and to the pervasive belief that moral judgments are necessarily relative.[45] Paradoxically, both factors are notable features of his own work. The difference is that there they are subordinated to the structure of a particular social order and viewed within the fabric of a particular vision. In the modern novel they have been extrapolated to take possession of the novel in their own right. Forster is not willing to venture into this uncharted sea. Since he must retire from his broader, more assured universe, he retires into the prepared position of devotion to people, and books, and places.

Such a position is still primarily defensive. Yet it is because the defences are so strong that he has attracted many readers of the present time, who have learned to present to their own moral and spiritual situation the same front of endurance and tolerance, backed by a similar cultivation of truthfulness and kindliness. Such readers see the novels as a working out in concrete situations of a philosophy which they find expounded in some of the later essays. They regard Forster as a highly articulate defender of things which they find it difficult to express without danger of misunderstanding—as (to quote Lionel Trilling's phrase again), 'one of those who raise the shield of Achilles, which is the moral intelligence of art.'[46]

Even if Forster now finds the ending of *Howards End* a less convincing solution than when he wrote it, therefore, his final symbol there remains apposite to the present age: the house which protects people and culture, but which faces the prospect of being surrounded and even engulfed by a tide of suburban houses.

The comparison with Lawrence becomes more sharply defined in this symbol. *The Rainbow* ends with Ursula Brangwen looking at '. . . the old church-tower standing up in hideous obsoleteness above raw new houses on the crest of the hill, the amorphous, brittle hard edged new houses advancing from Beldover to meet the corrupt new houses from Lethley . . . a dry, brittle, terrible corruption spreading over the face of the land . . .' But she is filled with hope in spite of everything:

> She knew that the sordid people who crept hard-scaled and separate on the face of the world's corruption were living still, that the rainbow was arched in their blood and would quiver to life in their spirit, that they would cast off their horny covering of disintegration, that new, clean, naked bodies would issue to a new germination, to a new growth, rising to the light and the wind and the clean rain of heaven.

Although this vision is not far from Forster's own, he would not offer his with the same assurance. His novels contain 'tonal' characters which help to provide them with vision and music: Lucy Honeychurch, Caroline Abbott, Rickie Elliot, Margaret Schlegel, Mrs Moore. But it is equally typical that they contain characters who survive in detachment and are left in isolation at the end: Cecil Vyse, Philip Herriton, Stewart Ansell, Margaret Schlegel again and Cyril Fielding. These characters provide the necessary note of defensive realism.

In other words, vision and realism co-exist to the end in Forster's work. The 'music' is the ultimate expression of his vision, the detachment a result demanded by his realism. Throughout his work he continues to present neither a full vision nor a complete imitation of reality but an interplay between the two.

Because of this interplay his achieved body of work stands partly in the main stream of our time, partly away from it. The devotion to persons and books and places which is its minimal content speaks to a civilization which in spite of its preoccupation with the dynamic forces of industrial development senses the need for more permanent values than the nebulous 'higher standard of living' and 'greater leisure' which technological advance offers it. And a technological society which needs smooth relationships between persons for the efficient running of its complicated organizations finds an immediate practical use for the virtues of kindness and tolerance.

If Forster's full vision is received sympathetically, on the other hand, the achievement of his novels is seen to extend correspondingly further. That wider 'realism' detects virtues and failings which survive the decay of the particular society within which he depicts them. The symbolism by which he interprets human life and love may sometimes oversimplify certain factors in human behaviour but carries the stamp of a psychological insight which can never be irrelevant to it. And the Hellenistic 'mythology' which is often the vehicle of this symbolism carries more weight because it is directly related to an actual historical civilization, which is thus invoked to criticize our own.

As Forster himself remarks, the progress of industrial civilization has been so swift in the last fifty years that even the middle-class culture which he satirized is now viewed nostalgically as more settled and peaceful than our own. But the ultimate paradox of his achievement lies deeper than this. It is that the very same technological civilization which finds a use for kindliness and tolerance in the interests of industrial efficiency and which finances research into psychology as 'the science of human adjustment' is continually engaged in isolating men more completely from those resources of the earth and the imagination which, according to Forster, are the twin sources of their fullest happiness.

Industrial society has its own momentum and even its own mythology: Forster's novels stand away from that current and in consequence the validity or otherwise of their total statement cannot finally be assessed at the present stage of the technological revolution. His immediate judgments may be verified day by day in human experience; his more basic principles may well be vindicated also in the course of time. Whatever the judgment of posterity, however, his works, the immediate social commentary and the wider, 'mythological' implications alike, stand by their insight and integrity: a completed corpus, a full criticism of life.

NOTES

(In the case of Forster's novels, the reference is to the pocket edition. The text is normally taken from the first edition, however. Abbreviations are explained in the Bibliography.)

CHAPTER I (pages 11-30)

1. G. Sampson, *The Concise Cambridge History of English Literature*, 1941, p. 969.
2. L. Trilling, *E. M. Forster*, London, 1944, p. 9.
3. AN, 40-1; 62.
4. R. Macaulay, *Writings of E. M. Forster*, 1938, p. 9; *The Listener*, 12.12.46, p. 847.
5. Trilling, *op. cit.*, 158.
6. MT, 29.
7. TC, 198.
8. AH, 236-7.
9. MT, 54 (one correction).
10. MT, 71.
11. LJ, xvi, 170; HE, iv, 24; HE, xli, 336. (In later editions, 'root' is misprinted as 'foot'.) The quotation is from Meredith's *Modern Love*.
12. LJ, xvi, 169.
13. AN, 214; *Writers at Work*, 1958, pp. 28-9; 30; 32. Forster refers to Peter Burra's preface to the Everyman edition of *A Passage to India*.
14. The visionary element in *The Ancient Mariner* is discussed in my *Coleridge the Visionary*, 1959, chapter v.
15. *Merchant of Venice*, V, i, 58-65.
16. Rex Warner, *E. M. Forster*, 1950, p. 28.
17. Text from Letter to Sara Hutchinson. Coleridge, *Collected Letters* (ed. Griggs), 1956, II, 796.
18. C. Connolly, *Enemies of Promise* (rev. ed.) 1949, 26-7.
19. M. D. Zabel, *Craft and Character in Modern Fiction*, 1957, p. 230.

CHAPTER II (pages 31-52)

1. MT, 271n.
2. MT, 269-70. Forster has left enough clues for the reader to be able to identify the exact situation of the house, if he wishes.
3. MT, 271-2.
4. HD, 87.
5. 'The Celestial Omnibus': CSS, 47-8, 55-6.

6. MT, 274-5. 'Blowdy Wags' was a cousin of Forster's.
7. LJ, xvii, 178-9.
8. GLD, 26; 35. LJ, i, 10.
9. GLD, 34.
10. CSS, 38-9; TC, 103; AH, 6; TC, 97; LJ, xiii, 146.
11. See Bibliography.
12. CSS, Introduction, v-vi.
13. L. Trilling, *E. M. Forster*, 1944, 19; 35; 49-50.
14. RWV, 87.
15. See, for example, 'The Music on the Hill'.
16. CSS, pp. v-vi.
17. TC, 366; 368.
18. TC, 368-9.
19. Wordsworth, 'Two Letters on the Kendal and Windermere Railway'. *Prose Works* (ed. Grosart), 1896, 385-405.
20. *The Listener*, 22.5.58.

CHAPTER III (pages 53-76)

1. RWV, ii, 36.
2. RWV, xi, 149.
3. RWV, xvii, 214.
4. RWV, i, 10; iv, 53; x, 143.
5. RWV, ii, 37; vii, 99; xvi, 203-4; xix, 239; xix, 246; 247; 248.
6. LJ, i, 16; xvi, 170.
7. AN, 93-106.
8. *Encounter*, Nov., 1957, pp. 56; 53.
9. RWV, xvii, 213.
10. RWV, xviii, 229.
11. RWV, iii, 44; xii.
12. RWV, xix, 244.
13. AN, 214-5.
14. RWV, iii.
15. RWV, xi, 149.
16. RWV, xv, 190.
17. RWV, xviii, 224; 230-2.
18. RWV, viii, 108-9.
19. RWV, iii, 35.
20. RWV, xii, 159.
21. RWV, ix, 122.
22. *Ibid.*
23. RWV, x, 143.
24. RWV, ix, 130.
25. RWV, vi, 85-6.

26. RWV, xix, 250.
27. RWV, xvii, 214.
28. RWV, vi, 74.
29. RWV, vii, 87-8.
30. WAF, iii, 47-8.
31. WAF, iii, 48.
32. WAF, iv, 71.
33. WAF, iv, 74.
34. WAF, v, 80.
35. WAF, vi, 139.
36. WAF, vii, 145.
37. WAF, viii, 168; 170-1.
38. WAF, ix, 192.
39. WAF, vii, 157.
40. WAF, viii, 179-80.
41. WAF, ix, 192.
42. WAF, x, 204.

CHAPTER IV (pages 77-100)

1. 'A View Without a Room.' *Observer*, 27.7.58, p. 15.
2. xiii, 142.
3. xiii, 146.
4. vii, 72-3.
5. xiv, 157.
6. xv, 166.
7. xix, 199.
8. The distinction seems first to have been made by Montgomery Belgion ('The Diabolism of Mr E. M. Forster'. *Criterion*, XIV, 70).
9. xxiv, 224.
10. *Encounter*, Nov. 1957, p. 56.
11. L. Trilling, *The Opposing Self*, 1955, 219-20.
12. xx, 201.
13. xxiii, 215.
14. xxvi, 234.
15. L. Trilling, *E. M. Forster*, 1944, p. 72.
16. iii, 49.
17. W. J. Harvey, 'Imagination and Moral Theme in E. M. Forster's *The Longest Journey*'. *Essays in Criticism*, 1956, VI, 431.
18. See above, p. 63.
19. ix, 96.
20. vi, 70; and above, p. 84.
21. Rose Macaulay, *Writings of E. M. Forster*, 1938, p. 50.
22. xviii, 192.

23. vii, 74.
24. xxvi, 235.
25. xv, 164.
26. Kenneth Young, 'A Dialogue with Durrell'. *Encounter*, Dec. 1957, p. 62.
27. HE, xxxiii, 282.
28. xxiii, 218.
29. xxxi, 278.
30. xxxiv, 311.
31. See above, pp. 46-8.
32. CSS, 163.
33. CSS, 174.
34. CSS, 117-8.
35. CSS, 156-7.
36. xxxiii, 302.
37. xii, 137; xv, 161; xx, 206; xxxv, 318.
38. See above, p. 89.
39. xiii, 150-1.
40. xxxv, 318; 319.
41. Preface to LJ (World's Classics edition), 1960.
42. GLD, 155.
43. George Eliot, *Middlemarch*, ch. lxxxi.
44. Preface to LJ (World's Classics edition), 1960.

CHAPTER V (pages 101-130)

1. 'A View Without a Room.' *The Observer*, 27.7.58, p. 15.
2. xliii, 352.
3. xx, 188.
4. xxii, 202-3.
5. See above, p. 20.
6. xi, 100-7 (one correction).
7. ix, 80.
8. iii, 23.
9. i, 2; xxix, 262-3; xliv.
10. i, 2; xxxiii, 288-9; xliv, 359. Tibby: xxxiii, 289; xxxiv, 295.
11. ix, 78.
12. viii, 74.
13. iv, 27.
14. iv, 28.
15. xix, 185.
16. xxvi, 234-5; xxix, 264.
17. xvii, 158.
18. xxxi, 275.

19. xiii, 114.
20. Blake, *Jerusalem*, 91.36-7. Forster's philosophy throughout this novel evidently owes a good deal to his reading of Blake.
21. xv, 138.
22. xxx, 283-4.
23. MT, 269-70.
24. MT, 188.
25. xliii, 349.
26. xxxiv, 296.
27. *Writers at Work*, 1958, p. 27.
28. xliv, 357.
29. AN, 113-4.
30. Quoted, Rose Macaulay, *Writings of E. M. Forster*, 1938, p. 114.
31. vi, 48; xiv, 121-2.
32. Frank Swinnerton, *The Georgian Literary Scene*, 1935, p. 415.
33. v, 34.
34. xiii, 121.
35. vi, 56-7.
36. xliii, 349.
37. See below, p. 168.
38. xxxviii, 325.
39. xxii, 196.
40. xxvi, 233.
41. xxviii, 254-5.
42. ii, 8.
43. xxviii, 257.
44. xl, 332.
45. xliii, 350-1.
46. xxxviii, 326.
47. xliii, 353.
48. xviii, 174; 175.
49. xxix, 263. C. Hoy, 'Forster's Metaphysical Novel'. PMLA, LXXV, 1960, 126-36.
50. xl, 333; xli, 341.
51. xxiv, 217-8.
52. xl, 331.
53. v, 34-5.
54. xxx, 270.
55. xxxv, 305.

CHAPTER VI (pages 131-165)

1. See above, p. 34.
2. *Writers at Work*, 1958, p. 27.

3. Nirad Chaudhuri, 'Passage to and from India'. *Encounter*, June, 1954, 19-24.
4. George Orwell, 'Rudyard Kipling' (1942) in *Critical Essays*, 1946, 103-4.
5. AH, 4-5.
6. v, 54.
7. xxxii, 293.
8. HE, xxiii, 206.
9. xxxiii, 297; HD, 109.
10. HD, 137-8.
11. AH, 5-6.
12. xxvii, 264.
13. xxvii, 260; HD, 63.
14. HD, 63.
15. xiv, 147.
16. HD, 89-90.
17. viii, 92-104.
18. HD, 155.
19. ii, 20.
20. iii, 32; 37-8.
21. xxxvi, 318-9.
22. xvi, 166.
23. Frank Kermode, 'Mr E. M. Forster as A Symbolist'. *The Listener*, 2.1.58, pp. 17-18.
24. vii, 79-80.
25. xii, 130.
26. TC, 340.
27. CSS, 143-4.
28. xxiii, 217.
29. vii, 83-4.
30. viii, 92.
31. xiv, 143.
32. xix, 186.
33. HE, 206.
34. Section xi. *Leaves of Grass*, 1907, p. 352.
35. GLD, 216.
36. xv, 158-9.
37. xxii, 206-13.
38. xxiv.
39. xxvi, 254-5.
40. See above, p. 47.
41. iii, 38.
42. xii, 129.
43. xiv, 144.
44. See above, p. 127.

45. xiv, 154; 156-7.
46. xxiii, 217.
47. Angus Wilson, 'A Conversation with E. M. Forster'. *Encounter*, Nov. 1957, p. 54.
48. xxiii, 218-9.
49. xxxiii, 298; 303.
50. Austin Warren, *A Rage for Order*, Chicago, 1948, p. 136; Gertrude White, 'A Passage to India, Analysis and Revaluation'. PMLA, LXVIII, 1953, 647; Virginia Woolf, *The Death of the Moth*, 1942, 108. These references are taken in the first instance from G. O. Allen, 'Forster's *A Passage to India*'. PMLA, LXX, 1955, p. 941. Allen cites Trilling as the critic who refers to the caves as 'wombs'. Forster's description brings out the womb-like quality of the caves (xiv, 153), and he describes them as 'engendering an event like an egg' (see below, p. 160), but I do not find this point in Trilling's study. On the contrary, Trilling, (*E. M. Forster*, p. 135) contrasts the caves with the room where Caroline Abbott found the baby, stressing the death-like quality of the first and reserving his image of the womb for the latter.
51. *Writers at Work*, 1958, pp. 26-7. The Marabar Caves are wrongly spelt 'Malabar' throughout.
52. Blake, *Milton*, 14.21-35.
53. See above, p. 133.
54. *The Listener*, 2.12.54, pp. 977-8; 5.12.40, pp. 801-2.
55. xxxvi, 329.
56. vii, 73.
57. xxix, 274.
58. Virginia Woolf, *The Death of the Moth*, 1942, p. 112.
59. D. A. Traversi, 'The Novels of E. M. Forster', *Arena* I, 36-9.
60. xxvi, 329.

CHAPTER VII (pages 166-176)

1. F. Scott Fitzgerald, *Tender is the Night* (1st vn.) ch. xiii. (*Bodley Head Scott Fitzgerald*, 1959, II, 129).
2. PI, xiv, 144; xxviii, 268.
3. PI, xxxii, 293.
4. E. Charteris, *Life and Letters of Edmund Gosse*, 1931, 324. Gosse was also moved by disgust at the 'preposterous morals' of the book, however.
5. AH, 29.
6. AG, 57.
7. PP, 79.
8. William Plomer, 'An Introduction to E. M. Forster'. *Penguin New Writing*, XX, 1944, p. 141.
9. Angus Wilson, 'A Conversation with E. M. Forster', *Encounter*, Nov., 1957, p. 52.

10. 'A View Without a Room.' *The Observer*, 27.7.58, p. 15.
11. *The Trial of Lady Chatterley* (ed. C. H. Rolph), 1961, p. 113.
12. LJ (World's Classics edition), 1960, p. xi.
13. Leonard Woolf, *Sowing, an Autobiography of the years* 1880-1904, 1960, pp. 171-2. C. Hassall, *Edward Marsh*, 1959, p. 522.
14. Virginia Woolf, *Roger Fry*, 1940, pp. 240-1.
15. TC, 130-1.
16. *The Listener*, 22.6.44, pp. 685-6.
17. TC, 79.
18. TC, 23; 21-2.
19. TC, 55; 58.
20. TC, 77.
21. Coleridge, *Biographia Literaria*, ch. xiii.
22. TC, 97.

CHAPTER VIII (pages 177-208)

1. Angus Wilson, 'A Conversation with E. M. Forster.' *Encounter*, Nov. 1957, pp. 54-5.
2. Letter of March 1959, quoted in Jonathan Spence, 'E. M. Forster at Eighty.' *The New Republic*, 5.9.59, p. 21.
3. LJ (World's Classics edition), 1960, p. xiii.
4. AH, 145.
5. MT, 127 (one correction).
6. MT, 255.
7. TC, 305-6.
8. *The Listener*, 9.3.38, p. 530.
9. AH, 225-33.
10. L. Trilling, *E. M. Forster*, 1944, p. 9.
11. Rose Macaulay, *Writings of E. M. Forster*, 1938, pp. 24-5.
12. *Ibid.*, 31.
13. HE, ix, 78.
14. HE, xvii, 163.
15. *Writers at Work*, 1958, p. 31.
16. Rose Macaulay, *op. cit.*, p. 97.
17. Lord David Cecil, *Poets and Story Tellers*, 1949, pp. 194-201.
18. PI, xxix, 272-6 and see above, p. 163.
19. PI, xxviii, 267.
20. HE, xi; xviii, 173; xli, 343.
21. AH, 11-12.
22. HE, xi, 104; and see above, pp. 103-5.
23. HE, xix, 185-6.
24. F. R. Leavis, *The Common Pursuit*, 1952, pp. 271-2.
25. See above, p. 34.

26. PI, xxvi, 257.
27. F. R. Leavis, op. cit., p. 274.
28. Shelley, 'Epipsychidion', 11.160-1; AH, 6.
29. RWV, vii, 93.
30. AN, 27-30.
31. Harry T. Moore, *Life and Works of D. H. Lawrence*, 1951, pp. 39-40, quoting Jessie Chambers. Lawrence's manuscripts might throw some light on this question.
32. D. H. Lawrence, *Letters*, 1932, p. 552.
33. HE, xxii, 196; D. H. Lawrence, *The Rainbow*, end.
34. *The Listener*, 30.4.30, pp. 753-4.
35. AN, 184-6.
36. R. Aldington, *Journey with Genius*, 1953, p. 286.
37. W. Tiverton (*ps.*) *D. H. Lawrence and Human Existence*, 1951, 83, paraphrasing D. Brett, *Lawrence and Brett*, 1933, 127 ff.
38. AN, 177.
39. *Writers at Work*, 1958, p. 31.
40. V. Woolf, *Death of the Moth*, 1942, p. 110.
41. AN, 210-7.
42. See his notes to the Everyman edition of *A Passage to India*.
43. TC, 258.
44. K. W. Gransden, 'E. M. Forster at Eighty.' *Encounter*, Jan. 1959, p. 77.
45. TC, 282-4.
46. See above, p. 14.

BIBLIOGRAPHY

WORKS BY E. M. FORSTER

(i) *Fiction*

'Albergo Empedocle.' *Temple Bar*, Dec. 1903.

WAF   *Where Angels Fear to Tread*. London, 1905. (Pocket ed., 1947.)

LJ   *The Longest Journey*. London, 1907. (Pocket ed., 1947.)

RWV   *A Room With a View*. London, 1908. (Pocket ed., 1947; World's Classics edition with introduction by the author, 1960.)

HE   *Howards End*. London, 1910. (Pocket ed., 1947.)

PI   *A Passage to India*. London, 1924. (Pocket ed., 1947; Everyman edition with an introduction by Peter Burra and some notes by the author, 1948.)

CSS   *Collected Short Stories*. London, 1947.

'Entrance to an Unwritten Novel.' *The Listener*, 23.12.48.

'A View Without a Room.' *The Observer*, 27.7.58, p. 15.

(ii) *Other Prose Works*

AG   *Alexandria, a History and a Guide*. Alexandria, 1922.

PP   *Pharos and Pharillon*. Richmond, 1923.

AN   *Aspects of the Novel* (The Clark Lectures). London, 1927.

GLD   *Goldsworthy Lowes Dickinson*. London, 1934.

AH   *Abinger Harvest*. London, 1936.

England's Pleasant Land, a Pageant Play. London, 1940.

TC   *Two Cheers for Democracy*. London, 1951.

HD   *The Hill of Devi. Being Letters from Dewas State Senior*. London, 1953.

MT   *Marianne Thornton, 1797-1887. A Domestic Biography*. London, 1956.

Also, numerous uncollected contributions to periodicals, including *The Listener, The Sunday Times, The Observer, The New Statesman and Nation, The Spectator*, etc., etc.

SOME INTERVIEWS

Writers at Work, The Paris Review Interviews. (1953.) London, 1958, pp. 23-34.

Angus Wilson, 'A Conversation with E. M. Forster.' *Encounter*, Nov. 1957.

K. W. Gransden, 'E. M. Forster at Eighty.' *Encounter*, Jan. 1959.

BIBLIOGRAPHY

SELECT BIBLIOGRAPHY OF CRITICAL STUDIES

I. A. Richards, *The Forum*, December, 1927.

Bonamy Dobrée, *The Lamp and the Lute, Studies in Six Modern Authors*. Oxford, 1929.

Katherine Mansfield, *Novels and Novelists*. London, 1930, pp. 237-9.

Montgomery Belgion, 'The Diabolism of Mr E. M. Forster.' *Criterion*, 1934, XIV, 54-73.

Frank Swinnerton, *The Georgian Literary Scene*. London, 1935, pp. 406-18.

Austin Warren, *A Rage for Order; Essays in Criticism*. Chicago, 1948.

D. A. Traversi, 'The Novels of E. M. Forster.' *Arena*, I, 28-40.

Rose Macaulay, *The Writings of E. M. Forster*. London, 1938.

F. R. Leavis, 'E. M. Forster' (1938) in *The Common Pursuit*, London, 1952, pp. 261-77.

Virginia Woolf, *The Death of the Moth*. London, 1942, pp. 104-12.

Lionel Trilling, *E. M. Forster; a Study*. London, 1944.

Noel Annan, *New Statesman and Nation*, 7.10.44, pp. 239-40.

Peter Ault, 'Aspects of E. M. Forster.' *Dublin Review*, Dublin, 1946.

Lord David Cecil, *Poets and Story-tellers; a Book of Critical Essays*. London, 1949, pp. 181-201.

Cyril Connolly, *Enemies of Promise*. Rev. ed., London, 1949, pp. 6; 26-7.

Rex Warner, *E. M. Forster*. (British Council pamphlet; supplement to *British Book News*). London, 1950.

E. K. Brown, *Rhythm in the Novel*. Toronto, 1950.

J. K. Johnstone, *The Bloomsbury Group, a Study of E. M. Forster, Lytton Strachey, Virginia Woolf and their Circle*. London, 1954.

G. O. Allen, 'Structure, Symbol, Theme in E. M. Forster's *A Passage to India*.' *PMLA*, 1955, LXX, 934-54.

W. J. Harvey, 'Imagination and Moral Theme in E. M. Forster's *The Longest Journey*.' *Essays in Criticism*, 1956, VI, 418-33.

M. D. Zabel, *Craft and Character in Modern Fiction*. London, 1957, pp. 228-52.

James McConkey, *The Novels of E. M. Forster*. Ithaca, N.Y., 1957.

Frank Kermode, 'Mr E. M. Forster as a Symbolist.' *The Listener*, 2.1.58, pp. 17-18.

G. D. Klingopoulos, 'E. M. Forster's Sense of History: and Cavafy.' *Essays in Criticism*, 1958, VIII, 156-65.

Glenn Pederson, 'Forster's Symbolic Form.' *Kenyon Review*, 1959, XXI, 231-49.

Jonathan Spence, 'E. M. Forster at Eighty.' *New Republic*, 5.9.59.

H. J. Oliver, *The Art of E. M. Forster*. Melbourne, 1960.

Cyrus Hoy, 'Forster's Metaphysical Novel.' *PMLA*, 1960, LXXV, 126-36.

F. C. Crews, 'E. M. Forster: the Limitations of Mythology.' *Comparative Literature*, 1960, xii, 97-112.

INDEX

(*Note*.—Abbreviations refer to the Bibliography. Entries in heavy type refer to important discussions of the topic. A fictional character is not entered except for references outside the chapter dealing with the novel in which he or she appears.)

I. EDWARD MORGAN FORSTER

I. LIFE (1879-   )

Childhood, 31-3
Schooldays, 33-4
University, 34-7, 173
Visits Greece, 37
Visits Italy, 38
Visits India, 131
In Alexandria, 168-9
Second World War, 169-71
Honorary Fellow of King's College, Cambridge, 170

Character, 15-21, 90, 169-76, 201, etc., etc.
Political opinions, 167-8, 171f
Religious opinions. *See* Religion in Index II

II. FICTION

A Room With a View (RWV), 21f, 38-9, **53-66**, 76, 87, 101, 123, 125, 171, 173, 183f, 192, 195-6 and n, 199, 203, 207
Where Angels Fear to Tread (WAF), 13, **66-76**, 128, 183, 199, 207, 215
The Longest Journey (LJ), 13, 19f, 22, 32, 33-7, 41, 57, **77-100**, 131, 148, 164, 177, 183, 199, 202f, 207
Howards End (HE), 13, 20, 23, 31, 41-42, 83, 95, **101-30**, 144, 146, 167, 170, 177, 182, 184-9, 194, 196, 199, 203, 205ff
A Passage to India (PI), 12, 19, 23, 41, 114, 130, **131-65**, 166, 173-4, 177, 189-92, 199, 202-4, 207
Arctic Summer (uncompleted), 114
Collected Short Stories (CSS), 97, 164, 173

'The Celestial Omnibus', 36, 50
'Co-ordination', 50
'The Curate's Friend', 50
'The Eternal Moment, 30, 49
'The Machine Stops', 50, 93-4, 145, 182
'Other Kingdom', 50
'The Other Side of the Fence', 49-50
'The Point of It', 46-8, 92-3, 153
'The Road from Colonus, 38, 43-6, 49-50
'The Story of a Panic', 37-8, 39-41
'The Story of the Siren', 51-2, 182

'Albergo Empedocle', 37
'A View Without a Room', 77, 101, 171

III. OTHER PROSE WORKS

Abinger Harvest (AH), 181-2
'The Difficulties of Mr and Mrs Abbey', 181
'Macolnia Shops', 181
'Notes on the English Character', 135, 138-9, 185
Alexandria, 168-9
Aspects of the Novel (AN), 11, 22, 57, 59, 192-4, 197, 201-2
Goldsworthy Lowes Dickinson (GLD), 34-6
Hill of Devi (HD), 131, 137-42
Marianne Thornton (MT), 16-17, 31, 171, 178-9
Pharos and Pharillon (PP), 168-9
Two Cheers for Democracy (TC), 174-6, 205
'Art for Art's Sake', 36
'Last of Abinger', 41-3
'Raison d'Etre of Criticism . . .', **174**

INDEX

II. GENERAL INDEX

Abinger, 41-3
Absolute, 112-16, 160, 167
Achilles, 46; Shield of, 14, 206
Airolo, 75
Alan, Miss (ch. III), 192
Allen, G. O., 160n
Ansell, 33
Ansell, Stewart (ch. IV), 207
Apollo, 99, 151, 168. *See also* Sun, Gods
'Armies of the benighted', 22, 55, 59, 148
Art, visual, 60-3, 72-4
Artemis, 96
Austen, Jane, 15-16, 115, 178, 180f; *Emma*, 203; *Mansfield Park*, 84, 111; *Pride and Prejudice*, 120; *Sense and Sensibility*, 15, 185

Baby, 53, 70-1, 72-3, 156
Barrie, J. M., 39
Bartlett, Miss (ch. III), 22; original of, 183
Bast, Leonard (ch. V), 20, 183f, 194
Bayreuth Festival, 32
Beebe, Mr (ch. III), 22
Beethoven, 15, 32, 50, 59-60, 117f, 120, 127, 171, 201
Belgion, M., 83n
Bellini, 72
Bennett, Arnold, 203
Bible, 17, 138, 175
Blake, W., 15, 26, 87, 110 and n, 156, 161, 172, 175
'Blowdy Wags', 33 and n
Bournemouth, 108
Brett, D., 198
British Museum, 46, 96
Brontë, C., *Jane Eyre*, 115
Bunyan, J., 172
Burra, P., 23 and n
'Business', 65, 68, 102-4, 125, 196

Caliban, 118f, 160
Cambridge, 34-7, 77-9, 88, 170, 173
Casualness, 142, 164
Cavafy, C. P., 168
Caves, 41, 130, ch. VI *passim*, 202, 215
Cecil, Lord David, 183
Characterization, 22, 198, 202-4, etc. *See* Flat, Round
Charm, 178-82

Chaudhuri, N., 133
Christianity, 99, 157, 161, 175, 178-9, 197. *See* Evangelical, Religion
Civilization, man of, 114
Clapham sect, 17-19
Coleridge, S. T., 15, 26, 29, 156, 175, 181, 198
Comedy, 16, 54, 120, 189, 198
'Connection', 111, 121-3, 135-7, 170, 204
Connolly, C., 30
Conrad, Joseph, 198
Conventions, 81ff
Culture, 118, 193-5, etc.
Crawford, Miss, 84

Dance, 146, 159-61
Death, 30, 40, 45-6, 46-8, 56, 68, 71, 79, 97, 106, 140-1, 159, 161, 184, etc.
Della Robbia, 53
Demeter, 96-7
Dent, Professor, 183
Desire, 48. *See* Passion
Detachment, 70-1, 199, 207
Dialectic, 36, 48, 83, 123, 135, 163, etc.
Dickens, 57, 192-4
Dickinson, G. L., 34-6, 99, 148, 173. *See* GLD
Dickinson, Misses, 183
Domestic comedy, 12, 51, 115f, 180, 184. *See* Comedy
Dostoyevsky, 197; *Brothers Karamazov*, 115
Dryads, 50, 78, 90. *See* Tree
Durham, Dean of, 168
Durrell, L. G., 90

Earth, 38-42, 82, 96-7, 105, 108f, 124-5, 136, 143-5, 164, 194, 208, etc.
Echoes, 23, 110, 113f, 129-30, 150, 156-159
Edwardians, 39, 50, 112, 116, 166, 170, 177-8, 183, etc.
Einstein, 167
Eliot, George, 27, 70, 119; *Middlemarch*, 98-9, 203
Eliot, T. S., 24, 30, 167
Elliot, Rickie (ch. IV), 19, 22, 32, 35, 36-7, 148, 199, 203, 207
Emerson, George (ch. III), 22, 87, 192; later life, 171

Emerson, Mr (ch. III), 21f, 76
Endymion, 75
Erasmus, 134
Eros, 55, 64
Evangelicalism, 17-19, 70f, 178-9, 184
Evil, 39, 41-2, 73, 145f, 156-8
'Experience', 79-80, 89
'Extraordinary', 143-5f

Failing, Mrs (ch. IV), original of, 183
Fielding, Cyril (ch. VI), 167, 184, 189-192, 199, 207
Fina, Santa, 67
First World War, 15, 37, 49, 99, 120, 166, 171, 205
Fitzgerald, F. Scott, 166
'Flat' characters, 57
Florence, 53-66 passim, 101, 171
Flux, 107, 109-11, 123, 126
Form, 112, 137, etc.
Forster, E. M. See Index I
Forster, Mrs (mother of novelist), 17, 31, 33, 179
French Revolution, 15
Freud, 14
Fry, Roger, 173-4

Galsworthy, John, 201
Gambier, Lord, 179
Gaskell, Mrs, 167; Cranford, 115
Gemini, 47
Genius loci, 23, 38, 41, 97, 110
Germany, 102, 121
Gibbon, Edward, 18
Giotto, 53, 61
Gluck, 60
'Goblin footfalls', 114, 117, 127, 129-130, 156
Godbole (ch. VI), 23
Gods (and goddesses), 74-6, 126, 145, 150-3, 202. See Apollo, Krishna, Phaethon
Goethe, 35
Gosse, E., 167 and n
Gransden, K. W., 205
Grasmere, 166-7
Greatness, 74-5, 105, 115
Greece, 16, 37, 43-6, 50, 54, 99; Mythology, 64, 74, 90, 207

Hamidullah (ch. VI), 189-92
Hardy, T., 27, 119, 198
Harvey, W. J., 87

Hayek, F., 174
Head and heart, 42-3, 55, 71, 100, 135-137, 152f, 159, 163-5, 171, 187
Heard, Gerald, 42
Heart, 85. See Head
Hegel, 102
Hell, 47, 93
Hellenism, 38, 99, 207. See Greece
Heroism, 32, 47, 91, 114-15, 117, 121, 127
Herriton, Philip (ch. III), originals of, 183, 199, 207
Hindu festival, 132-3, 143-4, 159, 161-162, 165, 202
Hindu temple, 133, 161, 199
Hinduism, 134, 161, 164, etc.
Hitlerism, 171
Holy Grail, 89
Honeychurch, Lucy (ch. III), 21f, 87, 148, 183, 203, 207; later life, 171
Honeychurch, Mrs, original of, 183
House, 31 and n, 41n, 67, 95, ch. V passim, 186, 196, 199, 206
Hoy, C., 125
Hulme, T. E., 167
Humanism, 11, 14, 44, 46-8, 75-6, 113-114, 172, 199, etc.
Humour, 15, 67-8, 178-83, etc. See Comedy
Hysteria, 19, 148, 153

Ibsen, 79
Idealism, 14, 36, 91, 102, 166f, 172
Imagination, 16, 22, 25-30, 37, 76, 78, 84f, 88f, 94, 97, 108, 125f, **175-6**, 201, et passim
Imperialism, 34, 102, 131, 133-6
India, 13, 32, 130, ch. VI, passim, 171
Infinity, 110, 112ff, 127, 144, 157, 160
Irony, 11, 104, 120, 180, 186-92, etc.
Italy, 38-41, 48-9, ch. III, passim, 102, 131, 137, 171

James, Henry, 23
Jewel, 87, 123, 188
Justice, 135-6

Kant, 102
Keats, 181, 197
Kermode, Frank, 144-5
Kindliness, 74, 99, 179, 206, 208, etc.
Kramrisch, S., 161
Krishna, 145, 164

Lamb, Charles, 111
Laski, H. J., 174
Lavish, Miss, 22; original of, 183
Lawrence, D. H., 112, 172, 184, 195-8
  and n; *Lady Chatterley's Lover*, 172;
  The Rainbow, 196, 206-7; *The
  Plumed Serpent*, 196
Leavis, F. R., 25, 188-91
Leitmotivs, 22-3, 59, 201-2. *See* Symbol-
  ism
Leonardo da Vinci, 22, 61-3, 65
Life, 22, 55, 63-4, 65, 67, 69, 89, 91,
  203, etc.
Light, 47, 63, 147, 157, etc. *See* Sun,
  Moon
London, 45, **108-10**, 113, 127, 170
Lorenzo di Credi, 72
Love, 20-1, 30, 35, 43, 47, 55-7, 64ff,
  75-6, 80, 87, 91, 106, 109f, 117, 122-
  125, 127, 142, 144-64 *passim*, 171,
  174-6, 202, 204, *et passim*

Macaulay, Rose, 12, 88, 181-2f
Madonna, 72-4, 128
Maeterlinck, 48
'Magic', 35, 80, 89
Marabar. *See* Caves
Marsh, Edward, 174
Melville, H., 197
Meredith, G., 20n, 41, 54, 59, 103, 201;
  Richard Feverel, 115
Micawber, Mr and Mrs, 57
Michelangelo, 61-2, 65
Miniver, Mrs, 179-80
Moment, 29-30, 48-9. *See* Visionary
  moment, Moral choice
'Monk and Beast', 122-3, 196
Moon, 143f, 147, 155, 158, 202, 204
Moore, G. E., *Principia Ethica*, 20, 36
Moore, Mrs (ch. VI), 19, 20, 23, 177,
  189-92, 204, 207
Moore, Stella (ch. VI), 199
Moral choice, moment of, 71, 80-1, 149
Morality, 13, 16, 19-21, 27, 30, 49, **57-
  59**, 76, 84, 118-19, 184-92, 195, 205,
  et passim
More, Hannah, 12, 18, 181
Mosque, 154, 158-9, 202
Motor-car, 102, 105, 109
Mozart, 60
'Muddle', 19-21, 22, **56-7**, 83, 103-5,
  122, 142, 149-53, 162-5, 185-7
Munt, Mrs (ch. V), 20, 187

Music, 23, 30, 32, 50, 51-2, 59-60, 69,
  86, 107, 117-18, 120-8, 201-4, etc.
Mystery, 20, 162-5
Mythology, 28, 38, 122, 207-8

Napoleon, 50
Nature, 41-3, 50, 109, 178, 197
Nightmare, 19, 29, 91, 156-9
'Now', 125-6
Nuclear weapons, 171

Orion, 47, 91-4
Orwell, G., 134
Oxford, 77, 105, 128

Pallas Athene, 55, 64
Pan, 39, 97, 164, 173
'Panic and emptiness', 14, 39-41, 97,
  106, 127
Paradise, 63, 86-8f
Passion, 16, 20-1, 55, 59, 64, 74-6, 79,
  83f, 88, 121-3, 125
Patriotism, 17, 34. *See* Imperialism
'Peevishness', 56-7, 105
Pembroke, Herbert (ch. IV), 19-21, 34,
  57, 131, 189
Personal, 103, 110, 153, etc.
Personal relationships, 17, 68, 106, 109,
  etc.
Phaethon, 64-5, 66
Place, Francis, 18
Place, sense of, 41-5, 106-11, 186, 205.
  See also Genius loci
Plato, 35-6
Plomer, William, 169-70
Plot, 11, 29, 74-6, 132-3, 183-4, 198ff,
  etc.
Plotinus, 169
Poole, 108, 187-8
Pound, Ezra, 167
Progress, 49, 102-14 *passim*, 134, 204-8,
  etc.
Prophecy, 198
Proportion, 137, 139, 149
Proust, 167, 201
Psychology, 19, 29, 82, 205, 208
'Puritanism', 172

Rainbow, 50, 122, 196-206
Realism (and reality), 12, 24, 25-30,
  36-7, 38-52, 66, 73, 76, 77-100, 101,
  116, 123, 126-7, 129-30, 147-8, 160,
  162-5f, 175-6, 188-9, 198-208, etc.

Reality, sense of, 15, 21, 37, 64, **77-100**, **148-59**, 187, etc.

Redemption. *See* Salvation

Refinement, 75

Reflections, 110, 114, 129

Reid, Forrest, 42

Relativity, 167

Religion, 109. *See* Christianity, Hinduism

Rhythm, 22, 201-2, etc.

Richards, I. A., 25

Rock, 144, 149, 154, 190. *See* Stone, Caves

Romanticism, 14, 25-7, 32, 99, 166-7, 175-6

'Round 'characters, 22, 57

Royal Academy, 168

Ruskin, John, 117

'Rutherford, Mark', 27

St Paul's, 113, 127, 129, 156

Sampson, George, 11

'Saki', 39

Salvation, 22, 57-8, 72, 75, 82, 99-100, 159, 178

San Gimignano, 67

Sargent, J. S., 168

Sawston, 13, 17, 19, 33, 66-100 *passim*, 131, 138, 148, 163, 191

Saxl, Dr, 161

Schlegel, Helen (ch. V), 183, 203; original of, 183

Schlegel, Margaret (ch. V), 182-9, 196, 199, 203, 205, 207; original of, 183

Schumann, 60

Scott, Walter, 60; *Heart of Midlothian*, 115

Second World War, 169, 171, 205

Shakespeare, 34, 189; *Merchant of Venice*, 27; *Tempest*, 118f

'Sheep and goats', 57-8 and n, 83

Shelley, 15, 26, 28, **35-6**, 98, 176, 191f

Signorelli, 72

Sky, 109, 137, 143-4, etc.

Snake, 140, 145, 149, 157

Socialism, 109, 167-8

Spence, Jonathan, 177

Spender, Miss, 183

Spirit, 82, 91-6, 105, 159, 162, 186

Splendour, 47-8, 93, 117, 127, 144, 152, 156

Stars, 28, 31-2, 40, 47, 90-4, 139, 143, 196, etc.

Stone, 47, 146, 159, 190. *See* Rock

Strachey, Lytton, 172f

Stream, 43-4, 46, 86, 92, 94-6, 123-6

Sun, 64-5, 67, 91, 124, 143ff, 147, 155-156, 161, 202, 204. *See* Apollo, Phaethon, Krishna, Gods and goddesses

Supernatural, 52, 141, 182-3

Swift, 191

Swinburne, 174-5

Swinnerton, Frank, 116-17

Swiss Family Robinson, 33

Symbolism, **22-24**, 26, 28, 82, 94, 101, 105, 117, 147f, 156, 162, 183, etc.

Taylor, Mr, 33

Technology, 178, 193f, 204-6

'Telegrams and anger', 106, 119

Thornton family, 112, 170

Thornton, Henry, 17

Thornton, Marianne, 17, 31, 171, 178-9

Time, 125-6, 155, 204

Times, The, 180

Tolstoy, *War and Peace*, 115, 202

Tonbridge School, 33

Tower, 67

Tragedy, 84, 119f, 127f

Traversi, D. A., 164

Tree, 23, 31, 43-6, 50, 78, 101-30 *passim*, 186

Trilling, Lionel, 11, 14, 23, 38, 84f, 160n, 181f, 206

Triumph, 50, 59

Truth, 47, 50, 54f, 74, 77, 82, 88, 90, 99, 146, 153f, 171, 206

U.S.A., 204

U.S.S.R., 204

'View', 62-6, 171, 200, etc.

Violence, 12, 15

Violets, 63, 67

Vision, 15-16, 25, 41-2, 74, 92, 120-3, 129-30, 158, 174-6, 184, 188-9, 197-208, etc.; 'negative vision', 127, 156-158

Visionary moment, 21-2, 45, 48-9, 68, 72-6, 86-8, 95, 101, 110-11, 120, 125-126, 200

Voltaire, 172

Vulgarity, 85, 117, 119, 194

Vyse, Cecil (ch. III), 22, 199, 207

INDEX

Wagner, 15, 23, 32, 50, 59f, 86f, 90, 167
Warner, Rex, 29
Warren, A., 160n
Wasp, 23, 143, 154-5, 159-60
Waste Land, 24
Waugh, Evelyn, 178; *Brideshead Revisited*, 111
Wells, H. G., 42, 50, 192-4
Whimsy, 17, 68, 138, 178-82, etc.
White, G., 160n
Whitman, Walt, 147
Wilberforce, William, 18, 179
Wilcox, Henry (ch. V), 182, 184-7, 196
Wilcox, Mrs, 184ff, 190

Will, 14, 46
Wilson, Angus, 57, 84, 170, 177
Wiltshire, 41f, 50, 77-100 *passim*, 172
Wonham, Stephen (ch. IV), 177, 183, 199
Woolf, Leonard, 142, 173
Woolf, Virginia, 160n, 164, 200; *Jacob's Room*, 203; *The Waves*, 202-3
Wordsworth, W., 27, 43, 197
World Mountain, 161
Worms, 145, 156-7

Yeats, W. B., 24, 26

Zabel, M. D., 30